SNAKES IN SUITS

REVISED EDITION

Also by Robert D. Hare, CM, Ph.D.

Without Conscience:
The Disturbing World of the Psychopaths Among Us

SNAKES IN SUITS

REVISED EDITION

Understanding and Surviving
the Psychopaths in Your Office

**Paul Babiak, Ph.D.,
and Robert D. Hare, CM, Ph.D.**

HARPER
BUSINESS

An Imprint of HarperCollins*Publishers*

HarperCollins books may be purchased for educational, business, or sales promotional use. For information, please email the Special Markets Department at SPsales@harpercollins.com.

First published in hardcover by HarperBusiness in 2006.

First revised edition published in 2019.

Library of Congress Cataloging-in-Publication Data has been applied for.

ISBN 978-0-06-269754-7

24 25 26 27 28 LBC 8 7 6 5 4

In loving memory of Joan Bedard

CONTENTS

Introduction   ix

The Case of Dave: Would a Snake Wear Such a
Nice Suit? Act I, Scene I—Grand Entrance   3

1. The Case of the Pit Bull   7

2. Who *Are* These People?   17

The Case of Dave: Act I, Scene II—
Off and Running   43

3. What You See May Not Be What You See   47

The Case of Dave: Act II, Scene I—
Hail-Fellow-Well-Met   69

4. Psychopathic Manipulation: How Did He Do That?   73

The Case of Dave: Act II, Scene II—
Plucking the Apple   89

5. Enter the Psychopath, Stage Left   93

The Case of Dave: Act III, Scene I—Panic Time   113

6. Pawns, Patrons, and Patsies: Roles in the
Psychopath's Drama   117

The Case of Dave: Act III, Scene II—
An Honest Mistake?   145

7. Darkness and Chaos: The Psychopath's Friends   149

The Case of Dave: Act III, Scene III—Let's Do Lunch 167

8. I'm Not a Psychopath, I Just Talk and Act Like One 171

The Case of Dave: Act IV—Doubts Dance Away 197

9. A Unique Empirical Study of Corporate Psychopathy 201

10. The B-Scan: A Measure of Corporate Psychopathy 219

11. Enemy at the Gates 231

The Case of Dave: Act V, Scene I—
Circle the Wagons 269

12. Personal Self-Defense 275

The Case of Dave: Act V, Scene II—
Unraveling the Puzzle 307

13. The Fifth Column: Psychopaths in Our Midst 313

The Case of Dave: Act V, Scene III
The Rise and the Fall 333

Acknowledgments 337

Appendix: Is There a Psychopathic Brain? 341

Notes 347

Some Recommended Documentaries 373

Index 377

INTRODUCTION

Most people are honest, loyal, law-abiding citizens who focus their energy on making a living, raising a family, and contributing to society. Others are more selfish, concerned only about themselves, and appear to lack a moral compass. These individuals display little regard for others, allowing their need for power and prestige to override their sense of fairness and equity.[1] Unfortunately, some individuals in the business world allow the responsibilities of leadership and the perquisites of power to override their moral sense. The recent increase in reports of abuse in major corporations and governments therefore should not be a surprise, given the increased access to unrestricted power, resources of startling proportions, and the erosion of ethical standards and values.

Perhaps leaders in business and government may experience this weakened moral sense of "right and wrong" in the face of excessive temptation and easy access to power. Others may feel justified in reaping the rewards in proportion to the size of the organization they lead, arguing that their extravagances seem excessive only to those who have little hope of achieving them. Some justify their success by embracing the self-serving mantra that "greed is good" and believe that success at any cost is both desirable and justifiable.

However, another group exists, one whose behaviors and attitudes potentially are much more destructive to organizations and employees, and to governments and citizens. This group, the subject of this book, displays a deep, dark personality rooted in lying, manipulation, deceit, egocentricity, callousness, and other potentially destructive traits. This personality is psychopathy.

What makes psychopathy unique is that its defining characteristics and traits lead to behaviors that conflict with the generally accepted norms and laws of society. Some people with psychopathic personalities are in prison because of their crimes, often violent, against people and property. Others are in prison for white-collar crimes, such as fraud, embezzlement, or stock manipulation. Yet many, if not most, of those who commit crimes rarely face prosecution or, if they do, typically serve light sentences before returning to a life of economic crime. As we indicate in Chapter 2, the instruments used to assess psychopathy identify a continuum that varies from no psychopathic traits to a heavy concentration of such traits. We refer to the latter as psychopathic or as psychopaths (see Figure 9.1 for a representation of the continuum). This is analogous to describing those with high blood pressure as hypertensive or hypertensives.

Many individuals with a heavy dose of psychopathic traits routinely bend or break the law but manage to avoid charges or convictions for their actions. Some researchers refer to such individuals as "successful psychopaths." However, it seems incongruous to us to refer to psychopaths as successful *merely because they manage to avoid prison*. Many of these individuals engage in a variety of parasitic, predatory, and socially deviant activities, such as flagrant traffic violations, sexual misconduct, spousal and child abuse, bullying, dishonest business practices, and other behaviors that result in serious psychological, physical, and financial harm to others, including family and friends. For many of these individuals, the subject of this book, their definition of success is the acquisition of power, prestige, and financial enrichment, without concern for the feelings or welfare of others. In this sense, some do succeed, but for others success is sporadic, transitory, and, in some cases, bordering on illusory.[2]

The scientific study of the criminal psychopath is extensive. However, at the time we wrote the first edition of this book, the empirical study of psychopaths in various organizations was scarce. For years, many experts believed that their very nature would make it difficult for them to function in society or to have long-term, successful careers in business and industry. At least that was the conventional wisdom until we did our research.

Over a decade ago, there was very little understanding of how psychopaths could operate "under the radar" in organizations such as for-profit businesses, non-profits, civil service, religious groups, academia, the military, and government agencies. The first edition of this book evolved out of our realization that the public needed more information about what constitutes psychopathic manipulation and deceit among seemingly successful psychopaths. As we wrote in the first edition: "The premise of this book is that psychopaths do work in modern organizations; they often are successful by most standard measures of career success; and their destructive personality characteristics are invisible to many of the people with whom they interact. They are able to circumvent and sometimes hijack succession planning and performance management systems in order to give legitimacy to their behaviors. They take advantage of communication weaknesses, organizational systems and processes, interpersonal conflicts, and general stressors that plague all companies. They abuse coworkers and, by lowering morale and stirring up conflict, the company itself. Some may even steal and defraud" (pp. 139–140).[3]

While the scientific literature on criminal psychopaths was extensive, and is still growing, it primarily involved forensic scientists, clinicians, and criminal justice professionals. By sharing our research, by using nontechnical language and actual case studies, we hoped to close some of the gaps in the understanding of psychopathy among business readers. We wanted to provide them with the experience of working right next to, and to recognize, a psychopath by presenting the kinds of real-life situations we have encountered in our work, including, in many cases, the actual dialog used by the players. Because a psychopathic coworker can harm your career in seen and unseen ways, we hoped that this knowledge would prepare readers to avoid the devastation of psychopathic abuse. Since that time, we have received numerous letters and emails from readers thanking us and sharing with us their own personal experiences with psychopathic coworkers, bosses, and even family members.

Unlike when we wrote the first edition, we now have a considerable number of empirical studies on corporate psychopathy, to which we will refer throughout the book. Although several of our suggestions concerning psychopathy in the workplace have been empirically studied and confirmed since then, the scientific study of corporate psychopathy is still in its infancy; there are many research questions in need of empirical field tests. For example, how do psychopaths manage to enter an organization? What impact do they have on the functioning and reputation of the organization and its personnel? Our goal in this revised edition of *Snakes in Suits* is to bring the reader up to speed on the current knowledge about psychopathy and share our continuously improving understanding of this phenomenon.

We approach this task by informing the reader about the nature of psychopathy and its impact on the workplace. In chapters 1 and 2, we explore in detail the many traits and characteristics that define the psychopathic syndrome. In chapters 3 through 10, we focus on the manipulation techniques psychopaths use to use and abuse their victims. In the third part of the book, chapters 11 through 13, we offer best practices, gleaned from our experience coaching and consulting with organizations that can aid readers who feel that they are dealing with a psychopath on the job.

To illustrate many of the concepts, we include case studies along the way. The first, The Case of Dave, is broken down into ten segments, written out as scenes in a stage play, so that the reader can not only see and feel the presence of psychopaths but also directly tie their machinations to the content presented in the related text. We also start with a full case, The Case of the Pit Bull, to illustrate the entire psychopathic manipulation process as it often plays out in real life. Then, throughout the book, we introduce other, shorter cases to illustrate specific points. (Note: with some exceptions, we do not use real names and have changed identifying details.)

Additionally, we have grouped the updated research notes as Supplemental Material, referenced in the text according to the chapter they are in, their position in the chapter, and a brief title. For example, the first Supplemental for Chapter 2 is S 2.1: *Nature? Nurture? Both!* The Supplementals are at the end of the chapter so that interested students of psychopathy can focus on the data while others can skip to the next chapter. We also have introduced Discussion Questions to provoke the reader to consider the finer points of the material; these are also suitable for classroom use or for book club discussions. The Notes section provides references for material discussed in the text, organized by chapters. There are many documentaries on psychopathy. We note some of the better ones in the *Recommended Documentaries* section. Readers also might wish to access www.hare.org for an updated list of books, chapters, and articles on psychopathy. In many cases, there are direct links to abstracts of articles. The web pages of the Society for the Scientific Study of Psychopathy (SSSP; www.psychopathysociety.org) and of the Aftermath: Surviving Psychopathy Foundation (www.aftermath-surviving-psychopathy.org) provide important information about research on psychopathy and survival techniques, respectively.

This book will introduce you to the way these "snakes in suits" manipulate others; it will help you see through their games and give you pointers on how to protect yourself, your career, and your company.

SNAKES IN SUITS

REVISED EDITION

The Case of Dave: Would a Snake Wear Such a Nice Suit?

GRAND ENTRANCE

One could imagine he was arriving for a *GQ* photo shoot, judging by his smooth, strong, and confident entrance. His suit was very well made, his smile broad, his shirt crisp, and, well, the whole package he presented was one of perfection.

"Hi, I'm Dave. I'm here to see Frank," he said to the receptionist.

"I'll ring him, sir. Please have a seat," she replied. "It's good to see you again." She smiled.

"Hi, Dave, good to see you again," rang Frank's voice from across the lobby. "How was the trip in?"

"Fine, pleasant," stated Dave, as he gave a firm handshake.

"We have a couple more interviews for you today," said Frank. "Just some human resources folks, and a meeting with my boss, our vice president, and then lunch and a tour of the surrounding community."

"Great, I'm ready to get started," Dave said enthusiastically.

Garrideb Technologies was one of those high-tech companies, born in a garage in the Midwest, that had skyrocketed to success beyond the wildest dreams of its founders. Because of the company's incredible growth, it sorely needed changes, not the least of which was the need to hire more staff. The management team sought the best talent available to keep up with the growing demands for their products and services. Few candidates had résumés with the specialized education and experience they needed, but Dave did.

The human resources interviews went better than these interviews usually go. HR types tend to probe more deeply into the motivations of people than do the department interviewers, asking for many details about past jobs and references, but Dave was polite and forthcoming. "I'll stay as long as you need me," he said, smiling, "so whatever you need, please, that's why I'm here." After they were through, the HR assistant escorted Dave to the senior executive wing.

"Welcome, Dave, I'm glad to finally meet you," said John, the vice president of new products, noting Dave's expensive suit and tie. "How was your trip in?"

"Excellent," stated Dave. "This is a beautiful part of the country. I can't wait to take a better look around. Your facilities are extraordinary; I've never seen such architecture."

"Thanks," responded John. "We try to make it comfortable for our staff. Success has its rewards, and we don't skimp on creature comforts."

"I've heard a bit about your strategic plan from Frank, and I've studied the company's website, but I'd like to get the details from you, as the major strategist of the company's success. How did you do all of this?" inquired Dave. Pleased with Dave's interest in the company's future, John took some slides from a binder on his bookshelf to show Dave some graphs. John launched into his exposition on his plan. "Unbelievable! You really have done a great job orchestrating everything," exclaimed Dave.

John was pleased to interact with someone who, despite his age, understood so well the intricacies of building a business. He pushed aside the suggested interview questions HR had prepared for him and asked Dave to tell him about himself. Dave obliged eagerly by describing his work history, giving plenty of examples reflecting John's respect for enthusiasm, hard work, and diligence. The extent of Dave's experience was—at age thirty-five—impressive, documented by a résumé and a portfolio most would work an entire career to achieve.

As the interview ended, Dave extended his hand, smiled, and said, looking straight into John's eyes, "Thank you so much for your time. I look forward to working closely with you; I know I can help you realize your strategic vision."

"The pleasure was mine; I hope to see you again." John's secretary escorted Dave back to the lobby to wait for Frank. *One could not ask for a better candidate*, thought John as he dialed up Frank with his approval.

Frank hung up with John and grabbed his jacket, but as he reached the door of his office on his way to pick up Dave, his phone rang again. "I'd like us all to get together later today to discuss Dave's candidacy," said the HR director.

"Oh, Melanie, that won't be necessary. John and I just agreed that Dave is the best person for the job; I'm going to take him to lunch and make him the offer."

"But we agreed to get all the interviewers together to discuss each candidate thoroughly; and we wanted to bring back Tom, the guy from New York, for a second look," she reminded Frank.

"That won't be necessary; clearly, one could not ask for a better candidate than Dave," he said as he hung up. Frank was happy to have found someone with the right fit for both the job and the organization, and he didn't want this one to get away.

Over lunch, Frank made the offer. Dave pushed back at the salary, which was actually high in the range, and Frank agreed to sweeten the pie with a sign-on bonus and review in six months.

Frank was very pleased when Dave accepted the enhanced package. Seeing leadership potential in him, Frank knew that Dave's style, intelligence, and technical expertise made him an ideal management development candidate in this successful, rapidly growing technology firm. Everyone who interviewed Dave thought he was perfect; one of the managers from the lab even stated that he was "too good to be true." Dave would start working for Frank in two weeks.

This scene is growing more common as companies accelerate their hiring practices to attract, hire, and retain new, high-potential talent before their competitors do. Gone are the days of the painstaking vetting process. Competition is fierce and qualified candidates are few. Business now moves swiftly, and common wisdom is that those who hesitate lose. However, was Dave a good hire?

We will follow Dave and others through this book, and explore what makes them so attractive, yet potentially so damaging to an organization. We will describe how they get in and how they move up the organization into positions of increasing power and influence, where the damage they can do to the organization and its members can be significant. We then offer suggestions to employees and coworkers who might be potential targets, and to managers and executives on how to secure the organization from unscrupulous manipulation.

DISCUSSION QUESTIONS

- How would you describe Dave's personality?
- Did Dave display any behaviors that would make you question the wisdom of Frank's decision to offer him the job?
- Did Dave say or do anything to make you suspicious?

1

The Case of the Pit Bull[1]

Fred led the group to O'Hare's tavern after work that night. He started a tab and ordered a round of drinks for everyone from the company. As more people arrived, there were cheers and high-fives as coworkers rejoiced about their good fortune. Fred raised his glass in a toast. Silence spread over the group as everyone turned toward him with a raised glass: "The Pit Bull is dead. Long live the Pit Bull!" he shouted to the glee of everyone there.

"Hear, hear!" they cheered and bursts of laughter and applause overtook the room. There was not a sad person in the place that night; quite a change from how most Friday nights at O'Hare's had been over the past two years.

In the early days, things at the company had been good. Raises were excellent, bonuses generous, working conditions pleasant, and the chance to work for one of the oldest and most respected names in the business was personally rewarding to many people. Nevertheless, as with all good things, there was change. Two years before, the CEO, "Old Man Bailey" to his friends (and most employees were his friends), had sold his financial services company to a bigger competitor. However, like so many entrepreneurs, he just could not see himself quietly fading away. He needed to keep his hands in the business, so he negotiated an interim consulting position on the board to assist with the transition.

The board welcomed his advice and felt comfortable with his occasional visits to his former company's (now a division) headquarters. Bailey wanted to keep the old values he had impressed upon his people alive in the company, and hoped that they would spread to the other parts of the bigger corporation, but this was not to be. The new parent corporation had many divisions and locations, and Bailey's little piece of the corporate world, as well as his ability to influence, was lessening with each acquisition. Each division had its own values, service lines, and way of doing things, and the corporate staff had their own ideas about what the overall company culture ought to be like.

Pitchers of beer and bowls of peanuts were spread out over the tables in O'Hare's back room. As staff from different departments mingled, those who had heard only some of the rumors sought out more information; others wanted to confirm what they had heard. It was great fun to collect different bits and pieces of the story and try to assemble a picture of the Pit Bull's termination.

Although he made a point of staying out of the day-to-day running of the business, one decision in particular that bothered Bailey was the promotional transfer of Gus into the top slot as COO of the division. Bailey saw Gus as a status-conscious suck-up who avoided confrontation, didn't hold people account-

able, and was rather susceptible to flattery and attention. Bailey thought Gus spent too much time socializing with the corporate folks and not enough time getting things done in his division.

Six months after Gus's promotion, all hell broke loose. For the first time in its long history, Bailey's division failed to meet its targets, so much so that the market analysts were starting to make unflattering comments, endangering the reputation of the whole corporation. Making things worse, there was also the risk of a hefty, very public, and humiliating fine for noncompliance on some government work—a fact that had not reached the newspapers yet, but was sure to make headlines if not averted quickly. Bailey felt that he ought to let Gus go, and offered to run the operation until a suitable, better-qualified replacement could be found. The board disagreed. Rather, in an effort to help Gus in his new role, they decided to create a new director of operations position reporting to him.

One person who caught their attention as the perfect candidate for the job was Helen. Helen had come along with one of the other acquisitions and was touted as a rising star. Her performance review praised her spirit, diligence, focus, energy, and leadership talent. She had a reputation for shaking things up, for getting things done, and for meeting deadlines. Bailey was not impressed, pointing out that there had been considerable collateral damage along the way and that her division was underperforming and consistently exceeding budget. However, that did not seem to have concerned her management team, who put her on the key executive potential watch list. Bailey was amazed at how the corporate folks could ignore these numbers and consider putting someone who was used to spending money in charge of a financial problem. But, these were no longer his decisions to make.

Helen did very well in her interviews with the search committee members. Her dynamic and engaging manner and her self-proclaimed ability to fix organizational problems made her an obvious choice for the spot. Outside analysts would also see the appointment of such an assertive, vibrant, and directive person to a failing high-profile division as a very firm commitment to resolving some of the division's performance issues. Her style and her manner matched what both the corporation and analysts wanted to see. The timing, the circumstances, and her abilities seemed like a good fit. With only one dissenting vote (Bailey's), the board decided to make her the offer.

Helen was disappointed. She expected that Gus would be fired and she would get the top job. Human Resources explained to her that the newly created director job was a high-profile development position, the key position responsible for improving the day-to-day workings of the division; all eyes would be upon her to see if she could help Gus turn the division around in short order. Stellar performance in her new role would go a long way to fast and significant promotions down the line.

Helen said that she would consider the job on the condition that she receive all the support she needed to succeed, a reasonable request by all accounts. The corporation was prepared to take whatever steps necessary, and approve any request in order to fix the problem. In sharp contrast to the financial controls elsewhere within the corporation, therefore, Gus and Helen could have pretty much whatever resources they requested. With these assurances, effectively a blank check, Helen agreed to take the job.

In a little over six months, the problems that had plagued the division seemed to disappear. The service level on the government contracts rose to 95 percent delivery performance, the errors (human, computer, and procedural) that had created the problems were identified and quickly corrected, and the regulatory compliance question went away quietly. Helen was singled out for public praise for saving the division. Even Gus spoke favorably about her, especially her ethical conduct, diligence, and dedication to the job. The board voted to place her on the executive succession plan.

Fred made the rounds of tables around the room, receiving new toasts as he moved in and out. Bits and pieces of heated conversation were audible through the overall din. Rick, from the mailroom, confirmed that the state police had been at the back door to keep everyone inside. "And there were these two guys in black suits carrying out computers, files, and the contents of the shred bin," he reported. Sheila, from security, confirmed that the call had come that morning, followed by the orders to put security staff by the front door. "Yes, handcuffs," she responded to the questions from the marketing staff.

No one was surprised when Gus was removed from his position—except, perhaps, Gus—after Helen made arguments to the executive committee members that implicated him in the original business letdown. Helen was profoundly competitive, dramatic in her engagement with others, and just loved to take center stage and the limelight. Turning the division around gave her the platform she needed for a great career at the company. Naturally, she was the choice to replace Gus, and was rewarded by a promotion to his position as COO.

The front door of O'Hare's opened slowly. There stood a rather large man in a long, black coat. He glanced at his wristwatch and moved toward the bar. O'Hare greeted the well-dressed man with a nod. Taking off his black gloves, the man ordered a ginger ale in a Scotch glass with a swizzle stick. O'Hare nodded and went to make the drink.

Most on Helen's staff did not trust her. She treated the junior colleagues with disdain and a measure of contempt, often deriding their abilities and competence. To those she found useful to her career, however, she was gracious, engaging, and fun. She had a talent for presenting her good side to those she felt mattered, all the while denying, discounting, discarding, and displacing anyone who did not agree with her decisions. Helen told the cor-

*porate staff what they wanted to hear, stage-managing meetings
with the executive team as if they were Hollywood productions.
Helen was a master at impression management, and she effectively manipulated higher-ups, intimidated direct reports, and
played up to key personalities important to her career.*

Picking up his drink, the man looked around the tavern. The
place was quiet except for the noise from the back room.

*With Gus out of the way, Helen let loose her domineering man-
agement style. Histrionics were common during staff meetings,
and participants often left bruised, battered, and humiliated.
She would stomp around the new office complex—which she
had leased because she wanted a bigger office—without ac-
knowledging others, barking out orders, and generally intimidating, frightening, and pushing people around.*

*This was a total departure from the management style
embodied in Bailey, a man whose door was always open, and
who routinely made the rounds of the staff, soliciting new ideas
to improve the business. Bailey valued his people and amazed
new staff with his ability to remember their spouses' names and
children's sports accomplishments. Bailey was a people person
who was not only extremely bright, but also knew how to make
money. He knew that his success—the success of the business—
rested with the quality of his staff, and he shared the glory as
well as the rewards with those around him.*

*Over the next few months, Helen hired in her own team to
replace many of the more vocal opponents on her staff. Relying
on her own gut-feel approach to talent acquisition, she would
offer large sign-on bonuses to entice young, bright executives to
leave their current jobs, but if she then decided—within weeks
and sometimes even days—that they were inadequate, incompetent, or not loyal enough, she fired them. There was no concern
about the damage she did to the careers and family lives of these*

people, or the legal problems she could potentially cause for the corporation. She also hired in a number of friends, often without consultation with human resources.

Helen seemed able to get away with whatever she wanted, including the purchase of the latest extravagance, whether this was a new car, expensive office furniture, corporate apartment, or the leasing of a corporate jet for her travels. Helen initiated a series of expensive management conferences, held in tropical locations, with prominent keynote speakers, in which she trumpeted the division's accomplishments with herself taking the spotlight. Her claims of success were at odds with a growing lack of cohesion, lowered morale, and increased stress within the division—but somehow those at the top did not notice this discrepancy.

Questioning Helen's behavior provoked intense reactions, as, for example, when she fired the executive coach hired by the corporation to help her smooth over her rough edges. She was never wrong and was interested only in hearing positive news. People resented the way she paraded about like a queen bee, showing off her status, power, and the executive privileges she assumed. Many on the staff were afraid of her; behind her back, they referred to her as the Pit Bull.

The man at the bar glanced at his wristwatch and looked around the room as if searching for someone. "They're in there," said O'Hare, nodding to the door to the back room. "I don't think they are expecting you, but I'm sure you can go right in."

What really irked the staff was Helen's increasing absence from the office. Her second in command, Ned—a close, personal friend appointed by her to a new business development post— was often absent at the same time, provoking unkind rumors. Other, more critical rumors had him running another business on the side, in spite of the prohibitions of company policy. Ned's presence was resented, but Helen protected him and no one dared contradict or question her.

Lynda, from accounting, sat at the back of the room sipping her wine. The raucous conversation of the colleagues who sat with her provided a soothing backdrop for her private thoughts. Just out of college with a degree in finance and accounting, Lynda was excited to be working for such a prestigious firm. She was also thrilled that Julie, the senior member of the audit team, let her introduce some forensic accounting techniques she learned in school to the department's internal auditing procedures.

"You should be happy, Lynda," said Julie. "You saw something and you said something, and the [expletive deleted] is gone."

Lynda took a drink and smiled shyly. The last few weeks had been a living hell. When Ned told the Pit Bull that Lynda was delving deep into the company's accounting database, she went ballistic on the entire finance department. She demanded Lynda be fired. Today was to be her last day.

"Listen, Lyn, the world is made up of all kinds of people, and you were unlucky to get a jerk, a criminal, on your first job. But most folks are honest and want to do a good job—you're one of them, and you're surrounded by friends—you did the right thing; you're our hero." A collective expression of support rose from the table, and Julie put her arm around Lynda, who smiled.

With glass in hand, the man in the black coat slowly pushed open the door to the back room. "Ned was found trying to escape through the cafeteria!" shrieked Sheila. "When they put the cuffs on him, he went nuts, demanding to call his lawyer!"

"What about the Pit Bull trying to escape on the jet?" questioned Sam, who was always the last to hear the latest gossip.

Seeing who had entered the room, Fred coughed loudly in an attempt to quiet down the group, but few heard him. Tapping his glass with his ring, he began to get the group's attention. Loud noise turned to whispers, and whispers to complete silence as more and more people took notice of the gentleman's arrival.

The fraud was as clever as it was brazen. No one suspected that most of the key accounts responsible for the turnaround and growth were completely phony. Little did those in the office realize that, using high-level access codes, Ned and the Pit Bull had also hacked the server and were able to make ever-so-small changes to several real customer accounts, gradually siphoning off assets to an offshore account. They could not imagine that they had been working right next to a couple of crooks.

The gentleman searched the faces in the room and smiled at those he still recognized. Seeing Shirley from accounting, he moved toward her table. Most of the folks had already risen, but Lynda, whose back was to the door, was still deep in her thoughts. As he moved forward, the crowd parted. Standing to her side, he asked, "Are you Lynda?" Surprised out of her reverie, she turned and saw who was standing next to her.

Few companies experience the high drama that unfolded that day. Ned, who by chance was in early that day, had seen the state police and several black vans pulling up and had had enough time to call Helen before he bolted out of his office toward the rear exit and into the hands of security. Helen was luckier. As the unmarked cars were coming down her street, she escaped out the back door of her palatial house and stole across the yard to the next street, where she always kept her second car parked and ready for just such an emergency. While they watched the corporate jet, few imagined that she also leased a private plane at a local airstrip on the other side of town.

"Yes, sir," Lynda said, timidly.

"I wanted to thank you personally for all your help. I really do appreciate your courage and honesty."

"Mr. Bailey," said Fred, coming up behind him, "it's great to see you. Welcome to our little celebration."

"It's good to see you, too, Fred. Looks like we've run out of beer," he hinted. "The party's on me, folks," said Old Man Bailey as he sat down next to Lynda. "Fred, could you get me another drink? O'Hare knows what I take."

DISCUSSION QUESTIONS

- How would you describe the management styles of Old Man Bailey, Gus, and Helen?
- How would you describe their personalities?
- Could one (or more) of them be a psychopath?
- Do gender and/or age factor into your opinion?

2

Who *Are* These People?

Novels and movies portray psychopaths in extreme, stereotypical ways. They appear as cold-blooded serial killers, stalkers, sex offenders, con men and women, or the prototypical evil, manipulating villain, such as Dr. No or Hannibal Lecter. Reality provides some support for this view, but the picture is actually quite a bit more complex than this. Part of the problem is that the public and many professionals treat *psychopathy*, *antisocial personality disorder*, and *sociopathy* as if they are interchangeable terms. They share some antisocial features but are not identical conditions.

- **Psychopathy** is a multi-dimensional clinical construct described by the personality traits and behaviors that form the basis of this book (see Table 2.1).[1] Psychopathy is not solely a product of social and environmental forces. Genetic factors play an important role in the formation of the personality traits and temperament considered essential to the disorder. However, its lifelong expression is the result of complex interactions between biological/temperamental predispositions and social forces. The traits and behaviors that help to define adult psychopathy begin to emerge early in childhood.[2] Psychopaths are relatively lacking in conscience and in the ability to experience empathy, guilt, or loyalty to anyone but themselves. About 1 percent of the population, and about 15 percent of incarcerated offenders, meet the research criteria for psychopathy described in this book. Some theorists and researchers consider psychopathy to be a disorder, the result of brain dysfunction or damage, whereas others argue that psychopathy is not a disorder but an evolutionary adaptation, a view that the second author finds compelling (see S 2.1: *Nature or Nurture? Both!*). The Appendix contains an overview of the use of neuroimaging for the study of psychopathy.

- **Antisocial personality disorder** (ASPD) is a broad diagnostic category introduced in the third edition of the American Psychiatric Association's *Diagnostic and Statistical Manual of Mental Disorders* (DSM-III; 1980), and continued unchanged in the fourth edition (DSM-IV; 1994).[3] Antisocial and criminal behaviors play a major role in its definition; in this sense, ASPD is similar to sociopathy, described below. A diagnosis of ASPD requires the presence of three of seven criteria: Failure to conform to social norms with respect to lawful behaviors; Deceitfulness; Impulsivity or failure to plan ahead; Irritability and aggressiveness; Reckless disregard for safety of self or others; Consistent irresponsibility; and Lack of remorse.

The difference between psychopathy and antisocial personality disorder is that the former includes personality traits such as lack of empathy, grandiosity, and shallow emotions (see Table 2.1) that are not necessary for a diagnosis of ASPD. ASPD is much more common than psychopathy in the general population and in prisons.

Because of dissatisfaction with the heavy emphasis of ASPD on criminal behaviors, the American Psychiatric Association planned to change the criteria for ASPD in the fifth edition of the DSM (DSM-5; 2013). Early in the development of DSM-5, the Personality Disorders Work Group for DSM-5 proposed to rename ASPD as *Antisocial/Psychopathy Type*. The intention was to incorporate the extensive theory and research on psychopathy into the diagnostic criteria for this personality disorder. By psychopathy they meant the clinical construct described so masterfully by psychiatrist Hervey Cleckley in several editions of *The Mask of Sanity* (discussed below) and measured with the *Hare Psychopathy Checklist* and its derivatives (Table 2.1, and below). However, after years of debate and poorly conceived field trials, DSM-5 retained the original diagnostic criteria for ASPD, listed above. Many prominent clinicians and researchers have commented on this failure to bring ASPD into line with the more useful construct of psychopathy.[4]

- **Sociopathy** is not a formal psychiatric condition, although in the 1930s some clinicians used the term for "psychopathic" features resulting from adverse social forces. Similarly, today, it refers to patterns of attitudes and behaviors that society considers antisocial and criminal, but are normal or necessary in the subculture or social environment in which they developed. For example, people raised in a subculture that is criminal, marginalized, or impoverished often will adopt the attitudes and mores of the subculture. The early work of psychologist David Lykken had a strong influence on Hare's research career.

He viewed sociopaths as a subgroup of ASPD, the product of unsocialized and/or incompetent parents.[5] Some sociopaths may have a normal or near-normal capacity for empathy, guilt, and loyalty, but their sense of right and wrong depends on the norms and expectations of their subculture or group. Some clinicians and researchers refer to these individuals as *secondary psychopaths*, or as having externalizing (acting out) behaviors. Many criminals and gang members fit this description. The prevalence of those we would describe as sociopathic is high.

Psychopathy as a Traditional Clinical Construct

Psychopathy is a multi-dimensional clinical construct that comprises a cluster of interpersonal, affective, lifestyle, and antisocial traits and behaviors. These include deception, manipulation, irresponsibility, impulsivity, stimulation-seeking, poor behavioral controls, shallow affect, a lack of empathy, guilt, or remorse, and a range of persistent unethical and antisocial behaviors, not necessarily criminal. Among the most devastating features of psychopathy are a callous disregard for the rights of others and high risk for a variety of predatory and aggressive behaviors. In *Without Conscience*[6] Hare described psychopaths as,

Social predators who charm, manipulate, and ruthlessly plow their way through life, leaving a broad trail of broken hearts, shattered expectations, and empty wallets. Completely lacking in conscience and in feelings for others, they selfishly take what they want and do as they please, violating social norms and expectations without the slightest sense of guilt or regret (p. xi). . . . Psychopaths make up a significant portion of the people the media describe—serial killers, rapists, thieves, swindlers, con men, wife beaters, white-collar criminals, hype-prone stock promoters and "boiler-room" operators, child abusers, gang members, disbarred lawyers, drug barons, professional gamblers, members of organized crime, doctors who've lost their licenses, terrorists, cult leaders, mercenaries, and unscrupulous business-people (p. 2).

We now know that both male and female psychopaths commit a greater number and variety of crimes than do other criminals.[7] Their crimes tend to be more violent and their overall behavior more controlling, aggressive, threatening, and abusive than that of other criminals. Further, their aggression and violence often are predatory in nature—cold-blooded and devoid of the intense emotional arousal that typically accompanies the violent acts of most people. It is *instrumental,* simply a means to an end, and is not followed by anything even approaching normal concern for the pain and suffering inflicted on others. On the other hand, much of the violence of most other criminals tends to be *reactive*—a response to perceived threats or situations. This type of violence is often described as *affective* violence, or as a crime of passion accompanied by an intense emotional state and typically followed by feelings of remorse and guilt for the harm done to others. Psychopaths also are capable of reactive violence, but without intense emotions other than anger or frustration.[8] The prevalence of psychopathy in the general population is relatively small, but the social, economic, physical, and psychological damage done by individuals with this disorder is far out of proportion to their numbers. Particularly alarming, from a public safety point of view, is that psychopathic criminals *reoffend* at a much higher rate, and do so much earlier, than do other criminals[9] (see S 2.2: *Psychopathy and Lethal Violence*).

Some psychopaths live in society and do not technically break the law—although they may come close, causing problems in hidden economic, psychological, and emotionally abusive ways.[10] They do not make warm and loving parents, children, or family members. They do not make reliable friends or coworkers. They take advantage of and often abuse the trust and support of friends and family. You could work for, work with, or be married to someone with a psycho-pathic personality and not know it. He can be a neighbor, friend, or family member whose behavior you may find fascinating, confusing, and repelling. Given their penchant for breaking the rules and push-ing the envelope of acceptable human behavior, it also is likely that some psychopaths in the workplace commit illegal acts that are covert or covered up by the organization in order to protect its reputation.

So how do psychologists and psychiatrists accurately decide if someone has a psychopathic personality? In the early days of scientific research on psychopathy (up to the late 1970s), there was no widely used standard of measurement. The psychiatric criteria for use in di-agnoses were vague, sometimes confusing, and could be interpreted differently depending on the personal experiences of the researcher or diagnostician. Various self-report scales that purported to measure psychopathy were unrelated to one another and to psychiatric diag-noses.[11] This dark and murky past has cleared up considerably over the last fifty years as psychopathy has grown into one of the most re-searched and well-understood clinical/forensic variables. The clinical framework and inspiration for much of the current research on psy-chopathy stems from descriptive and theoretical accounts provided by many early clinicians, particularly Hervey Cleckley.

From Clinical to Empirical

Science depends on the availability of accurate, standardized in-struments to measure phenomena of interest. For example, clin-ical observations of a cardiac patient's symptoms are useful as a starting point in determining the patient's condition. However, the physician also uses scientific measurement tools, such as an elec-trocardiogram and an angiogram to provide empirical, biometric information about the state of the patient's cardiovascular system. With respect to psychopathy, psychologists Drew Westen and Joel Weinberger described the transition from *the clinical to the empiri-*

cal study of psychopathy as follows: "An emerging body of research suggests that clinical observations, just like lay observations, can be quantified using standard psychometric procedures, so that clinical description becomes statistical prediction." Further, "Virtually all current research on psychopathy . . . presupposes the observations of a brilliant clinical observer [Cleckley 1941] whose clinical immersion among psychopaths over 60 years ago still provides the foundation for the measure [the PCL-R] considered the gold standard in psychopathy research." [12]

Hervey Cleckley (1903–1984) was an influential American psychiatrist whose detailed and insightful descriptions of psychopathy and its manifestations played a crucial part in current conceptualizations of psychopathy. He also influenced the development of what now is the international standard for the clinical and forensic assessment of psychopathy, the PCL-R. [13] Initially best known for the book *The Three Faces of Eve*, co-authored with Corbett Thigpen in 1957, his greatest legacy is his body of early writings and prescient views on psychopathy.

In the 1930s, as today, some offenders with mental illness ended up in forensic psychiatric hospitals for treatment. As a young psychiatrist, Cleckley had the opportunity to study his patients carefully, and he realized that many of them did not display the usual symptoms of mental illness, but instead seemed "normal" under most conditions. He watched them charm, manipulate, and take advantage of other patients, family members, and even hospital staff. To Cleckley's trained eyes, these individuals were *psychopaths*, previously a vague psychiatric concept with a troubled and controversial history, going back more than a century.

Based on his experiences, Cleckley wrote a classic clinical textbook on psychopathy: *The Mask of Sanity*. Published in 1941, this seminal book was the first attempt to present a clear and detailed clinical picture of psychopathy and its manifestations. The fifth edition of *The Mask of Sanity* appeared in 1976. [14] Cleckley noted that these patients had normal intelligence but often made poor life judgments. They did not learn much from their personal experiences, causing them to repeat dysfunctional or unfruitful behaviors. They lacked insight concerning themselves and the impact of their behavior on others, but this seemed not to concern them as they did not understand or care for the feelings of others. They were noticeably unreliable, even about important things relevant to their current situation, and seemed to have no real life goals or plans. They were insincere, although often appearing to be very sincere to those with little experience interacting with them, particularly new staff members and patients. Most obvious of all, these patients were consummate liars.

Cleckley never intended his observations to be a formal checklist for diagnosis, and he never tested his model statistically. He simply, though persuasively, reported those traits that seemed to him to characterize the syndrome. Confirmation of his observations and the development of scientific methods for assessment, therefore, became a primary endeavor for Hare and his team of students and colleagues throughout the 1970s and 1980s. A recent article described this historical period as one in which Cleckley and Hare encouraged one another to continue their respective efforts to understand psychopathy: "Without the correspondence between Cleckley and Hare, the fifth edition of *The Mask of Sanity* and Hare's career as a psychopathy researcher might never have come to fruition." [15]

The problem that Hare and other researchers faced in the 1970s was the lack of a standard and reliable assessment instrument to measure what Cleckley and other early clinicians had described. During this period, he and his students conducted scores of studies on psychopathy, using "rating" systems based on Cleckley's work, detailed interviews with offenders, and an in-depth review of their file information. [16] While these ratings were useful, there remained a need to create a measure of psychopathy that was reliable, valid, and psychologically and psychometrically sound. Collecting a large number of known descriptors of psychopathic traits and behaviors, and using statistical analysis techniques, Hare, with the collaboration of his colleagues and students, set out to resolve what were the most common and specific traits and behaviors that define psychopathy. The initial result was a 22-item scale, scored from interview and file/collateral information, which combined personality traits with antisocial behaviors, in line with clinical tradition.[17] The comments of other researchers, and the extensive experiences of Hare and his colleagues over a decade, led to a revision of the scale, published as the *Hare Psychopathy Checklist–Revised* (PCL-R) in 1991. A second edition appeared in 2003.[18]

On a personal note, in 2005 the Society for the Scientific Study of Psychopathy created the *R. D. Hare Lifetime Achievement Award*, with Hare as its first recipient. The award went to David Lykken in 2007 and to Hervey Cleckley in 2011, in each case, posthumously. Hare considered it a singular honor to be associated in this way with the two scholars primarily responsible for the launching of his career.

The Clinical/Forensic Measurement of Psychopathy

THE PCL-R

Though it is the instrument of choice for reliable and valid assessments of psychopathy, users of the PCL-R must have appropriate experience and training, and professional qualifications used in accordance with the ethical and professional standards of their discipline.[19,20] Clinicians and researchers use a semi-structured interview and extensive file/collateral information to rate each item according to the extent to which the individual matches specific scoring criteria listed in the Manual: 0 = item does not apply; 1 = item applies to a certain extent; and 2 = item applies to the individual. PCL-R scores thus can vary from 0 to 40. The total score represents the degree to which the individual matches the traditional, prototypical psychopath. For research and "diagnostic" purposes, a PCL-R score of 30 typically indicates that the individual is highly psychopathic, perhaps warranting the label "psychopath." Note, however, that this threshold score is somewhat arbitrary, and that all instruments of this sort are subject to errors of measurement. Moreover, statistical analyses indicate that the items measure a multi-dimensional construct, not a discrete category. As Table 2.1 (left half) indicates, they fall into four correlated domains, dimensions, or factors: *Interpersonal* (how we present ourselves to others); *Affective* (how we feel emotionally); *Lifestyle* (how we live in society); and *Antisocial* (our propensity for antisocial behaviors). Items 19 and 20 in the PCL-R and PCL: YV are scored only if the individual has a criminal conviction.

THE PCL: SV

To our knowledge, only one study has used the PCL-R in a large study of corporate psychopathy (see Chapter 9). *The Psychopathy Checklist: Screening Version* (PCL: SV) is more suited for the assessment of psychopathy in the community and the workplace. It is shorter and easier to use than is the PCL-R, but uses the same scoring procedure.[21,22] The mean score can vary from 0 to 24, with a score of 18 being more-or-less equal to a PCL-R score of 30. The average person scores between 0 and 3, whereas criminals on average score around 13. As depicted in Table 2.1 (middle part), the items fall into the same four dimensions found in the PCL-R. The structure and psychometric properties of the PCL-R and the PCL: SV are very much the same. The two scales are virtually equivalent in their measurement of psychopathy. Because we discuss research on adolescent and childhood psychopathic traits later in this book (p. 348), we list the items in the *Psychopathy Checklist: Youth Version* (PCL: YV). It has much the same structure and properties as do the other PCL scales.

The problem is that few human resources (HR) personnel have the experience or training for their routine use. This is unfortunate because most HR persons rely on various self-report instruments designed to measure general personality traits, many of which have

Table 2.1

The Four-Factor Model for the Hare PCL Scales

PCL-R	PCL-SV	PCL-YV
Interpersonal	*Interpersonal*	*Interpersonal*
1. Glibness/superficial charm	1. Superficial	1. Impression management
2. Grandiose sense of self worth	2. Grandiose	2. Glibness/superficial charm
4. Pathological lying	3. Deceitful	4. Pathological lying
5. Conning/manipulative		5. Manipulation for personal gain
Affective	*Affective*	*Affective*
6. Lack of remorse or guilt	4. Lacks remorse	6. Lack of remorse
7. Shallow affect	5. Lacks empathy	7. Shallow affect
8. Callous/Lack of empathy	6. Doesn't accept responsibility	8. Callous/Lack of empathy
16. Failure to accept responsibility		16. Failure to accept responsibility
Lifestyle	*Lifestyle*	*Behavioral*
3. Need for stimulation	7. Impulsive	3. Stimulation-seeking
9. Parasitic lifestyle	9. Lacks goals	9. Parasitic orientation
13. No realistic, long-term goals	10. Irresponsibility	13. Lack of goals
14. Impulsivity		14. Impulsivity
15. Irresponsibility		15. Irresponsibility
Antisocial	*Antisocial*	*Antisocial*
10. Poor behavioral controls	8. Poor behavioral controls	10. Poor anger control
12. Early behavioral problems	11. Adolescent antisocial behavior	12. Early behavior problems
18. Juvenile delinquency	12. Adult antisocial behavior	18. Serious criminal behavior
19. Revoke conditional release		19. Serious violations of release
20. Criminal versatility		20. Criminal versatility

Note: PCL-R = Psychopathy Checklist-Revised. PCL: SV = Psychopathy Checklist: Screening Version. PCL: YV = Psychopathy Checklist: Youth Version. Reprinted with permission from R. D. Hare and Multi-Health Systems. Raters score each item with reference to the formal criteria contained in the published manuals. PCL-R items 11 (Promiscuous sexual behavior) and 17 (Many short-term marital relationships) contribute to the Total score but do not load on any factors. Some researchers use a two-factor model: **Factor 1** = Interpersonal and Affective. **Factor 2** = Lifestyle and Antisocial.

little bearing on psychopathy and are subject to faking and positive impression management by psychopathic individuals.[23] It is possible that clinical ratings and self-reports provide different perspectives on the same construct, and that their joint use may help us better to understand psychopathy. It also is possible that they represent conceptualizations of different or weakly related constructs, albeit using the same name (the "jingle fallacy").

Nonetheless, throughout the text, we will describe and comment on research with self-reports to assess corporate psychopathy, where appropriate. Among the most popular measures are various versions of the *Dark Triad*, consisting of psychopathy, Machiavellianism, and narcissism. See S 2.3: *The Dark Triad*.

Am I a Psychopath?

Reading a list of psychopathic features frequently evokes concern or a superficial flash of insight. "OMG, my boss is impulsive, irresponsible, and lies to your face. Maybe he's a psychopath!" Alternatively, "I'm a risk taker and I sleep around a lot. Am I a psychopath?" Perhaps so, but *only* if a lot more of the relevant traits and characteristics are present.

Think of psychopathy as a multi-dimensional continuum consisting of the interpersonal, affective, lifestyle, and antisocial features described in Table 2.1. The number and severity (density) of these features range from zero to abnormally high (40 on the PCL-R and 24 on the PCL: SV). Most people fall at the very low end of the continuum, with few if any psychopathic features. We refer to those at the upper end of the range as psychopathic; they have an extremely heavy dose of the interpersonal, affective, lifestyle, and antisocial features that define psychopathy. Those in the midrange have a significant number of psychopathic features, but they are not psychopaths in the strict sense of the term. Their diagnosis would depend on the particular mix of the key defining features they have. Certainly, many in the middle range will not be model citizens or very nice people, but others variously are hard driving, fun loving, entitled, aggressively ambitious, seriously pragmatic, or difficult. Some may be aspirant psychopaths, presenting themselves as the real deal, usually not convincingly. Over his career, Hare received hundreds of emails and letters from people who claim to be psychopaths ("the next stage in evolution," as some have asserted), many of whom offer to be research subjects.

For plots of the distribution of PCL: SV scores in a community sample and in a corporate sample, see Chapter 9.

Perhaps They Improve with Age

Research indicates that for some psychopathic offenders, aging is associated with a reduction in their PCL-R score. However, this reduction occurs only with Factor 2 traits and behaviors (e.g., impulsivity, sensation-seeking, poor behavioral controls). Factor 1 traits (e.g., grandiosity, pathological lying, deception, conning/manipulative, lack of empathy and remorse) remain relatively stable with age.[24] We know little about the effects of aging for "white-collar" psychopaths, most of whom tend not to display high levels of Factor 2 traits and behaviors. But, in his book *Without Conscience*, Hare had this to say:

> *In July 1987, in response to an article that appeared in* The New York Times *summarizing my work on psychopathy, I received a letter from Assistant District Attorney (ADA) Brian Rosner of New York. He wrote that he had recently spoke at a sentencing hearing of a man who had been convicted of a multimillion-dollar international bank fraud. "Your words, as reported in the article, described this defendant to a 'T.'...* *In the Frauds Bureau, our stock-in-trade is, to paraphrase your words, the shyster attorney, doctor, and businessman. Your work,*

I think, will assist us in convincing courts to understand why educated men in three-piece suits commit crime and what must be done with them at sentencing. For your interest, I've enclosed some material from this case. If ever you needed facts to confirm a theory, here they are." Accompanying the letter was a package of materials describing the exploits of a thirty-six-year-old John Grambling, Jr., who, with the help of a cohort, defrauded not one or two but many banks into freely and confidently handing over millions of dollars, although the two had no collateral whatsoever.

Rosner's book *Swindle*, and the package he sent to Hare, described in astonishing detail the exploits of a man born into privilege but who chose a life of unbridled, cold-blooded predation.[25] As Rosner put it, "He has littered this nation with broken careers and aspirations. The monetary destruction he has caused can be calculated. The human suffering and psychological damage cannot [be calculated]" (p. 86). Rosner and his colleagues concluded, on the basis of an extensive report on Grambling's family relations, that they had never "seen a more comprehensive analysis of the white-collar criminal mind: the relentless drive to accumulate wealth; the use of people to obtain that end; the abandonment of all emotion and human attachment other than self-love" (p. 361). We encourage everyone to read Rosner's brilliant account of a psychopathic white-collar criminal.

In 1986, Grambling was thirty-six years old, which makes him about sixty-eight now. Perhaps he has burned out, mellowed, or found Christ, as many criminals do. Not so! In 2012, the United States District Court in Kentucky issued a $6,900,000 judgment against Grambling and his companies for breach of contract and "fraudulent and negligent misrepresentation" concerning promises to raise money for the plaintiff.[26]

Hare recently contacted Rosner about Grambling's current activities. His response was that every six months or so, he gets a call from someone who, with variations, says, "You won't believe it, this guy tried to borrow funds/sell me something, it did not seem right,

I went to the Internet, is this him?" With respect to the topic of this discussion, Rosner made an interesting comment: "Sad because some people are wired in an unfortunate way that just does not change, which, I suspect, may be an observation consistent with your work." [27]

DISCUSSION QUESTIONS

- Do you know anyone who seems to display psychopathic-like features?
- What features have you observed in a given individual?
- Do you know any people whose psychopathic features decreased with age?
- What psychopathic features did *not* change or mellow in Grambling as he aged?

S 2.1
Nature? Nurture? Both!

Are psychopathic features the product of nature or nurture? A better question is, "To what extent do nature and nurture jointly influence the development of the traits and behaviors that define psychopathy?" The answer to this question is becoming clearer with the application of behavioral genetics to the study of personality traits and behavioral dispositions.

Behavioral Genetics
Psychologists Waldman, Rhee, LoParo, and Park reviewed twin and adoption studies and found convincing evidence that genetic factors play an important role in the development of psychopathic features.[28] This does not mean that the pathways to adult psychopathy are fixed and immutable, but it does indicate that the social environment will have a tough time overcoming what nature has provided. Nature, and possibly some unknown biological influences on the developing fetus and neonate, provide

the elements needed for the development of psychopathy—such as a profound inability to experience empathy and the complete range of emotions, including fear. As a result, there is a reduction in the capacity for developing internal controls and conscience, and for making emotional "connections" with others.

A complicating factor in understanding the nature-nurture issue is the recent evidence from behavioral epigenetics that environmental events can turn genes on or turn them off. "Epigenetic mechanisms are molecular events that govern the way the environment regulates the genomes of organisms. Epigenetic processes lead to individual differences in appearance, physiology, cognition, and behavior—the group of traits known as the *phenotype*" (p. 588).[29] For example, if someone has the gene (or genes) for a psychopathic feature, it is possible that early childhood experiences or trauma will turn the gene on.

Early Trauma

Perhaps the most logical candidate for the influence of epigenetics on the development of psychopathy is early trauma, particularly child abuse: physical, emotional, sexual, and neglect. However, the dynamics of child abuse are so complex and specific to a particular family context that researchers, particularly those who use self-reports of childhood experiences, have difficulty coming to general conclusions about the impact of early abuse on later psychopathology and behavior.

Several studies indicate that child abuse (physical, emotional, sexual, neglect) is associated with some components of adult psychopathy, as measured by the PCL-R. However, the associations typically are weak and apparently dependent on the type of abuse involved, and on the dimension or factor of the PCL-R. For example, in a study of female offenders, researchers found that self-reported child abuse (physical and sexual) and suicidality were associated with antisocial and criminal behaviors (Factor 2 traits) but not to manipulation, deception, grandiosity, callousness, shallow affect, and lack of empathy (Factor 1 traits).[30] A later study of potentially traumatic events (PTE; childhood trauma), post-traumatic stress disorder (PTSD), and female psychopathy obtained similar results.[31] The researchers reported that the Interpersonal factor (e.g., grandiose, manipulative, and pathological lying) and the Affective factor (e.g., lack of empathy, remorse or guilt, and shallow emotions) of the PCL-R were unrelated to both PTE and PTSD. The Lifestyle factor (e.g., impulsivity, need for stimulation) and the Antisocial factor (e.g., poor behavioral controls, early behavioral problems, antisocial activities) each was associated with PTE. The Antisocial factor was uniquely associated with PTSD symptoms. Other researchers found that childhood abuse among sex offenders evaluated for civil commitment was primarily associated with the Antisocial dimension of the PCL-R.[32]

Similarly, a recent report concluded that early physical abuse was related to the Antisocial factor of psychopathy but not to its Interpersonal or Affective factors in male offenders.[33] The authors suggested that in some cases, "the parents' inability to cope with a child's potentially psychopathic temperament could lead to mutual destructive interactions." That is, it appears that childhood trauma is more predictive of a range of antisocial and externalizing (e.g., acting out, aggression) behaviors than of the personality features of psychopathy.[34]

Disorder or Adaptation

Evolutionary psychology provides reasons for the nomadic lifestyle of many psychopaths: the search for multiple sex partners, the need for new and stimulating people and opportunities to exploit ("waterholes"), and becoming too well known by the community as a problem. Psychopaths engage in many casual sexual relationships that are devoid of genuine, long-term emotional and personal attachments to partners. Frequent liaisons, the use of sex as a weapon, and the callous treatment of intimates are common features of psychopathic individuals, both male and female.

Recent theory and research in evolutionary psychology suggests that there are genetic reasons for such attitudes and behaviors. In this model, psychopathy is a heritable, adaptive life strategy in which the goal—reflected in the early emergence of aggressive sexuality—is to provide genetic continuity. There are several ways of passing on one's gene pool, including the careful nurturance of a small number of offspring.[35] The psychopathic pattern appears to be quite different, but equally (or even more) effective: the production of a large number of children, with little or no emotional and physical investment in their well-being. Some psychopathic men and women may see their offspring as extensions of themselves, but such extensions are self-serving (power, control, possession, welfare checks, and so forth), devoid of real affection and a nurturing environment, and expressed in the context of physical and emotional neglect, and abandonment.

This pattern involves the use of a persistent and callous pattern of deception and manipulation to attract potential mates, a readiness to abandon them and their offspring, and the need to move on to fresh mating grounds. More generally, psychopaths may be the product of evolutionary pressures that, through a complex interaction of environmental and genetic factors, lead some individuals to pursue a life-history strategy of manipulative and predatory social interactions."[36,37]

These interactions may involve a *cheater* strategy (e.g., manipulation, deception, and selfishness), a *warrior-hawk* strategy (e.g., impulsivity, aggression, callousness, violence), or both: a *cheater-hawk*.[38] Presumably, psychopaths differ among themselves (and across context and time) in the relative use of manipulative or aggressive strategies. From this perspective, psychopaths are interpersonal cheaters and social predators with access to physical, psychological, and reproductive success with minimal investment. A brilliant series by the Public Broadcasting System (PBS) points out that these deceptive, cheating, aggressive, and psychopathic-like behaviors are common in many animal species.[39] A related issue is whether psychopathy is a mental disorder or an evolved life-history strategy. Some researchers argue that if psychopathy is a mental disorder it should exhibit the indicators of developmental instability and evidence of intellectual, operational, or reproductive disadvantage.[40] However, it does not exhibit these features of mental disorder. These researchers note, "Although psychopaths differ from others in brain function and structure, *difference* is not isomorphic with *dysfunction*," a point repeatedly made by Hare,[41] who put it this way:

> My view is that psychopathic individuals have an intellectual understanding of the rules of society and the conventional meanings of right and wrong, and know enough about what they are doing to be accountable for their actions. Like Iago in Shakespeare's *Othello*, they choose which rules to follow or to ignore, based on their own self-interest, a calculating appraisal of the circumstances, and a lack of concern for the feelings or welfare of others. They lack empathy, guilt or remorse for their actions, and are emotionally "disconnected" from others. But, they do not ignore or break every moral or legal code, nor do they make everyone they encounter a victim. There is little doubt that many psychopathic features are associated, in theoretically relevant ways, with a variety of brain structures and functions that differ from those of the majority of other individuals . . . This does not necessarily mean that they suffer from a neurological deficit or dysfunction. Indeed, psychopaths might claim that because they are not encumbered by emotional baggage they are more rational than are most people. As a psychopathic offender in one of our research projects put it, "The psychiatrist said that my problem is I think more with my head than with my heart." He did not see this as a problem, and went on to say that he was "a cat in a world of mice."

This unintended but succinct allusion to the evolutionary view of psychopathy as an adaptive life strategy implied that he merely was doing what nature intended him to do. Whatever the merits of this particular view, we should consider the possibility that the actions of psychopaths reflect cognitive, affective, and behavioral processes and strategies that are different from those of other people, but for reasons other than neuropathology or deficit, in the traditional medical and psychiatric sense of the terms.

I say this because it is tempting—for experts and lay-
persons alike—to explain the callous, manipulative, and
remorseless behaviour of psychopaths in terms of "something" that doesn't work properly. Such explanations are
understandable when the observed differences between
psychopathic and other individuals involve brain regions
and circuitry that are related to emotional, social, and executive functions that characterize psychopathy. And it is
not surprising that many observers view clinical descriptions and empirical findings through a prism of dysfunction
when dealing with adjudicated criminals, particularly those
who are violent. It is more difficult to do so with respect to
psychopathic entrepreneurs, stockbrokers, financial consultants, politicians, clinicians, lawyers, academics, and so
forth (pp. vii–viii).

The debate continues, as it always does in science. The standard, but apt, cliché is that we need more research. See the
Appendix for an outline of neuroimaging and psychopathy.

S 2.2
Psychopathy and Lethal Violence

Psychopathy is a major contributor to all forms of antisocial and
criminal behavior.[42] Indeed, sociologist Matt DeLisi[43] has argued
that psychopathy is "the unified theory of crime." However, the
level of psychopathy—as measured by one of the PCL scales—
among homicide offenders is about the same as it is among
general offenders.[44,45] In a very detailed and sophisticated analysis, Fox and DeLisi analyzed homicide data and found that the
strength of the psychopathy-homicide association depends very
much on the *type* and *severity* of the homicide.[46] "In other words,
as the homicide type became more violent, extreme, or horrific
[general, sexual, sadistic/mutilation, serial, multi offences] the
relationship between psychopathy and the homicide sub-type

became stronger" (p. 75). Factor 1 (see Table 2.1) was the major contributor to this association. Psychopaths often described killing "in a casual, matter-of-fact, blame externalizing, almost clinical manner, as if the act of killing was as trivial and mundane as running errands." In a meta-analysis of 19 studies and 5161 male offenders,[47] O'Connell and Marcus reported that *both* PCL-R Factor 1 and Factor 2 were associated with sadism. Sadism "may involve both a lack of empathy for others and willingness to exploit others for one's pleasure or gain (Factor 1), as well as a pattern of impulsive rulebreaking behaviors (Factor 2)."

Cold-blooded is a term many researchers use to describe the violence of psychopaths.[48,49] As outlined by Hare, "Their violence is callous and instrumental—used to satisfy a simple need, such as sex, or to obtain something he or she wants—and the psychopath's reactions to the event are much more likely to be indifference, a sense of power, pleasure, or smug satisfaction than regret at the damage done. Certainly, nothing to lose any sleep over" (p. 71).

These findings are relevant to the topic of this book, not only because of the potential for psychopathic violence (see S 3.2: *Red-Collar Criminals*), but because psychopathic personnel are more likely than others to be involved in the most serious of corporate misbehaviors, such as fraud and embezzlement, and to inflict the greatest damage to others in the organization.

S 2.3
The Dark Triad

In 2002, Paulhus and Williams introduced the notion of the *Dark Triad*, a concept that includes three dark personalities: narcissism, Machiavellianism, and psychopathy. We describe narcissism and Machiavellianism in Chapter 3 of the present book.

In studying the three personalities that compose the Dark Triad, Paulhus and Williams explain, "Despite their diverse origins, the personalities . . . share a number of features. To varying degrees, all three entail a socially malevolent character with behavior tendencies toward self-promotion, emotional coldness, duplicity, and aggressiveness" (p. 557).[50] However, the authors concluded that these personalities are not equivalent. What are the common traits associated with these dark personalities? There is evidence that the self-serving components in Hare's PCL-R Factor 1 (e.g., Manipulation, Deceit, and Callousness/Lack of empathy) are at the core of the Dark Triad personalities.[51] From an evolutionary perspective (see S 2.1), these components are "indicators of a stable and adaptive strategy directed toward immediate rewards and gratification, which, in turn, are associated with reproductive and survival benefits for an individual."[52]

It is important to note that, of these three, psychopathy seems to be the most dishonest, treacherous, and destructive. Although these statements apply to psychopathic individuals in the general population, we believe it to be also true in the workplace.

Supplemental S 12.2 describes several additional dark personality traits.

S 2.4
Gender, Ethnicity, Culture

It is likely that psychopathy is universal in nature, found in all racial, ethnic, and cultural societies, and in males and females.[53] However, some of its behavioral manifestations may stem from differences in the behavioral norms and expectations that a particular society has for its members. For example, many societies have explicit or implicit *expectations* about how women and men should behave. Similarly, some societal expectations depend on its members' race, ethnicity, religion, politics, socioeconomic status, and so forth. As indicated below, factors such as these may influence procedures designed to measure psychopathy. Here, we focus our brief discussion on the PCL-R and its derivatives. Detailed discussions that include other measurement tools are available elsewhere.[54,55]

Gender

Many studies indicate that females (adults and adolescents) score lower on psychopathy measures than do their male counterparts.[56,57] Females may be less psychopathic by nature than are men. However, it also is possible that the difference is due to sex-role expectations and cultural factors that inhibit or modify the expression of certain behaviors, especially those that are antisocial or aggressive. In general, the empirical evidence indicates that the interpersonal and affective (Factor 1) features of psychopathy (e.g., grandiose, deceptive, manipulative, callous, lack of guilt or remorse) are reasonably similar in men and women. However, there are sex differences in the expression of the impulsive, antisocial features (Factor 2) of psychopathy, with females having fewer early behavioral problems, and less, or different forms of, aggression and violence than do males. In their comprehensive review of this issue, psychologists Verona and Vitale[58] suggested that in the assessment of female psychopathy it may be useful to consider indicators "that tap uniquely female expressions of antisocial-externalizing (Factor 2) tendencies, such as prostitution, sexual risk-taking, [interpersonal violence], self-directed aggression, and relational forms of aggression such as friendship betrayal and backbiting." We note that the PCL-R item Promiscuous Sexual Behavior already measures prostitution and sexual risk-taking.

The above differences notwithstanding, a given North American PCL-R score (say 20–30) reflects approximately the same level of psychopathy in females as it does in males.[59] Moreover, adult and adolescent males and females share much the same four-factor structure of psychopathy, as measured by the PCL instruments.

Ethnic/Cultural

In many respects, the issues concerning female psychopathy are similar to those having to do with ethnicity/race and culture. For example, cultural factors, economic conditions and opportunities, high-crime regions, and so forth may help to elevate scores on some of the antisocial features of psychopathy. Following publication of the PCL-R in 1991, some clinicians and researchers were concerned about potential bias against African-Americans and, in Canada, against Aboriginals. In each case, their total and Factor 2 PCL-R scores are higher than they are for Caucasians. However, the psychometric properties, factor structure, and predictive ability for crime and violence are more-or-less the same.[60,61] Similar conclusions hold for a wide variety of countries and cultures.[62] Indeed, the PCL-R and its derivatives are the research standards for the assessment of psychopathy in North America, many European countries, several Middle Eastern, South American, and Asian countries, as well as in Mexico, Australia, and New Zealand.

As a final point, we note that the results of a global survey of psychopathic features and their correlates argue for the broad generalizability of the psychopathy construct.[63] The study involved 11 regions, 58 nations, and 33,016 participants (58 percent females). Because it was not feasible to use the PCL-R or PCL: SV, the measurement scale was a self-report version of the PCL-R, the SRP-E, translated into local languages.[64] Across the regions, the proportion of participants with high self-reported psychopathy was lower in women than in men. However, the factor structure was the same for women and men, and consistent with the four-factor structure described in Table 2.1. As expected, there were gender and regional differences in the prevalence of high psychopathy total and factors scores. In general, the patterns were consistent with expectation, but too complex to report here. It was clear that culture affects the expression of SRP-based psychopathy. However, the pattern of male and female factor scores was similar across world regions, "suggesting some universality in terms of *how* culture may affect the expression of psychopathy."

The Case of Dave

ACT I, Scene II

OFF AND RUNNING

Dave's first day on the job created much excitement as he was shown around the department and introduced to the staff. There was a buzz about the new person who had been hired away from a larger player in the industry, someone who would help them regain some of the lost ground resulting from the problematic new product introduction cycles. Everyone came out to greet Dave and all who met him immediately liked him. He had an engaging personality, good looks, and projected rock-solid confidence, not to mention his strong technical background in the company's major research area.

After introducing Dave around, Frank took him to his new office. "Oh," muttered Dave, disappointed in what he saw. "I thought it would be a little closer to the action," he paused, "and a tad bigger."

"Well, we're growing very rapidly and office space is at a premium," offered Frank, wondering why he was feeling apologetic, "but you'll be moving around soon enough as we're always shuffling staff around. In fact, it's quite the joke here."

Dave wasn't amused, but as he turned to face Frank, he threw on a smile and said, "That's great! So, I better settle in and start being productive!"

Frank returned to his office and continued with his schedule of meetings, report writing, and phone calls. He would pick up Dave around 1:30 and take him to lunch in the company cafeteria— actually a high-quality restaurant offering free food to employees. And perhaps, if he could, he would take him over to the executive wing and introduce him to Jack Garrideb, founder and CEO, if he was available.

The morning went quickly as Frank immersed himself in his work. Marge, his secretary, startled him when she came to the door about 1:15. "Frank, Victoria from Mr. Garrideb's office called; he'd like you to come over right now," she said, adding before his next question, "she didn't say what it was about." Frank picked up his project book and calendar, and grabbed his suit jacket from behind the door, putting it on as he hurried down the hall. He decided to look in on Dave as he passed his office to tell him that their lunch might be postponed a bit. Dave wasn't there, so Frank continued, his thoughts returning to what projects he had outstanding and what Jack might need of him on such short notice.

Arriving at the executive suite, which was at the other end of the complex, Frank went to Victoria's desk. "Hi, Vicki, so am I in trouble again?" he joked.

"You know you're never in trouble when it comes to Mr. Garrideb. You're still his favorite," she joked back. Vicki and Frank started with Garrideb Technologies on the same day, many years ago, and they had been friends since. The company culture was friendly, relaxed, and informal, but the executive wing was always daunting because of the big-company aura everyone thought they had to project to visitors or potential clients.

Jack Garrideb saw Frank standing at Vicki's desk through his open door and waved him in. Frank noticed that Jack had someone sitting in his office, but couldn't see much of him in the plush leather chair. "Hey, Frank, I've just been talking to one of yours," said Jack. Dave got up and turned around. "Another good choice!" continued Jack. "Things in R&D are going to really start rocking if your new associate has anything to do with it!"

Frank was startled to see Dave in the CEO's office. "Well, Jack, we have to keep up with the marketing guys who keep promising customers products that don't exist yet."

"Good luck, Dave; you're now working for the best person in the business," said Jack, as Frank and Dave took their leave.

"Nice guy," said Dave as they headed down the hall toward the cafeteria.

Frank's thoughts were already back on the project report he had been writing when Victoria's call interrupted him. "You're lucky that he was in today; he travels too much."

DISCUSSION QUESTIONS

- Would you visit the company CEO, uninvited, the first day on your job?
- Should Frank be worried or just glad that Dave showed such initiative?

3

What You See May Not Be What You See

Ellyn picked up her small daughter and headed out to work. The bus dropped her and her daughter off at the brightly lit main square where the midday crowds of tourists walked and talked. Her job depended on these people, and she was looking forward to a good afternoon.

A crowd had formed at the corner of Main and First, blocking her way. Winding through the crowd she saw that a game of three-card monte was in progress. Tourists are warned to avoid this swindle, but there is always someone in the crowd who is sucked in. The game works like this: The dealer has three cards face-up on a small table; one is a face card, either a king, queen, or jack, and the other two are number cards. He (or sometimes she) flips them over, facedown, moves them around quickly on the tabletop, and then stops. The dealer, using a nonstop and entertaining patter, invites crowd members to bet on which one of the cards is the face card. Eventually, some onlooker decides that his or her eye is quicker than the dealer's hands and places a bet. No one but the dealer ever wins this game.

After every couple of hands, the onlookers reshuffle and those at the back get up to the front near the table. Ellyn made it to the front. The dealer smiled and began talking directly to her daughter. "You're such a pretty girl; and smart too, just like your mommy! I bet you're going to go to college someday!" This playful chatter continued with others near the front when unintentionally a card bounced over and back, briefly revealing its face. The dealer quickly tried to move the cards about, but Ellyn and a few others saw every move.

"I'm in!" shouted Ellyn nervously. "I want to bet."

"How much?" asked the dealer tentatively, as the crowd moved in closer to see what was going on. Ellyn had her rent money with her, and doubling at least some of it would surely help with the bills. She thought and thought. "Are you going to bet or not?" shouted the dealer.

"Yes, yes, a hundred dollars!" Those closest to the action held their breath. Ellyn didn't look like she had a hundred dollars to her name, let alone the ability to bet that much on a street game. The dealer balked—he would have to double her money if she won—but the crowd spoke up. "Let her play!" some shouted. "Yeah, take the bet!" more joined in. The dealer looked nervous.

"Okay, okay," he said, "show me your money." Ellyn looked nervous. "Go ahead, show him your money," someone said from the crowd behind her. Reaching into her shirtfront, she pulled the hundred-dollar bill out and held it in front of her. "Pick your card," he said, and Ellyn did.

It seemed like slow motion, but in reality, the next few moments happened very, very quickly. The dealer flipped the card Ellyn chose and it was the seven of diamonds; he flipped the one next to it and it was the king of clubs. Ellyn had lost. Then someone from the back of the crowd yelled, "Cops!" The dealer snatched the hundred-dollar bill from Ellyn, quickly folded his card table, and disappeared with his accomplices into the moving horde of tourists and visitors. Ellyn just stood there. She was in shock. Tears welled up in her eyes. "My rent money!" she whimpered. Some in the crowd left shaking their heads. An elderly woman in an old blue coat tried to comfort Ellyn and patted her little daughter on the head. She took a ten-dollar bill from her purse and gave it to Ellyn. A few others did the same, but these gestures of altruism and goodwill could not make up for all the lost rent money or the shame of having fallen for one of the oldest scams around. This con, as with many others, skillfully uses basic human nature against the unsuspecting target.

The fact that between 1 and 2 percent of the population have psychopathic personalities suggests (perhaps almost guarantees) that most of us will come across at least one psychopath during a typical day. However, the ability of clever psychopaths to hide their true nature makes it difficult to tell them from others one might meet on the street. Although we actually observed the events described in the case above on a street corner in a major American city, we lack the information needed to determine if the person is a psychopath or just a crook. For all we know, this is a case of a petty criminal (three-card monte is illegal in this eastern US city) conning the curious and the gullible into parting with their money. While tourists may find that such "slice of life" experiences make interesting stories to tell friends back home, the fact is that a crime was committed.

Are Psychopaths More Skillful than the Rest of Us?

INTERACTIONS WITH A PSYCHOPATH

Our point is that several abilities—skills, actually—make it difficult to see psychopaths for who they are. First, they have a talent for "reading people" and for sizing them up quickly. They identify a person's likes and dislikes, motives, needs, weak spots, and vulnerabilities. They know how to play on our emotions. We all have "buttons" that can be pushed, and psychopaths, more than most people, are always ready to push them (we will speak more about this in a subsequent chapter). Second, many psychopaths have excellent oral communication skills. They can jump right into a conversation without the social inhibitions that hamper most people. They make use of the fact that the content of a message is less important than its delivery. A confident, aggressive delivery style—larded with jargon, clichés, and flowery phrases—makes up for the lack of substance and sincerity in their interactions with others. This skill, coupled with the belief that they deserve whatever they can take, allows psychopaths to use effectively what they learn about a person *against* the person as they interact with him or her—they know what to say and how to say it to exert influence. Third, they are masters of managing the impressions of others; their insight into the psyche of others combined with a superficial—but convincing—verbal fluency allows them to change their personas skillfully as it suits the situation and their game plan. They have an ability to don many masks, change "who they are" depending upon the person with whom they are interacting, and make themselves appear likable to their intended victim. Few will suspect that they are dealing with a psychopath who is playing up to their particular personality and vulnerabilities. In the great card game of life, psychopaths know what cards you hold, and they cheat.

Researchers who interact with known psychopaths regularly describe them as social chameleons. Chameleons, of course, have the capacity to assume the coloration of their environment in order to survive. When clinging to either a leaf or branch, they turn green or brown, using their ability to change the color of their skin to blend into their surroundings. Thus, using nature's protection, they can remain invisible to their enemies, yet can sneak up on unsuspecting insects that make up their diet. They are the perfect invisible predator. Like chameleons, psychopaths can hide who they really are and mask their true intentions from their victims for extended periods. The psychopath is a near-perfect invisible human predator.

This is not to say that most people cannot be charming, effective, socially facile communicators and still be honest—of course, they can. Many people use impression management and manipulation techniques to influence others to like and trust them, or to get what they want from people—very often subconsciously, but sometimes as the result of training, practice, and planning. However, wanting people to like and respect you (and doing what it takes to achieve this) is not necessarily dishonest or insincere—the need for approval and validation from others is normal. Social manipulation begins to be insincere if you really do not care about the feelings of others or you try to take unfair advantage of others. The difference between the psychopathic approach and the non-psychopathic approach lies in *motivation* to take unfair and callous advantage of people. Psychopaths simply do not care if what they say and do hurts people as long as they get what they want, and they are very good at hiding this fact. Given his or her powerful manipulation skills, it is little wonder why seeing a "psychopathic personality" beneath a charming, engaging surface is so difficult to do. See S 3.1: *Using What You Have.*

Not all psychopaths are smooth operators, though. Some do not possess enough social or communicative skill or education to interact seamlessly with others. Instead, they rely on threats, coercion, intimidation, and violence to get what they want. This book is less about them than about those who are capable of and willing to use their "deadly charm" to con and manipulate others. However, if the charming approach does not work, psychopaths readily escalate into both covert and overt intimidation. See S 3.2: *Red-Collar Criminals.*

PSYCHOPATHY AND NARCISSISM

It is important to note that psychopathy is a personality disorder, and that personality disorders are *not* the same as mental illness. At a basic level, a person with a personality disorder has a limited range of stereotyped "solutions" that are applied to most of the problems encountered in life. Those without a personality disorder are able to apply a *variety* of behaviors, depending on what best suits the situation.

Individuals with a personality disorder sometimes have trouble in life because of their limited perspective and somewhat inflexible approach. They have difficulty navigating through a world that does not operate in the one-way fashion they prefer, while those who know them may see them as closed-minded, predictable, and sometimes, unfortunately, annoying.

There are ten personality disorders recognized by the DSMs, including *narcissistic personality disorder* and *histrionic personality disorder*, which are important to understand, as they relate to psychopathy.

For example, narcissistic personality disorder involves an excessive need for admiration and a sense of superiority, among other traits. DSM-5[1] describes someone with narcissistic personality disorder as displaying a pervasive pattern of grandiosity (in fantasy or behavior), need for admiration, sense of entitlement, and lack of empathy.

Narcissists think that everything that happens around them, in fact, everything that others say and do, is or should be about *them*. In social situations where this is not the case, they will take action to become the center of attention, such as hogging the conversation or belittling others while praising themselves. Narcissistic people lack other choices in their behavioral repertoire, like paying attention to the needs and wants of others, "sharing the floor," and negotiating with others for attention and feedback. Being narcissistic is not necessarily a bad thing, according to true narcissists, as they see pathological self-admiration as merely a natural reaction to their obvious perfection. After all, "What's not to like about me?" Some narcissists even may complain that their talent and beauty are burdens they must bear!

Narcissists have difficulty learning alternative behaviors; but over time, and with some assistance, they can learn to moderate their behaviors and the negative effect they have on others. The real problem for others is when narcissistic features, especially a sense of entitlement and a lack of empathy, shade into antisocial and destructive behaviors. When this happens, the pattern may be aggressive or malignant narcissism, which is difficult to distinguish from psychopathy.

Histrionic personality disorder also shares some traits and characteristics with the psychopath, the two most salient being emotionality and a need for approval that others find excessive. These individuals come across as overly dramatic, emotional, and possibly theatrical. They sometimes dress and act flirtatiously in an attempt to garner attention. Unlike the narcissist, though, they do not always need to feel superior—they will accept a supportive role, if available, which can provide them with the psychological support they crave.

The number of individuals who can be diagnosed with true narcissistic (only 1 percent of the general population) or histrionic (2 to 3 percent) personality disorders is small. In fact, many more individuals appear as "narcissistic" or "histrionic" to those around them than actually have these disorders. Unfortunately, we view some psychopaths as narcissistic or histrionic because of the self-centered or emotional features they display in public rather than their hidden side, which takes much longer to discern. This makes diagnosis difficult and often confusing for those with limited face-to-face experience with these individuals. Even psychologists or psychiatrists trained in the diagnosis of personality disorders can struggle with differentiating psychopathy from other personality disorders that share overlapping traits.[2] It is only after considerable analysis that the other features that define the psychopathic syndrome can be discerned beneath the overt narcissism and drama.

Note: The above is a simplified explanation of personality disorders. We direct interested readers to the DSM-5 for a more complete discussion of similarities and differences among personality disorders.

The Psychopath in Motion

Psychopaths are master manipulators and game players; they will use every trick in the book to achieve their goals. The traits and characteristics noted by Hare and Cleckley serve them well, particularly if explained in the context in which they play out in their daily lives. Understanding how they perform in public and how they interact with others—which we label the psychopath in motion—can help one begin to catch a glimpse of the real person behind the charming façade and, we hope, will help the reader mount a defense against their clever manipulations.

We begin by looking at the strategies and tactics used as part of a three-phase psychopathic manipulation process, a natural manifestation of their personality that often is more automatic than consciously planned out.

PHASE 1: ASSESSMENT

Psychopaths like to play games with people. The chance to con and manipulate others is a primary motivator. They often are on the lookout for individuals to swindle or scam, and this first phase of psychopathic manipulation involves identifying and then assessing targets or prey. Most psychopaths are opportunistic, aggressive predators who will take advantage of almost anyone they meet, while others are more planful, lying in wait for the perfect, innocent victim to cross their path. In either case, the psychopath is constantly sizing up the potential usefulness of individuals they meet as sources of money, power, sex, or influence. People who have power, celebrity, or high social status are particularly attractive. See S 3.1: *Using What You Have.*

In the business world, it is relatively easy to spot those in power— big offices and fancy titles are obvious ways to help us identify who's who in an organization. However, do not think that just because you *don't* have a big office or title you lack power or assets that a psychopath might find useful. Are you a secretary who controls access to your boss and his or her calendar? Are you a union representative who can smooth over employee conflicts and difficulties? Are you plugged into the grapevine in your company, and do you have access to information circulated to everyone in the know? Alternatively, maybe you are the person in the mailroom who goes the extra mile to make sure important documents reach their destinations on time. These are examples of *informal* power, which a clever psychopath can leverage to further their larger, self-serving objectives.

In addition to assessing the potential utility of others, psychopaths assess their emotional weak points and psychological defenses in order to work out a plan of attack. Individual psychopaths do this in different ways and to varying degrees because their own personal style, experience, and preference play a role in this assessment as well. Some psychopaths enjoy a strong challenge, such as that posed by a confident, uber-wealthy celebrity or an astute professional or executive with a strong ego. Others prefer to prey on people who are lonely, in need of emotional support and companionship, the elderly on fixed incomes, the underage and naive, or those recently hurt or victimized by others. Although the usefulness of this latter group may not appear to be obvious from a strictly monetary standpoint, their perceived "ease" of approach makes them attractive to the criminal psychopath who weighs the investment in time and energy.

Several psychopathic traits and characteristics are apparent in this phase. On the surface, psychopaths generally come across in public as being at the top of their game, wearing the suit of success. However, they are actually playing out a *parasitic* lifestyle. They prefer living off the work of others rather than their own efforts, so actually being a drifter, moocher, or wastrel is a common lifestyle choice despite a façade to the contrary. They have no misgivings about asking for and often demanding financial support from other people. Sometimes, the target is a family member or friend, but it can easily be a stranger whom they seduce or con into providing food, shelter, and a source of income. Now, it is not unusual, or wrong, for people to rely on the help of others, including public aid, during rough times in their lives, but psychopaths remorselessly use others even when able-bodied and capable of supporting themselves. Not all psychopaths are unemployed, of course. Indeed, we have conducted much of our recent research in businesses and government. However, as we shall see, even psychopaths who have jobs mooch off others in overt and covert ways; they take from coworkers and employers alike.

Characteristically, the economic and emotional impact of their parasitic behavior on others is irrelevant to them, in part because they believe everyone in this dog-eat-dog world is as greedy and unfeeling as they are. They also seem unable to construct an accurate picture of others' emotional depth, wrongly assuming that the emotional life of everyone else is as shallow and barren as their own. In psychopaths' mental world people do not exist except as objects, targets, and obstacles. This is one of the most difficult features of the psychopath's mind for most people to come to grips with (or said another way: wrap their minds around). They truly lack the emotions of guilt, remorse, and empathy. Some might suggest that psychopaths are such effective predators because they are *not* plagued by doubts and concerns raised by a conscience.

In addition to their parasitic nature and lack of an emotional life, there is evidence that psychopaths need considerable novel stimulation to keep from becoming bored. This need, which recent research suggests may be rooted in their brain physiology, often leads them to search for new and exciting opportunities and to move casually from relationship to relationship, and job to job. Most people are able to endure tedium and hard work over long periods in order to do significant things in their lives, such as completing a college degree, apprenticing, or working at an entry-level job in hope of a promotion. Psychopaths search for easier routes to the same ends; they have very poor frustration tolerance. A surprisingly large number do manage to graduate from college or obtain professional credentials (many in our research possess graduate school, medical, or law degrees, among others), but in most cases their credentials are gained less through hard work and dedication than through cheating, getting others to do their work, and "working the system."

This trait is visible on the job, as they tend to avoid tasks that become monotonous or difficult, or that need some long-term, serious commitment to complete. They cannot imagine how or why anyone would work hard—or wait their turn—for anything they wanted. Their need for stimulation is apparent in a penchant for high-risk, thrill-seeking behaviors. Many non-psychopathic people seek the adrenaline rush associated with such behaviors, especially in sports activities, but unlike psychopaths, they typically do so by evaluating the risks to themselves and to others, and without putting others in harm's way. Sadly, for society, the psychopath's need for stimulation shades easily into antisocial and criminal behavior.

Psychopaths have a great sense of superiority and entitlement. Their grandiose sense of self leads them to believe that other people exist just to take care of them and think nothing of helping themselves to property that belongs to others. Because they see most people as weak, inferior, and easy to deceive, psychopathic con artists will often tell you that their victims deserved what they got. Sometimes their sense of superiority is so great that they will say that they are conferring a *gift* by letting their victims support them. This is obvious in the many cases of cult leaders who are charlatans or outright psychopaths, but is visible in more subtle cases as well. This condescending air toward others comes across as cocky and egotistical to many observers, but, as we will discuss below, some may find this behavior somewhat charming, even charismatic.

PHASE 2: MANIPULATION

Following the identification of individuals who may be useful to them and assessing their vulnerabilities, psychopaths begin to weave a shroud of charm and deceit that we have labeled the *psychopathic fiction*. This is the beginning of the Manipulation phase.

Their first goal here is to gain the trust of the target individual. One of the most effective skills psychopaths use to get the trust of people is their ability to *charm* them through ingratiation and various impression-management techniques. They have an engaging manner and make great first impressions on people. With this first

impression, they begin to build an elaborate fictitious persona. We
will go into greater detail later explaining how this is done, but, in
general, psychopaths can come across as strong, naive, dominant,
honest, submissive, trustworthy, worldly, or whatever they believe
will get others to respond positively to manipulative overtures. Some
rely on social stereotypes to help them create a useful façade. For
example, they might foster impressions of a suffering artist, a mis-
understood spouse, a successful businessperson, a celebrity, a member of a respected profession, or a person with connections to the
rich, the famous, or the infamous.

Granted, some psychopaths lay the charm on too thick, coming
across as glib, superficial, and unconvincing. However, the truly
talented ones have raised their ability to charm people to that of an
art, even priding themselves on (and often bragging about) their
ability to fool people by presenting a fictional self that is convincing.
Psychopaths do naturally what some politicians, salespersons, and
promoters have to work hard to achieve, such as getting people to
believe what they say. In criminal cases, it is sometimes only after
the authorities uncover some heinous crime or masterful deceit that
they question a psychopath's charming mask of sincerity, integrity,
and honesty. In less dramatic cases, it may still take a lot of daily
exposure before the façade becomes transparent to a few studious
observers, but this rarely happens with most people with whom they
interact as their targets become more and more enthralled with their
psychopathic fiction.

What contributes significantly to their success in engendering
trust in their victims is their almost pathological ability to *lie* with
impunity, without any hesitation. Unencumbered by social anxieties,
fear of being found out, empathy, remorse, or guilt—some of nature's brake pedals for antisocial behavior in humans—psychopaths
tell tales so believable, so entertaining, so creative, that many listen-
ers *instinctively* trust them.

One might think that a long series of lies would eventually become transparent, leading to unmasking the psychopath, but this

is rarely the case. The reason most observers do not see through the lies is that many psychopathic lies serve both to allay the doubts or concerns of the victim and to bolster the psychopathic fiction. Their often theatrical, yet convincing stories reinforce an environment of trust and genuine delight, leading most people to accept them exactly as whom they appear to be—and almost unconsciously excuse any inconsistencies they might have noted. If someone challenges them or catches them in a lie, psychopaths are not embarrassed. They simply change or elaborate on the story line to weave together all the misarranged details into a believable fabric. Well-practiced oral communication skills make this endless stream of disinformation seem believable, sensible, and logical. Some psychopaths are so good at this that they can create a veritable Shangri-La view of their world in the minds of others, a view that they almost seem to believe themselves.

Surprisingly, psychopaths can lie convincingly to people who already know the truth about what they are saying. Victims often come to doubt their *own* knowledge of the truth and change their *own* views to believe what the psychopath tells them rather than what they know to be true. Such is the power of psychopathic manipulation. Some psychopaths are proud of this expertise, making fun of their victims' gullibility and often bragging about how they fooled this person and that person. To give the devil his due, in many cases, this self-praise is justified.

It is not clear to researchers whether psychopaths lie because it is an effective tactic to get what they want or the act of lying itself is pleasurable, or both. It could be that psychopaths fail to learn the importance of honesty in their youth, and learn, instead, the utility of lying to get what they want from others. However, in the typical child, lying and storytelling lessen with age, while psychopaths continue through adulthood. They do not see the value of telling the truth over lying unless it will help get them what they want; it is a business decision.

The difference between psychopathic lies and those told by others is that the latter typically are less calculated and destructive. They also are far less pervasive (you may only tell an occasional lie) than psychopathic lies. For example, men trying to talk a woman into going on a date, adolescents working their parents over to obtain permission to go to a party, a businessman trying to close a deal, and a politician trying to get elected may use a variety of lies (white and black lies) to attain their goals. However, unlike psychopaths, cynical, facile lying is not an integral, systemic part of their *personality*, and it does not coexist with the other features that define psychopathy.

Another characteristic of psychopaths is an ability to avoid taking responsibility for things they do that go wrong; instead, they blame others, circumstances, personality clashes, fate, and so forth. They have an impressive supply of excuses for why *they* are not to blame for anything that they have said or done to hurt someone else. Interestingly, pointing the finger at others can also serve their manipulative plan well, especially if well executed, as it can be used to elevate their own image while spreading disparaging information about rivals and detractors. They do this by positioning their blame of others as a display of loyalty to the listener. That is, psychopaths appear to be helping or protecting the individual from harm by passing the blame on to a third party. In many organizations, there are coworkers who distrust the company or are angry about something that happened to them. By joining in blaming of the system, the company, or even society as a whole, for things that have gone wrong, psychopaths can garner support for their own agenda.

Not surprisingly, even those psychopaths who admit to involvement in a crime will minimize the negative impact on the victims and may even blame them for their own misfortune, offering convincing reasons why they got what they deserved!

As the manipulation phase forms the bulk of the psychopath's machinations, we will spend considerable time in subsequent chapters drilling down into the strategies and tactics that they use.

PHASE 3: ABANDONMENT

Once psychopaths have drained all the value from their victim, they abandon that victim and move on to someone else. Abandonment is typically abrupt—the psychopath just disappears one day—and it often occurs without the current victim even realizing the psychopath has been looking for someone new to use.

In crimes such as identity theft, credit card fraud, and construction swindles, the psychopath typically reappears with a new identity in another geographic location to prey on new victims. The arrival of the Internet has made the psychopathic criminal's life easier, as running and hiding occur at the flip of a switch, and targets are plentiful, readily accessible, and anonymous.

To be able to abandon people in such a callous and harmful manner, one must be immune to the feelings of those one hurts. Psychopaths can easily do this because they develop poor or weak emotional and social attachments with others. Most people feel at least a twinge of guilt or regret if they have hurt someone. Psychopaths have only a vague appreciation of these concepts, and sometimes find the idea of guilt or remorse an amusing weakness the rest of us possess—something that they can use to their advantage. It also makes it easy for psychopaths to move others around as if they were objects or pawns. Psychopaths are better at understanding the intellectual or cognitive lives of others than they are at understanding their own emotional life. Consequently, people have value only for what they can provide. Once used, discard them.

Over the course of their lifetime, the Assessment-Manipulation-Abandonment process leads to predictable outcomes. First, psychopaths have many short-term relationships over the course of their lives. They may approach many individuals offering "commitment," but then leave when their usefulness has expired. This results in a series of traditional and common-law marriages, short-term live-in relationships, and so forth. They often leave behind a trail of jilted lovers, possibly abused ex-spouses, and unsupported children. Occasionally, this pattern of behavior leads to a reputation as a "player," and some psychopaths will even promote these reputations themselves to build up their status and mystique. Unfortunately, for the psychopaths' partners, these relationships are one-sided and often plagued by intimidation, abuse, and violence. Sadly, as many as one in five persistent spouse abusers have psychopathic personalities. Many avoid prison by taking part in court-mandated treatment programs that do them or their partners no good. Others quite effectively manipulate attorneys, judges, therapists, and court-appointed guardians and get away scot-free.

Second, despite the claims to the contrary, psychopaths typically do not have practicable long-term career or life goals. Rather, a series of unconnected, randomly selected jobs defines their work history. Despite the lack of a real career, psychopaths will claim all sorts of goals and achievements, and weave a career "history" so convincing that others believe the success they profess to have attained in their lives. In the business world, these fictitious achievements find their way into a memorialized résumé filled with self-generated letters of commendation (using the names of friends as references) and fake awards. Even psychopaths who choose a *criminal* career lack clear goals and objectives, getting involved in a wide variety of opportunistic offenses rather than specializing in the way that typical career criminals do. This is an outcome of their impulsivity, poor behavioral controls, and low frustration tolerance.

To summarize, first psychopaths assess the value or utility of individuals, and identify their psychological strengths and weaknesses. Second, they manipulate the targets (turning them into victims) by feeding them carefully crafted messages (the psychopathic fiction) designed to build and maintain control. They then drain them of psychical, psychological, emotional, and financial resources. Third, they leave the drained and bewildered victims when they are bored or otherwise through with them.

DISCUSSION QUESTIONS

- Have you ever had an experience in your personal or professional life with someone who appears to be following the Assessment-Manipulation-Abandonment model?
- Do you have any friends who have been manipulated and then abandoned by someone with whom they thought they had a solid relationship? What details have they shared with you?
- Do you know anyone who seems to lack basic human emotions, someone whom you can describe as "cold and empty" inside?
- Have you ever tried to "fake" emotions when a situation called for them? Which ones? Were you successful?

S 3.1
Using What You Have

If they happen to be intelligent, "well bred," and physically attractive, psychopaths can have a devastating impact on the people they meet.

For example, Caroline is a very attractive and intelligent fifty-year-old British woman. Her father was a barrister and her mother a successful stage performer. Caroline went to several of the best schools but seldom stayed at any one of them for very long. She got into some minor difficulties on occasion—for example, she was unable to account for some missing money during her volunteer work for a charitable organization—but was always bailed out by her parents. She moved in fashionable circles, where she had many brief affairs.

By the age of thirty, Caroline was part of a pseudo-religious cult, and her "direct line to the saints" helped her to manipulate elderly people into "buying their own little piece of heaven." Later, she met an international smuggler and this led to her first prison term, a three-year sentence for diamond smuggling. She is a delightful conversationalist, exuding an engaging charm and wit that keeps you captivated for hours. Her description of her current circumstances and the events that led up to them has an almost romantic quality. Caroline likes the fast life and loves excitement. For the past two decades, she has been combining those interests as a diamond smuggler, making regular runs between Johannesburg, New York, Tel Aviv, and Amsterdam, and packing thousands of dollars' worth of diamonds on each trip.

Caroline's unusual occupation—simply the latest in a long string of profitable scams and cons—rewarded her in two ways: it provided her with a substantial income to support her lavish lifestyle, and simultaneously was a constant source of excitement. Caroline stated that walking through an airport with thousands of dollars' worth of smuggled diamonds was a tremendous thrill, "an incomparable rush." When first caught, by a married customs agent, she was able to convince him not to turn her in and ended up having a brief affair with him. She later turned him in as part of a plea bargain when she was caught a second time. Although he lost his family, his job, and his reputation, she was unmoved: "He had a good time; now the party's over."

Her only regret was that her days as a runner were probably over now that Interpol knew about her. She had vague plans to become a stockbroker or a real estate agent. Meanwhile, she was working on a scheme for deportation to England, in hopes that it would lead to a reduced sentence. In a letter to a British official about this matter, Caroline suggested that his wife or girlfriend might like a "little sparkling something on her finger," and that she "could easily arrange this for him." The ploy failed, and she managed to avoid legal action for bribery. Her current situation and whereabouts are unknown.

S 3.2
Red-Collar Criminals

In May 2003, I (Hare) was just about to begin an invited address to the Western Psychological Association Conference in Vancouver. The title of the address was *Snakes in Suits: When psychopaths go to work* (a prescient title!). Del Paulhus had introduced me as moving my research from prisons to the workplace. Before I could start, two sheriffs approached and asked if I was Dr. Robert Hare. I confirmed that I was, and they promptly served me with a subpoena. I didn't have my reading glasses on, but could make out the number $250,000. I commented to Del that perhaps he had been premature in where I would take my work. The subpoena was from an attorney in the United States, imprisoned for embezzling money from his client and then killing her to cover up his fraud. I had described the case in *Without Conscience*, and the attorney used this as a basis for suing me because the judge, sheriff, and prosecutor in the case had referred to the passage to support their opposition to the attorney's request for a transfer to a minimum-security facility. The attorney had drawn up the subpoena himself in October 2002, but it was not delivered to me until May of 2003. As it turned out, the attorney had died in December. The court decided that the case was without merit.

I mention this because the crimes of the attorney are in line with recent research on what criminal trial lawyer and fraud researcher Frank Perri refers to as *red-collar criminals*.[3] The term refers to white-collar criminals who commit fraud on a client and then resort to homicide to prevent the victim from detecting or reporting the fraud. Perri presented many cases of this sort of homicide, and concluded that most of the perpetrators were highly psychopathic. Based on an examination of their backgrounds, Perri and his colleague argued that these persons did not act out of character when they committed murder.[4] "In fact, quite the opposite holds true: the capacity to kill without remorse was a seed inherent in the red-collar criminal that germinated when the proper conditions surfaced" (p. 21).

The Case of Dave

ACT II, Scene I

HAIL-FELLOW-WELL-MET

Dave drove around the parking lot looking for a space. He had overslept and was running late. Normally in and at his desk before Frank arrived, Dave swore to himself and headed for the visitor lot, where he knew there would be openings available. Not that there weren't plenty of spaces in the "north forty," the nickname of the employee parking lot on the far side of the complex, but he hated to walk when he could park much closer. *I should have asked for a reserved spot*, he thought, eyeing Dorothy's new Lexus in the "employee of the month" spot right next to Jack Garrideb's space. He knew her reputation as the hotshot marketing associate. *I should head up marketing*, thought Dave as he pulled into the first available visitor's spot, grabbed his briefcase, and opened the door.

Todd, from site security, was making his rounds. He worked the

early morning shift, which suited him just fine. Being a people person, he liked waving and greeting the other employees as they arrived
for work, and at a company like Garrideb Technologies, he got great
benefits—much more than he would have gotten down the road,
working security for some of the other companies in the area. He
spotted the red sports car heading for the visitor's lot and decided to
investigate. "You're a Garrideb employee, aren't you?" he confronted
Dave after noticing his employee decal on the window.

"What? Yes, I'm late for a meeting with the executive committee," Dave said, continuing to get out of his car. "I'm Dave S. from
research; I have the plans for the new product line," he said, raising
his briefcase into the air, "and it wouldn't look good for me or you if
I'm late for this meeting."

"Employees park in Lots B, C, and D, sir," Todd reminded
Dave. "I'm afraid I'll have to ask you to move your car over to the
employee area."

"Listen, Todd," said Dave, eyeing Todd's name from his badge.
"I told you, I have a meeting and it's very important."

"Sir, you can't park here," Todd countered sternly. Dave gave
him a mean look, closed his car door, and started to walk toward the
building entrance. "I'm going to have to ticket you, sir," said Todd,
speaking to Dave's back as he moved away.

"Do what you have to do, Todd. I don't care, and I'm certain
some important people won't either after I present my material,"
said Dave loudly as he walked away. "New products pay your salary,
Todd, don't forget that!" shouted Dave as he hustled off without
turning around.

"Hi, Dave," chimed Debbie from accounting, who made it a
habit to be walking down the hallway toward the lobby every morning, just to bump into Dave. Today, she had already walked this
route four times and was beginning to wonder if Dave was coming
in or not.

"That asshole," muttered Dave under his breath, but loud enough
that Debbie could hear him.

"Are you all right?" she inquired, drawing closer and hoping to engage him in conversation. Dave looked up.

"Yeah, I'm okay, just flew in on the red-eye from the coast," said Dave, as he passed her by in the hall. *He's seen me almost every day for three months now, and he's yet to give me more than a "good morning" and a wave!* thought Debbie sadly, as she walked over to the cafeteria to re-refill her cup.

Dave got to his office and threw his briefcase onto the credenza. Grabbing his notebook, he headed for the cafeteria for coffee. "Hi, Marge," he beamed as he passed by her desk. "Is the big guy in today?" he said, peering into Frank's office and noting his briefcase wasn't there.

"Off-site executive committee meeting; don't expect any of them back until Wednesday. How was your weekend?" she asked.

"Oh, the usual, I stayed late Friday afternoon to finish that report for Frank; probably the one he's giving to the committee at the off-site." *The meeting I should be presenting at*, he thought.

On the way to the cafeteria, Dave always made it a point to stop by every desk. In his brief three months, he had met and introduced himself to almost every employee. He had his lists. There were the losers, of course. *Guess I met another loser in the parking lot*, he thought, chuckling. But Dave also took note of who the winners were, and the wannabes, of course—there were several of them in this fast-growing company.

As he entered the company café, he noticed Dorothy at the coffee urn. *Nice*, he thought, smiling. "So, the employee of the month drinks coffee like the rest of us?" said Dave, coming up behind her.

"Oh, hi, yes. I know, the parking spot," Dorothy said, turning. "It's embarrassing, actually. I'd like to think I'm just . . ."

"I'm Dave, pleased to finally meet you."

"Likewise," she said smiling.

"Can I buy you some coffee?" he said jokingly.

"Sure, anytime."

DISCUSSION QUESTIONS

- What lie did Dave tell Todd? Debbie?
- What possible psychopathic traits or characteristics did you notice in Dave's interactions so far?
- What manipulation phase(s) is Dave in with Todd, Debbie, and Dorothy?

4

Psychopathic Manipulation: How Did He Do That?

The group that had formed on the lawn collectively gasped as the police led Ted, their neighbor, away in handcuffs. Ted's wife, holding their young daughter, was crying and fumbling in her pocketbook to find the keys to the car. She glanced at the neighbors, who looked away out of respect and embarrassment. Ted yelled back to her, "Don't worry, Hon, just a mix-up. Call our lawyer; his number is in my desk, he'll take care of this." Behind Ted and the officer were others carrying file boxes and a computer plus some garbage bags filled with stuff from Ted's house.

"Can you believe it?" whispered Martha quietly to her neighbor, Sarah. "No, I can't," joined Ed, moving closer to the front of the growing crowd to get a better look. Ted was chairperson of the block association that helped to protect the residents from burglars and their children from predators. He attended church when he was in town—his job required a lot of travel. His wife baked cakes to raise money for the building fund and was just a delightful person. No one could fathom the reason for this. "Here comes Ralph; let's see what he found out."

Ralph played softball with some of the people on the police force and checked in with one of his friends, who sat in the cruiser blocking the road just in case Ted tried to flee. "Stole lots of money from his company," he said. "Embezzlement, big time. They think he's been doing this for about two years, and it only came out recently. Apparently he was able to hide everything from them."

"Oh my God," gasped a few folks in the group. This was such a quiet neighborhood filled with professionals, many with small children. It didn't make sense that something like this could happen. "It must be some mistake," offered Sarah, "maybe—"

"I don't think so," interrupted Ralph. "Apparently, his real name isn't Ted," he looked around and lowered his voice, "and Sheila isn't his only wife."

"Oh my God!" gasped the group collectively.

Psychopaths, Psychopaths Everywhere?

Andrew Cunanan, a restaurant employee in San Diego, had moved to Miami and was trying to enter the social scene when he allegedly met famous designer Gianni Versace at a party. While accounts suggest that Mr. Versace might have snubbed him, this is unlikely, given the gracious, social nature of Versace. For reasons not fully explained, Cunanan, who had already allegedly brutally murdered two lovers in Minnesota, a real estate developer in Chicago, and a caretaker in New Jersey, was able to elude authorities by moving to Miami, despite an arrest warrant, newspaper coverage, and a manhunt. In Miami, he approached Versace, who was returning home after a morning walk, and fatally shot him at point-blank range. The police discovered Cunanan hiding out in a houseboat less than three miles from the murder scene. After five hours and several rounds of tear gas, the SWAT team entered and found Mr. Cunanan's body, an apparent suicide. There has been no explanation of the tragedy created by this "spree" killer; there only are questions. How had Cunanan conned his way into Versace's social circle? Was Cunanan a psychopath or "merely" an emotionally disturbed individual whose crimes, though reprehensible, were explainable?

Uncovering the truth behind someone leading a double life is big news, as improved forensics, coupled with more knowledge about psychopathic manipulation, have increased law enforcement's ability to unmask frauds. An Oprah Winfrey program (March 3, 2005) discussed a book titled *Blood Brother: 33 Reasons My Brother Scott Peterson Is Guilty* by Anne Bird. Dr. Keith Ablow, a forensic psychiatrist, noted that Scott Peterson, the man found guilty of the brutal murder of his wife and unborn child, fit the profile of a sociopath (see Chapter 2 for a discussion of the difference between a sociopath and a psychopath). Peterson was able to convincingly present the face of a concerned husband, even participating in the search for his missing pregnant wife, all the while planning a future with his (unsuspecting and innocent) girlfriend. In home movies, he came across as a normal, fun-loving husband and soon-to-be father. Anyone can appreciate the *real* Scott Peterson by watching his television interviews or listening to the taped phone conversations his girlfriend made once she discovered that he was married and that his wife was mysteriously missing. In these audio and visual documents, he shows no apparent concern, empathy, remorse, or even sadness at his wife's disappearance. Despite (or perhaps because of) a major police investigation, he attempted to leave the country, outfitted with new hair color and a pocket full of cash. Clearly, the evidence amassed by the authorities was sufficient to erase any doubt in the minds of those who counted in the end, as a jury of his peers convicted him of the brutal murder and, in 2005, sentenced him to death.

Is it ever possible to discern the potential for cold-blooded violence before it is too late? As far as we know, neither Andrew Cunanan nor Scott Peterson exhibited any murderous tendencies early on. Were there other signs? Perhaps with more information about their personality and interactions with others over the years, their crimes might become less inexplicable. Even so, psychological "autopsies" are more useful for generating hypotheses about behavioral patterns than they are for providing causal explanations of an event. Furthermore, even if family members, close friends, and associates *had* noticed that not all was right with these individuals, they would not necessarily have appreciated the potential significance of the information, and they might not have known how to act on it. What we can say, however, is that even if we cannot predict specific events, the behavior of psychopathic individuals does not occur out of nowhere and seldom is out of character. The problem is that without prolonged and perceptive interactions with these individuals, we typically are not sure what this character is, particularly when obscured by a charming physically and socially attractive exterior.

Merely having a mental checklist of the traits that define psychopathy does not guarantee success in spotting the psychopath. In fact, well-trained researchers in this field of study are not immune from the deceit and manipulation of those known to be psychopathic. This is because psychopaths are very effective at masking their true selves from those they wish to con and manipulate.

Although psychopaths invest a lot of mental energy in identifying and manipulating their victims, they do not spend much energy trying to uphold a mask for those with little utility to them. Your chances of recognizing psychopathic manipulation increase if you do not appear to be valuable or a threat. This puts you in a good position to watch psychopathic individuals manipulate others. With the knowledge of how they operate, you may be able to get glimpses behind the mask.

People learning about psychopathy for the first time sometimes begin to see psychopathic traits in people that they know or have known. Bosses, ex-spouses, politicians, public officials, teachers, family members, and friends often become suspects if they happen to display some of the behaviors that are on Hare's list of psychopathic traits. Students new to the field will begin to see psychopathic traits in themselves, much like doctors in training who sometimes think they are experiencing the symptoms of the diseases they are studying. That said, awareness of one's own tendency to attribute psychopathy to those displaying some of its features, including oneself, is important in perfecting one's skill in spotting the real thing.

Let the Games Begin: Forging the Psychopathic Bond

Once the psychopath decides you have utility, the next item on the psychopath's agenda is figuring out the inner workings of your personality. While this assessment progresses, the psychopath begins to focus efforts on building a close, personal relationship on which later manipulations will rest. Their true power lies in their ability to "psyche out" your personality.

Sales representatives, human resources staff, and other professionals who spend much time interacting with people become good at judging personality traits and characteristics. Psychologists and psychiatrists trained in doing personality assessments can usually see a bit more of the underlying personality dynamics. So do poker players looking for "tells" leaked by other players. But to their credit, psychopaths have the deserved reputation of being good judges of the personalities of others—perhaps because they work hard at it— and have the uncanny ability to project the most effective persona, depending on the situation, to get what they want. How do they do it? To psychopaths, your face, words, and body language are your autobiography, printed in large type. See S 11.2: *Politics and Poker: A License to Lie.*

Personality: The Three Faces of You

To understand how psychopaths manage to manipulate people so easily, it is fruitful to explore some basics about personality. There are many books and theories about personality, its development, and the ways in which it differs from person to person and reveals itself in one's behavior. However, regardless of the particular theory of personality favored, there are three common ways to experience your personality. All are relevant to understanding psychopathic manipulation, because in addition to being astute students of human nature, psychopaths are willing to use what they have learned for their own selfish purposes. They may not all have textbook learning about personality theory, but they have an intuitive feel that they put to good use: they use their knowledge of personality to control your view of them and ultimately to control you. The clever psychopath has three avenues of attack.

PRIVATE SELF

First, there is the internal or *private* personality—the "me" that we experience inside ourselves. Our private or inner personality is complex and made up of our thoughts, attitudes, perceptions, judgments, drives, needs, preferences, values, and emotions. Our private self also includes our fantasies, hopes, and ambitions, all positive traits and characteristics that we believe truly represent who we are. We want others to appreciate these traits, and we can get very upset if someone suggests they are not true.

Our private self also includes personal characteristics we *do not* like, which, typically, we do not want others to see. While we may try to improve some of these characteristics, we would just prefer to ignore some others altogether. These unpleasant or darker traits include harmful things we do to people, illicit or violent thoughts and fantasies we have, our general insecurity, greed, and illusions about our place in the world. Getting angry and losing control, being excessively rude or annoying to others, acting coarsely to those around us, and being depressed or despondent are examples of things we might do that reflect the darker (but normal) side of our personality. During a typical day, we spend quite a lot of mental and emotional energy building up and enhancing the positive or bright side of our private self and minimizing or controlling the dark side. In fact, to preserve our internal emotional balance and to avoid excessive anxiety, we *need* to believe that our positive self-evaluations are accurate, and we will invest energy in fighting doubts as they arise.

As long as our self-image is mostly positive, and we accept the less positive side of ourselves as a normal part of being human, we conclude that we are okay people. Feeling all right about oneself comes across as self-confidence and inner strength.

PUBLIC SELF

Second, there is the projected or *public* personality, sometimes called the persona—the "me" that we want others to see, the "self" that we present to others when we are in public. Your public self is how you want those around you to see "you." Your persona is a subset of your private self—a carefully edited version, to be sure, of your private personality that you reveal to others in order to influence how they see (and judge) you. Anyone who has ever tried to make a positive impression on another—perhaps on a date or during a job interview—understands how difficult it can be to maximize the positives and minimize the negatives of your personality. Despite our best efforts to control what we reveal to others, we do unintentionally reveal private personality traits to others on occasion, but, overall, our persona reflects the personality we want others to see.

REPUTATION

This brings us to the third view of personality: how *others* view and describe *us*. This is the *reputation* others attribute to us based on their interactions with us. Unfortunately, despite our best efforts to present a positive persona, people form their own opinions, both correct and mistaken, based on what we do, how we look, the clothes we wear, and whether they agree with our values and beliefs. This all filters through their *own* biases, stereotypes, likes, and dislikes.

Unfortunately, the filters people use to evaluate us may distort the picture people get of who we really are. The problem is that all of us form first impressions of others very quickly, perhaps during the first seconds of meeting someone for the first time. Once formed, we solidify these first impressions by filtering out new information that contradicts the early impressions, and preferentially let in supportive information. The people we like right off become even more likable, and those we do not care for remain so. For example, you may feel an affinity for those of a similar religion or political party and generalize this to other aspects of their makeup. Feeling affinity for someone makes us more accepting of the things we like about him or her, and more forgiving of those things that we might dislike. Consistency between a person's words and deeds also plays an important role in reinforcing his or her reputation. Consistency leads us to see people as honest—even if we do not totally agree with their views—while inconsistencies we notice may leave us wondering about them. All of these filtered perceptions cause problems, of course, *if we misjudged the persona of a person when forming a first impression.*

In an ideal world, all three views of the personality would line up. We would be happy with our private self, feel comfortable revealing it through our persona, and feel safe in the knowledge that those with whom we interact come to know us for who we truly are. However, the world is not such a perfect place and people are not perfect beings. The best that we can hope for in most social situations is that our persona reflects the things we want to share with others, and that observers are open-minded enough that their attributions about us, and our reputation, are accurate.

Mind Tricks

As a psychopath interacts with you, he carefully assesses your persona, which paints a picture of the traits and characteristics you value in yourself. Your persona may also reveal, to an astute observer, insecurities or weaknesses hiding in your private self. The psychopath will then gently test the inner strengths and needs that are part of your private self and eventually seduce you (through words and deeds) into a psychopathic relationship or bond using four key messages.

MESSAGE ONE

The first message is that the psychopath likes and values the strengths and talents presented by your persona. In other words, the psychopath positively reinforces your self-presentation, saying, in effect, *I like who you are.* Reinforcing someone's persona is a simple, yet powerful, influence technique, especially if communicated in a convincing and charming manner. Unfortunately, many people we deal with in our personal and professional lives are so self-absorbed and narcissistic that they rarely see our persona because of the preoccupation they have with their own. So finding someone who actually pays attention to us, who *really* appreciates and "sees" us, is refreshing; it validates who we are and makes us feel special. The psychopath quickly fulfills this need and we begin to let down our guard.

MESSAGE TWO

We invest considerable mental energy in presenting our persona every time we interact with someone. Still, behind our outward presentation, and sometimes mixed in with it, are aspects of our private self, both positive and negative, that we like to *keep* private. We rarely want to share parts of our private self with business associates and acquaintances; we reserve this for close friends and serious relationships. However, the psychopath, on meeting us for the first time, can often surmise some of the issues or concerns that exist in our private self. The psychopath uses this information to craft a fake persona—a mask—that mirrors or complements these characteristics. To do this, the psychopath subtly, through clever banter, begins to share bits of personal information, seemingly letting down his or her *own* guard with us. These conversations resonate with us because someone is sharing personal details that reflect values, beliefs, and issues *similar to our own*. The psychopath seems to trust you (and you are a trustworthy person, are you not?). The psychopath's second, powerful message is *I am just like you.*

MESSAGE THREE

The psychopath takes advantage of the fact that in the real world meeting someone who shares our personal values, beliefs, and life experiences is not very common, so it is wonderful when it does occur. It is so much easier to open up to someone like this, and soon we are sharing more and more of our inner thoughts and feelings. To our great pleasure, we want to believe that this person understands us at a much *deeper* level than anyone else we have met. Having parts of our private self understood and accepted by someone means we can relax, let down our guard, and begin to trust that *this* person is different— he or she truly likes us for who we *really* are, behind our own mask or persona. Happily and with relief, consciously and subconsciously, we conclude that the psychopath will not pose a psychological threat; in effect, the psychopath's third message is *Your secrets are safe with me.* Safety or security is one of our most basic psychophysical needs; the psychopath willingly fulfills this need.

MESSAGE FOUR

When the psychopath convinces us that he or she understands and accepts our weaknesses and personal flaws, then we begin to believe in the potential of the relationship to go further; we believe this person will be a true friend. True friends, of course, share information—often intimate information—about themselves with each other. Relationships develop and mature as people share more and more of their private lives with their partners, including their inner desires, hopes, and dreams. Some of it is personal, other topics are mundane, but all of it is relevant to manufacturing a picture that fulfills our deep psychological needs and expectations. The psychopath is all too ready and willing to fulfill these needs. Because a psychopath—our new true friend—is an excellent communicator, she easily picks out topics that are important to us and reflects sympathetic points of view, sometimes complete with enthusiasm or "emotion" to reinforce the spoken words. The psychopath uses glib verbal and social skills to build a firm *reputation* in our mind of someone whose strengths we wish we had and weaknesses we understand. The deep, psychological bond that results capitalizes on our inner personality, holding out the promise of greater depth and possibly intimacy, and offering a relationship that is special, unique, equal—forever. This is not easy to carry out, but the psychopath exerts notable effort communicating that she is *exactly* the person we have been looking for. The psychopath's fourth message is *I am the perfect friend, lover, partner for you.*

Once this is accomplished, the psychopathic bond is in place and your fate is sealed. Subsequent interactions merely reinforce the foundation formed during this early part of the manipulation process.

What makes this psychopath–victim relationship any different from a real bond formed between two people who meet each other and find that they have a lot in common? For one thing, the persona of the psychopath—the "personality" we are bonding with—*does not really exist*. It is a façade built on lies, carefully woven together to entrap us. It is a mask, one of many, custom-made by the psychopath to fit our particular psychological needs and expectations. It does not reflect the true personality—the psychopathic personality—that lies beneath. It is a convenient and potent fabrication.

Also, informed choice is not the basis for these relationships. The psychopath chooses his or her target and then moves in. Friends may see what is really going on, but we tend to discount their observations, often spending considerable energy convincing them that this person is different and special.

And because the psychopathic bond is fake, it will not last like genuine relationships. While genuine relationships can change over time—love may turn to hate, marriages end in divorce—the initial starting point was information and impressions formed at the time. In addition, there is often a commitment (on both sides) to work on repairing any rifts, typically couples counseling. The psychopath, though, will not invest more than minimal energy in maintaining the relationship unless we can offer something *very* special, which is not usually the case. Hence, when the relationship ends, we wonder about what just happened.

Finally and most importantly, the relationship is one-sided because the psychopath has an ulterior—some would say "evil"—motive. This victimization goes far beyond trying to take advantage of someone during a simple business transaction. The victimization is predatory in nature; it often leads to severe financial, physical, or emotional harm for the individual. Healthy, real relationships form from mutual respect and trust and from sharing honest thoughts and feelings. The mistaken belief that the psychopathic bond has any of these characteristics is the reason it is so effective.

This bonding can take place very quickly, even during the space of one cross-country airplane ride. There are two payoffs: the psychopath wins the immediate game by gaining the person's trust, and the victim, now in the grip of the psychopath's power, will soon give up whatever the psychopath requests or demands.

We have worked with many individuals involved in long-term relationships with psychopaths. Many referred to their psychopathic partners as their "soul mates" and reported how much they believed they had in common with the psychopath. The more they interacted with the psychopath, the more they felt drawn in or mesmerized by the façade. It is even more disturbing to hear some victims' reports—especially if their partners already had cut them loose during the Abandonment phase—that they *miss* the relationship and want the psychopath *back* in their lives. It is just so difficult for many to believe the relationship never really existed, that they were ensnared in a one-sided, dysfunctional, destructive psychopathic bond.

DISCUSSION QUESTIONS

- Consider your public self, your private self, and your reputation: What would you share with a close friend or partner?
- What would you not share?
- Have you ever shared something personal that you later wished you had not?

The Case of Dave

ACT II, Scene II

PLUCKING THE APPLE

The sun had long set and the cleaning staff had all left the building. Dorothy enjoyed her work and putting in long hours did not bother her. She sat hunched over her laptop studying the recent report from the focus groups on the new project. She liked what she read and smiled to herself. Garrideb had always supported "skunk works" by their top employees, and Dorothy's recent promotion gave her the authority to proceed. Engrossed in her thoughts, she had not noticed what time it was.

"Burning the midnight oil again," came a voice from the doorway.

"Oh!" She jumped, turning around. "Dave, you startled me!"

"Sorry, just passing through and saw your light on," he said, approaching. "Must be something good, judging by your concentration."

"Oh, just something I'm playing with," she said, nervously shuffling some papers on her desk.

"Personal business? On company time?" he joked.

"Hardly. More like company business on personal time." She smiled back playfully.

"And I thought I was the only one overworked here," he said, leaning over her desk to take a look at her computer screen.

"Sorry, can't look," she said, lowering her screen to block Dave's view.

"Excuse me," he said, pretending to pout and backing off. "I thought you trusted me! We've known each other for a month now—and I always buy you coffee in the morning."

"The coffee is free, Dave. You're going to have to do better than that," she quipped.

Dorothy and Dave had gotten to know each other pretty well since he first approached her in the cafeteria. The morning coffees had turned into the occasional lunch, and they had drinks together once after a company function. They shared stories about the company and laughed about some of the more colorful staff, but nothing out of the ordinary or inappropriate. Dorothy's focus was always on her work and career, and her dad's advice about not mixing business with pleasure was etched in her mind. Not that she didn't find Dave attractive—all the women did—but she really didn't know much about his personal life, and felt that she should never cross that line.

"Do you really think they're going to support you on this?" he asked probingly.

"Well, Jerry said he would consider anything I come up with as long as I have the data."

"Yes, but Jerry's not the decision-maker here," countered Dave.

"Well, who is, you?" she laughed.

"Frank's really the one you have to convince. He's the roadblock here, you know. He only likes ideas he comes up with, and regardless of what marketing says, unless development approves it, it's history. Jerry just doesn't have the in with the big boys like Frank. Frank will quash it the first chance he gets."

"I think he'll like my idea," she said, feeling a bit defensive, "and Jerry will make a good pitch for it."

"I would line up a few more ducks before I float anything to Jerry," Dave suggested in a paternalistic tone.

"So I guess Frank hasn't liked any of your ideas yet," she said pointedly. "You've been here a long time by Garrideb standards; what's your track record?"

"Boy, you get feisty at times, don't you," said Dave, defusing the growing tension in the room.

"Sorry, it's just that I've been working on this for over a month now, and I don't want to think that politics is going to stand in the way."

"This is a big company now, Dorothy. There's going to be politics. And," he said, interrupting her before she could respond, "you're not very comfortable with things political, I'd say."

"We're not all big shots like you, Dave. I'll get this through on my own."

"I'm just suggesting that sometimes it's wise to work with others. One hand washes the other, you know."

"Please," she said, dragging the word into two syllables and rolling her eyes. "I know, you're going to make me an offer I can't refuse, right?" she said, turning back to her computer screen.

"Well, maybe . . ."

DISCUSSION QUESTIONS

- What aspects of Dorothy's personality (public, private, reputation) can you discern?
- What manipulation techniques is Dave using on Dorothy?
- What "messages" is he sending her?

5

Enter the Psychopath, Stage Left

Lawrence took the collection plates down the stairs to the church basement. He poured the money onto the table in the kitchen and the committee members began separating the bills and coins into piles for counting and depositing in the safe. The normally talkative members of the collections committee always grew silent as they counted. When everyone finished, the committee members rotated two positions to the left around the table in the church's kitchen and then recounted the piles of bills and coins for accuracy. They collected the totals, written on small notes, and handed them to the new church treasurer, who made the entries into the ledger.

As the group rolled the coins into paper wrappers, the treasurer added up the numbers. "This is a good week; there's enough to cover the mortgage payment and utilities, plus some left over for the restoration fund."

"Amen," sighed the others. This had been a rough month for the parish. Many were shocked about what had happened, but all had come to the painful realization that they had been taken in by one of their own.

The detectives had explained to the congregation during a parish meeting that they were victims of what experts call an "affinity" fraud—a deception in which a person uses the appearance of shared personal beliefs and values to con a group into investing in phony business deals. Sam had been that person. He had joined the church nine months earlier and had become an active parishioner. He was bright, well liked, and, above all else, trusted. So much so that several members had invested their own money in some business deals he had going. These "opportunities" seemed safe and profitable. The early dividends were sizable—and had been for some time, judging by the high-quality clothes Sam wore, the luxury car he drove, and the big house he owned across town.

Sam's approach was always the same, according to the detectives. He would move into town, join a church or temple with a large congregation and several donation-funded community outreach programs, and then become increasingly active as a volunteer. Newcomers always attract attention and stimulate curiosity, and Sam's seemingly endless energy, unwavering sincerity, and positive outlook led many parishioners to seek him out for friendship. Conversations would naturally turn toward how he made a living, and Sam would share his story. In so many words, Sam explained that he was once a high-flying investment banker who realized the shallowness of his chosen profession only after his young wife and infant daughter died in a horrible car accident. His resulting bout with depression, alcohol, and pills finally led him to understand the Creator had something more in store for his life. Sam quit his job and moved out of his fancy penthouse apartment to fulfill his newly found purpose. Because he continued to do well with his investments, he didn't have to work, but could dedicate his life to helping others, and give back to the community in the name and spirit of his lost family.

Eventually, folks from the parish approached Sam, seeking personal financial advice. Some invested in the programs he managed, and after the dividends started coming in, many more followed. His obvious skill at managing money made him a natural candidate for church treasurer. Soon the congregation voted to invest money from the building fund and the after-school tutoring program in Sam's programs. They had grown tired of no-interest savings accounts and high-interest loans eating away at their weekly intake from parishioners. Sam's generosity and willingness to help others was the opposite of all that was bad about the banking industry. Financially, things could not get better.

Then, one day, Sam disappeared. He didn't show up for services, and no one had heard from him for a week. When the mortgage company called to say the last payment check had bounced, people grew concerned. Discovery of the emptied bank account and safe-deposit box led them to call the local police. Few suspected that theirs was the fourth religious group he had targeted during the past three years.

Sam, now living in a different state, clicked the computer mouse on the latest headline about "Sammy the Slimeball" ripping off innocent churchgoers. Sam kept up on the progress the police were making—or not making—in tracking him down by reading the press coverage on the Internet. "We want to thank our generous neighbors, especially those of differing religious beliefs in our community, for their spiritual support and financial contributions in our time of need. Our children's education program and food for the elderly programs have continued with their help, and our treasury restoration fund is growing," reported John, the new treasurer.

Sam smiled as he put on his tie, picked up his suit jacket, and headed out for Friday services.

AFFINITY GROUPS

Affinity groups—religious, political, or social groups in which all members share common values or beliefs—are particularly attractive to psychopaths because of the collective trust that members of these groups have in one another, and they can rely on the common belief system of the group members for an easy cover simply by espousing these beliefs. Most people join affinity groups to associate with those who share their values, beliefs, and interests. Psychopaths join to take advantage of them by hiding within a well-defined set of personal expectations that they easily mimic and that guarantees a large cadre of targets. Religious belief groups, in particular, have the added benefit of often offering forgiveness for past transgressions, which the psychopath sees as a kind of insurance policy against being uncovered. See S 5.1: *"On Sunday he prayed on his knees . . ."*

This type of fraud is disturbing because of the ease with which a social predator can con and manipulate. It also is a testament to the power of style over substance. However, not all members of a given affinity group are so gullible. Indeed, informal observation of a number of such groups suggests that something like the one-third rule may apply. For example, when a con makes his move on an unsuspecting religious group, perhaps a third of its members will see him as convincing or charismatic, a third will be suspicious ("he makes my skin crawl"), and a third will reserve judgment. The interesting part is that when the scams, deceptions, and depredations are revealed, many of the initial opinions remain *unchanged*. Those who were impressed at first still believe they were right and that there must be a mistake or misunderstanding. Those who were suspicious at first now feel vindicated ("I knew he was bad news"). The remaining third still are on the fence ("what happened?").

Most organizations not created primarily to foster a shared belief system offer greater challenges to the psychopath because of the great diversity of members and the complexity of relationships. When trying to manipulate several people simultaneously in these organizations, there is a risk that someone will suspect the truth, raise doubts, and put in jeopardy the psychopath's plans. Because it takes a lot of effort to maintain multiple façades in a group, each one custom-designed for the intended victim, many psychopaths focus their manipulations on one person at a time or affinity groups (where there are more similarities than differences). Some psychopaths, however, *enjoy* the challenge of running several different deceits concurrently and are adept at assuring that their victims never share information with other targets, or better yet, never even meet one another.

FORENSIC SETTINGS

Administrators and staff in prisons and psychiatric hospitals are painfully aware of how psychopaths operate in groups. In these structured settings, it takes little time for psychopaths to figure out the two main dynamics in the power structure—inmates versus guards and patients versus doctors or staff. Given this knowledge, they effectively make use of the role expectations of the different players. For example, some psychopaths are able to manipulate prison officials to get themselves transferred to a forensic hospital, where they believe—often mistakenly—that they will enjoy more freedoms. The more creative ones can fake psychological test scores—some psychopaths are as test-wise as many psychologists and psychiatrists—in order to convince staff that they are "crazy" and do not belong in prison. Once in the hospital, they manage to manipulate and control some of the forensic hospital staff and the other patients. In many cases, the psychopath is so troublesome that staff do all they can to arrange a transfer back to prison, often a difficult task.[1]

BUSINESS SETTINGS

Business organizations pose the next level of challenge for the psychopath. They are different from affinity groups, forensic hospitals, or prisons in their purpose, complexity, and structure. Although they can potentially present severe constraints to psychopaths wishing to misuse coworkers, managers, or the company itself, they do offer tremendous opportunity.

To start, business organizations have a fundamentally different reason for existence than other groups. They combine the labor of many people into a product or service sold for financial gain. For example, a local bakery will employ bakers to produce the pies, cakes, and breads; an office manager who orders supplies, hires the help, and handles the bookkeeping; and salespeople who will describe the various pastries and breads, hand out samples, pack the customers' selections, and handle the cash. Although it is not out of the question that some psychopaths work in a small neighborhood bakery, most tend to take on jobs in companies where they can take advantage of others, make a big killing, *and* hide as well. A neighborhood bakery, usually run by family members, would not offer them the opportunities they require, at least not as long as it remains small and tightly controlled.

However, what if the bakery grew into a major, national player in the baked goods industry? Initially, the owners may decide to open a second shop across town. They will need to staff this one and train the new help in their business processes. They may hire a maintenance person to keep the increased number of ovens and other kitchen appliances running, a phone operator to handle telephone orders, an IT person to handle the computerized ordering and inventory systems, and specialty bakers who can create new and different treats to help differentiate this bakery's products from those of competitors. Eventually, the owners may decide to buy or lease trucks so they can deliver large orders to commercial customers, hire a full-time accountant to do the books, bring on cleaning staff, a marketing team, and so forth. Managing all this growth is not easy. To the degree that all the people, all the functions, and all the equipment work together and cooperate toward the same end, the business will run smoothly and evolve to meet increasingly complex business demands. In a perfect world, everything *would* run smoothly, but this is rarely the case. Without strong leadership and organizational development, our hypothetical family-run business would grow uncontrolled, quickly running off the track.

How does an organization manage growth? Increased size and business complexity brought with it, out of necessity, *bureaucracy*, a model of business that typically involves a lot of rules and regulations in the form of systems, processes, procedures, and controls. The recipe for sourdough bread, which used to reside in the mind of the baker, is now in a "batch sheet." The original owner's insistence on "using only high-quality ingredients" now becomes "following good manufacturing practices." While this standardization of things is necessary for success, it does cause a lot of stress for management and employees alike.

Most Psychopaths Would Not Fit

We doubt that psychopathic individuals would last long, or be very successful, in a highly structured traditional bureaucracy, for several important reasons. First, psychopaths are generalized rule breakers; rules and regulations mean little to them. The sheer number of policies governing how companies must act, as well as the fact that managers and supervisors are responsible for enforcing them, makes them inhospitable to those prone to psychopathic behavior. It is unlikely that they would even consider working for one, unless they knew the boss/owner and could get away with getting a paycheck without actually producing any work.

Second, we know that psychopaths are not team players. They are far too selfish to work with others toward common goals. Effective manipulation relies on three important conditions: (1) the psychopath needs one-on-one access to the individual, (2) the fostered relationship is private, and (3) there can be no means to bring their deviant behavior to the attention of management. In bureaucratic organizations, where teams do much of the work, it would be diffi-

cult to gain such restricted access to useful individuals, and for clan-
destine manipulation and serious counterproductive behavior to go
unnoticed. All employees are *expected* to be productive, focused on
achieving objectives, and not abusive toward their colleagues. Given
that prosocial behaviors and attitudes are difficult for those with a
psychopathic personality to maintain in any consistent way, how
could they possibly survive?

Third, psychopaths have little genuine interest in the short- or
long-term goals and objectives of the organization. Any suggestion
that their efforts should take into account the good of the company
would be foreign to them. They are much more likely to be motivated and guided by relatively immediate needs and gratifications—
a quick score—than by the possibility of uncertain future goals and
rewards, particularly if they require hard work.

Fourth, bureaucratic organizations do not offer an easy means
to hide. Counterproductive work behaviors that are visible to others
and reported to management often are dealt with through human
resource policies. Internal auditors typically investigate suspicions
of fraud or theft. If proven true, these may eventually lead to legal
action by the organization against the employee. Often, termination
and a negative employment reference result.

Fifth, psychopaths do not share the same work ethic of most
other workers, believe in an honest day's work for an honest day's
pay, or value long-term employment. It is difficult to imagine that
a psychopath would work diligently from nine to five in the hope
of becoming manager in five or six years. This does not mean that
psychopaths never work in routine jobs or in trades or professions that would seem to require training and experience. Many
do, but it is very likely that their qualifications are questionable,
their performance self-serving, and their actions may be even illegal. Think of high-pressure sales representatives, predatory repair
people, "pump and dump" stock promoters, Internet scammers,
fraudulent counselors, and shady professionals of all sorts, to name
but a few.

What about the so-called *successful* psychopaths? How do they survive and thrive in a big company, especially one that is highly bureaucratic? The fact is that many modern organizations are prime feeding grounds for psychopaths with an entrepreneurial bent and the charisma and social skills to fool many people. Like all predators, psychopaths go where the action is, which to them means positions, occupations, professions, and organizations that afford them the opportunity to obtain power, control, status, and possessions, and to engage in exploitative interpersonal relationships.

There is the opportunity to make a lot of money and to gain status and power. The psychopaths' ability to take advantage of a company while being in its employ requires more sophistication than the simple social manipulation they present out in public. However, they face challenges.

To succeed in an organization, psychopaths would have to operate covertly, cognizant of the policies, rules, regulations, and official codes of conduct, but able to circumvent them for a significant amount of time. They would have to manipulate many coworkers and managers into believing their lies, while *neutralizing* the negative impact of any coworkers who discover (and threaten to uncover) their lies and deceit. To manipulate coworkers, compliance systems, and management observations consistently would be very difficult indeed, possibly beyond the ability of all but the most talented and persistent. Few psychopaths would have the wherewithal to try it, and those who did would fail quickly. Or so we once thought.

The Corporate Psychopath

To understand the success of the corporate psychopath, we must realize that textbook-perfect bureaucracies rarely exist and in modern times seldom survive. Instead, organizational structures, processes, and culture are always evolving and developing toward an ideal whose picture is, at best, unclear and forever changing. This constant change and uncertainty causes stress for most employees and managers, but opens the door for the psychopath.

Babiak has shown that psychopaths may have little difficulty influencing others even on the job, where their manipulations may attract more attention. We can best understand this in the context of a case. During a long-term consulting assignment, many years ago, Babiak had the experience of working with a psychopath without knowing it at the time.

> *A project team that was experiencing a decline in its overall productivity and a significant increase in conflict asked me to work with them. Some team members had even asked for a transfer to other projects, despite the prestige associated with working on this high-performing team. When questioned by management, the team leader and some members said they did not know what was causing the difficulty. We launched a team-building program for the team members in an attempt to isolate the problems and help the team regain its previous high-performance levels.*
>
> *Interviews with team members, observations from coworkers in other departments and other management, and review of relevant human resources documents provided a preliminary picture of what was happening. Many members of the team felt that one of its members was the primary cause of its problems, but were afraid to come forward. They reported to me, privately, that this individual circumvented team processes and procedures, caused conflict, acted rudely in meetings, and did more to derail progress than to promote it. He often showed up late to meetings, and when he finally would arrive, he had not completed the tasks assigned to him, routinely blaming others for his failures. Some suggested that he bullied, even threatened, team members who did not agree with him. At every turn, he*

undercut the leader's role on the team, who also happened to be his boss.

Some other members of the team felt differently, though. They told me that he was a solid performer whose ideas were both creative and innovative. This group of supporters said that he was a true leader and contributed toward the team's objectives. A few members of the management committee even commented that they thought this person had the potential for promotion into a management position someday. Depending on whom you were speaking with, you would get a different picture of this person. It was as if these groups of coworkers were describing two different people instead of one. The behaviors of this individual and the different reactions of the various team members—the split between supporters and detractors—suggested that something more than mere office politics and interpersonal conflict was going on behind the scenes. However, what?

A subsequent review of this person's record by the personnel department revealed that he had lied on his résumé and did not have the essential experience or education that he claimed to have. The security department also discovered that he routinely took home company supplies of significant monetary value for personal use; the auditing department also found several suspicious inconsistencies in his expense account. The division between the supporters' view and the detractors' view became even wider as more and more information was forthcoming.

Local management reviewed much of this information, but, unfortunately, before it could take any action, senior management reorganized the departments involved, and disbanded the team. The team leader moved to another location and the individual who was at the center of the controversy received a promotion—into his boss's job—and a leadership role in the department. His questionable behaviors were swept under the rug.

I considered this case for a long time after the business relationship ended but was unable to explain satisfactorily all *the discrepancies (only some examples reported here). One day, while rereading a copy of Cleckley's book, I realized that the controversial team member might have a psychopathic personality. My field notes and documents contained many examples of behaviors similar to those mentioned by Cleckley and studied by Hare. Perhaps psychopathy would explain most of the conflicting observations made by so many people so close to the individual. Using the information available, I completed the Psychopathy Checklist: Screening Version (PCL: SV) on this person, with Bob Hare's guidance, just as an experiment. The results were startling.*

This individual came out very close to the PCL: SV cut score for psychopathy—a score much higher than that expected even for most serious offenders. The PCL: SV also yields four subscores that reflect psychopathic features in four areas: Interpersonal, Affective, Lifestyle, and Antisocial. Known criminal psychopaths tend to score high on all four, while those like the reader score low on each one. The individual who caused such controversy on the team scored high on the first two factors and moderately on the other two. This profile indicated that he was grandiose, manipulative, deceptive, and lacking in empathy and concern for others, but also that he was less impulsive or overtly antisocial than most psychopaths. He had not broken the law or seriously victimized others, at least as far as we knew at the time.

During the next few years, employees who felt that they were victims of coworkers brought several individuals working in other businesses to my attention. Business executives and human resources professionals, following public speaking engagements and education sessions about psychopathy, also shared war stories with me about individuals whose behaviors had caused some difficulties at their companies. In some cases, I had enough information to complete the PCL: SV on them. Some exhibited the same profile as the individual noted above, but some did not—they were merely problematic employees engaged in counterproductive or deviant work behavior for reasons un-related to psychopathic personality. I wondered how best to tell the difference.

Over the years, we were able to collect more information on how some of these individuals, now variously referred to in the literature as industrial, corporate, successful, or social psychopaths, interacted with coworkers and management over extended periods. Gradually, a consistent pattern emerged, a pattern eerily similar to the parasitic lifestyle described earlier. Based on all our observations, it is now clear that a small number of individuals with psychopathic personality features are in business, religious, non-profit, medical, legal, criminal justice, civil service, and government organizations. Some highly motivated individuals with psychopathic personalities (as assessed by the Hare PCL-R or PCL: SV) were able to enter an organization, evaluate strengths and weaknesses in its culture (processes, communication networks, corporate politics), use and abuse coworkers, "deal with" opposition, and climb the corporate ladder. How they did it, and more important, why they were so successful, took a number of studies and a bit of time to fully understand and answer. Subjects came from companies with which the authors consulted. When we compared cases side by side, many similarities emerged, with almost every psychopath following a similar career progression. These individuals were able to enter the corporation, adapt to its culture, and manipulate coworkers and executives, as described in detail below and in the next chapter.

Task 1: Enter the Corporation

The initial challenge for any psychopath trying to join a company is, of course, to be hired. Like psychopaths who easily enter people's personal lives, corporate psychopaths are able to join organizations more easily than one might expect. This is because many people are aware of the standard techniques used to screen out underqualified individuals; they are little match for the psychopath's lying and manipulative skills.

Much of an organization's success or failure depends on its human assets: what knowledge, skills, and attitudes they bring to their work; how well they understand the company; how well the company understands them; and how well they get along with each other. The selection process is very important to the ultimate success of the company, but it is not always easy to find individuals who are a good match for the company and its objectives. Likewise, it is not easy to identify individuals who will grow and prosper with the company over time.

The typical selection process involves reviewing the résumés of job candidates for the knowledge, skills, and attitudes needed to do a good job. On the surface, the process seems quite straightforward, but it is not foolproof. For mid-level and lower-level jobs, lists of requirements often come from current employees who exhibit outstanding performance. However, when the job is new, with no incumbents, supervisors and human resources professionals create the lists based on research from other, similar companies. Once there is a clear sense of what the interviewers expect of the job applicant, then interviewers can evaluate the candidate through detailed probing and questioning.

This process is especially effective for sourcing candidates for technical jobs such as those found in research, development, and finance, or lower-level staff positions. However, as one moves up the corporate ladder into jobs with greater scope and less clear responsibilities, the task becomes more difficult. "Strategic planning," "critical thinking," "freedom to act," "leadership," and other variables must be added to the list—and these are much more difficult to quantify. This makes selecting the most qualified job candidate difficult, and "gut feel" or "chemistry" begins to take on more of a role in decision-making. The less clearly defined—or higher level—the job, the more companies rely on subjective, rather than objective, measures, running the risk of misjudging the qualifications of a candidate.

It is common knowledge among executive recruiters that 15 percent or more of the résumés they receive contain distortions or outright lies. Psychopaths are quite adept at creating written documentation—résumés, letters of recommendation, citations, and awards—out of whole cloth. They can fabricate a work history custom-tailored to the job requirements, and back it up with phony references, job samples, and appropriate jargon. This is especially easy in the Internet age as virtually all of the information the psychopath needs to craft a successful application is readily available online.

Psychopaths have an advantage in person as well as on paper. This is most evident during face-to-face interviewing, *exactly* the place where the psychopath shines (see S 5.2: *The Dark Triad and Face-to-Face Negotiations*). They can talk a good game during the interview, coming across as smooth, talented, bright, sensitive, self-confident, and assertive. Their storytelling abilities reinforce their résumé "data," and the whole package they present can be quite compelling. Unfortunately, if the interviewer bases hiring decisions on easily faked résumés and on the ability to convince the interviewer that you know what you are talking about, the company runs the risk of hiring someone who is a fraud.

A further complicating factor is that the hiring process has many objectives beyond merely adding new employees or replacing those who have left. It is very common, especially in rapidly growing companies, to hire people based primarily on *perceptions* of their management *potential* or future contributions to the company. That is, the company hires some people because they might fit the requirements for the next job or beyond, not necessarily for the one for which they originally applied. Unfortunately, it is easy for the unsuspecting interviewer to believe that a psychopathic candidate, because of his or her convincing communications style, may have leadership potential beyond the technical knowledge, skills, and abilities listed on the résumé. A clever psychopath can present such a well-rounded picture of a perfect job candidate that even seasoned interviewers can be caught up in the excitement of convincing the individual to join the company (as illustrated in The Case of Dave).

The role of charm in persuading the interviewer that one possesses the characteristics most often sought in new employees cannot be overstated. When we question managers about the traits they look for in high-level employees, they often state they want individuals who are bright, conscientious, honest, and socially skilled. Unfortunately, these *same* traits were ascribed to the corporate psychopaths we studied by those who liked and supported them. Interestingly, these are also the characteristics victims report seeing in con men and women, before they realized that they were the victims of a scam and deception.

DISCUSSION QUESTIONS

- Have you ever worked with someone who talked a good game, but rarely delivered the goods?
- How did they get away with it?
- Have you ever known someone who initially came across as honest and sincere, but who you later realized was quite the opposite?
- What initially fooled you?
- What tipped you off to their deceit?

S 5.1
"On Sunday he prayed on his knees.
On Monday he preyed on his fellow man."

Bryan Richards wheedled his way into a religious community by convincing its members that he was "one of them." He is a member of a line of distasteful predators who attached themselves to religious, ethnic, cultural, or special-purpose groups in which the members share common interests and typically are very trusting of others who profess to share their beliefs. Many Christian groups, for example, readily open their hearts to any newcomer, especially those who profess to have "found Christ." Unfortunately, these groups often also open their wallets, unwitting players in affinity fraud.

As described by Douglas Todd and Rick Ouston in the *Vancouver Sun*, Bryan Richards, whose real name was Richard Bryan Minard, was a smooth-talking, woman-chasing, Net-scamming evangelist who blew into a small Canadian town with a convincing line that he was a Christian, just like the members of the unsuspecting group he had targeted. "Don't despair. God's always there."

He ran a local low-wattage radio station and described himself as "the rock jock who spins for Jesus." He also ran numerous frauds, including selling members time-shares in resorts that he didn't own, vacation packages he never paid for, and pirating music for his thirty-minute *Christian Power Hour* program. He also ran a Christian dating service, had numerous girlfriends, and "chased the unmarried women." He attempted, and often achieved, "instant intimacy" by spinning a bewildering line of tall tales that many found exciting and fascinating. His checks bounced.

As one of his victims said, "My feeling right now is that if [he] weren't on this earth, it would be a better place." He died in 2012 (cause unknown). One woman left flowers.

Con man for Christ: https://vancouversun.com/news/staff -blogs/con-man-for-christ

S 5.2
The Dark Triad and Face-to-Face Negotiations

Supplemental S 2.3 described the Dark Triad (psychopathy, Machiavellianism, and narcissism), and indicated that its members share several common features, including the callous and unempathetic ability to deceive, manipulate, and control others.

Several studies indicate that the manipulative behaviors of members of the Dark Triad put them at an advantage in face-to-face settings in the workplace. For example, in an online study, researchers[2] asked participants, many of them students, to complete a brief self-report measure of the Dark Triad, and to answer a series of questions about their use of face-to-face manipulation tactics at work. Those high on "psychopathy" tended to use *hard tactics* (e.g., threats and overt manipulation). Those high on Machiavellianism used both hard and *soft tactics* (e.g., charm, ingratiation, compliments, and promises of reward), while those high on narcissism tended to use soft tactics.

Psychologists Crossley, Woodworth, Black, and Hare[3] conducted a study in which pairs of participants (one a seller and the other a buyer) negotiated over a pair of concert tickets, with four issues in mind: ticket price, band merchandise, seat location, and backstage access. They conducted the negotiations either face-to-face or via a computer link (the chat feature on Skype, without visual contact with one another). Individuals with high scores on the Dark Triad performed better when the negotiations were face-to-face than when they were online. Conversely, those with low scores on the Dark Triad performed better during online than during face-to-face negotiations. It is important to recognize that the members of the Dark Triad share a common set of interpersonal and affective features, namely Factor 1 of the PCL-R.[4] These features presumably are most effective when used in front of a live audience. The authors of this article also noted that psychopaths (in this case assessed with the Self-Report Psychopathy Scale-III)[5] were adept at mimicking the facial expressions of the other participant, thus appearing credible and genuine during face-to-face negotiations.

As noted in Chapter 9, self-report measures provide general, but useful, information about the role of dark personalities in the workplace. However, those who interpret such measures must recognize the issues related to their use.

The Case of Dave

PANIC TIME

Frank left the meeting exhausted but happy that it was only 7:00 on a Friday night. Most days he left the office much later. "Another important meeting, Mr. Frank?" asked Marissa, the night cleaning crew supervisor.

"Yes, always meetings. But this one was useful; we actually got some things done." Marissa smiled and Frank continued down the hall toward his office. He flipped on the light and saw the folder Dave had left for him in the center of his blotter. Opening it, Frank saw the report Dave wrote, the printout of the slides Dave had prepared, and the thumb drive with the files. *Excellent*, he thought as he put the folder in his briefcase, added some other files from his desk, and then closed it up. Turning to the door, Frank sighed and thankfully headed home to a great dinner with the family, a Saturday at the zoo with the kids, and a Sunday flight to the meeting where he would make his presentation.

The aroma of pancakes, bacon, and eggs filled the kitchen as Frank served up breakfast for the family. Frank enjoyed this Sunday morning ritual with the kids and loved to spend the day with them, but today he had an afternoon flight and needed to finalize his presentation. He had completed most of it and just needed to integrate Dave's data and then he could get on with the packing. Sally herded the kids into the car and drove off for church, lunch with Grandma, and a return home in time to see Frank off on his trip.

Silence, thought Frank, smiling, as he carried his coffee into the den. The schedule was to have him speak to the executive board's strategic planning meeting on Monday morning. He had worked out the last-minute details with the other presenters during the Friday meeting. He was confident that the board would support his new product proposals—they always had in the past. This time he had Dave's research, which would augment his presentation.

Frank opened Dave's folder, loaded the files from the thumb drive, and began reading the report and looking at the charts. Frank read and read. He studied the charts. He sipped coffee. He opened the folder to see if he had forgotten to take out part of the report. Growing concerned, Frank searched the drive for more files. There was nothing else; he had all the material there on his desk. Frank started getting nervous and then angry. "This is crap!" he said aloud as he picked up the phone and dialed Dave's home number. The phone rang and rang. There was no answer. Rummaging through his briefcase, he found his phone book and dialed Dave's cell phone number. The call went straight into voice mail. Getting control of himself, Frank firmly and clearly left a message telling Dave that he didn't have the full report and asking Dave to get back to him as soon as possible with the numbers he needed.

Frank reread the material, and it dawned on him how familiar it was. His anger slowly turned to fear as he realized where he had read this material before. This was from an article he had read in an industry magazine a few weeks back—an article written about their chief competitor. He turned his briefcase upside down on the floor. There among his stuff was the magazine. He flipped through it to the article. "Oh, my God!" exclaimed Frank as he realized that Dave had taken paragraphs from the article and retyped them into his report. The charts were the same, except he had changed the product labels and the legend to say Garrideb Technologies, and had increased the figures 12 percent across the board. There were no new data, no real projections, and no new product presentation!

Frank realized what he had to do. He logged on to the corporate computer and began searching through databases. He knew he still had the flip charts in the closet from the off-site planning meeting that he had run himself before he handed the project over to Dave weeks before. He furiously emailed requests for information to his staff, hoping that they, being the compulsive folks he knew them to be, were at home working, as well. Finally, he called his travel agent and got her to change his flight to the later one that night. He would miss the cocktail party and dinner, but there was no other way. He had to finish his presentation—his reputation and career depended on it.

Frank tried to sleep on the plane, but frantic thoughts kept running through his mind. When his cab pulled up in front of the hotel, he jumped out and quickly headed for the registration desk. Turning toward the elevators, Frank spotted John, his boss, walking through the lobby bar. Before he could duck into the elevator, John waved him down. "Frank, Frank, glad you made it. We were worried; how are things at home?"

"Oh, John, fine. I just had to change flights because of a family thing. Sally's mother called . . ."

"No problem, Frank, I understand. Look, I really love your presentation. I think it's a winner. You've really knocked the ball out of the park this time," said John enthusiastically, patting Frank on the back and pulling him back into the bar.

"You do?" asked Frank, not knowing about what presentation John was talking.

"Yes, the ideas are so fresh; just what we need to pull us out of this slump and rebuild the board's confidence," said John as he ordered two martinis. "You know, you're pretty sly, Frank. You never mentioned any of this to me on Friday—wanted to surprise me at cocktails before the meeting?"

"Well," squeaked Frank, wondering what was really going on. "John? Which version of my presentation did I send you?"

"Oh, I just assumed it was the final one," said John as the bartender put down their drinks, and John signaled him to start a tab. "I got it from Dave, earlier this evening."

Frank reached for the glass and downed half his martini before he said, "Dave?"

"Yes, he called and told me you had some issue at home and weren't sure you would make it to the meeting. So he went ahead and sent the latest version, knowing you were preoccupied." John paused. "You know, he's really got the right stuff, hasn't he?"

"I . . . I," stuttered Frank.

"And you, putting in a whole slide thanking Dave and the team for their input. A bit much, Frank—the picture, I mean—but a nice thought nonetheless." Frank finished his drink and smiled weakly.

"You look like you've had a rough day, Frank. Would you like another?"

DISCUSSION QUESTIONS

- What just happened here?
- Did Frank have the wrong report?
- Did Dave pull a fast one on Frank (and John)?

6

Pawns, Patrons, and Patsies: Roles in the Psychopath's Drama

"There'll be two of us," said Ron to the host who greeted him at the door.

"Okay, follow me," she said, picking up two menus and indicating for Ron to follow her. "Is this okay?" she asked.

"This is great," said Ron, smiling, as he took a seat facing the door and placed the paper bag under the table next to his feet. The host positioned the menus on the table and removed the extra tableware, leaving two place settings.

"Gloria will be with you shortly," she said, smiling. "Can I get you a drink while you're waiting?"

"Two martinis, one dirty and one extra dry," said Ron, not looking up from the menu. Ron was the best salesperson the company had ever seen. He was a master of the face-to-face sale and had gotten customers who had had long-term relationships with competitors to switch to his company. Ron had a carefree lifestyle, enjoying many benefits at work such as a company-leased luxury car (significantly above the standard allowed for a field salesperson at his level) and an expense account for entertaining clients. Everyone seemed to look the other way when Ron's expense reports came in for processing. Occasionally, the liquor bills, visits to gentlemen's clubs, and other obviously out-of-the-ordinary things were questioned, but with his boss's signature on the reports, there was little the accounting department could do, other than roll their eyes and joke about how the West Coast handled business dealings. The few times Ron's boss, Joe, the regional sales manager, pushed back, Ron simply talked his way around it, promising a big sale down the road. Ron was very persuasive and knew how to play Joe very well.

Joe arrived shortly, a bit out of breath, and found Ron perusing the menu.

"Hey, Ron, you're looking great—sorry I'm late. Traffic, as usual," said Joe, extending his hand.

"Joe, good to see you," responded Ron, rising briefly to offer Joe a firm handshake. "There's a New York strip special today; hope you're hungry."

"More thirsty than hungry," he started to say, just as the server returned with the drinks. Ron indicated which drink was Joe's and waved the server off.

"To another great month," Ron said loudly, raising his glass. They both sipped their drinks and got down to business. Ron pulled out his latest call report and handed it to Joe. Despite the lack of sales for this month, Ron had made a significant effort "beating the bushes," meeting almost daily with potentially large clients. "And here's my expense report," said Ron, handing it to him with a pen on top. Joe pretended to read it, merely glancing actually, as he signed the report. "Thanks, Joe," said Ron, reaching under the table for the bag and sliding it across the floor toward Joe.

Ron waved to the server, indicating that they needed two more drinks as they continued discussing baseball scores, the weather, and Joe's grandchildren. Sipping his second martini, Joe said, "Ron, I have some news for you."

"Oh?" questioned Ron, motioning to the server.

"Ron, I've decided to take my retirement; I'll be leaving the company at the end of this month."

"Joe, that's great. Congratulations! What made you decide?" asked Ron.

"Well, they've offered me a package, and with our last kid now out of college, my wife and I decided to sell our house and move up to the lake. The stress is getting to be too much for me, as you know, and I guess they realized it, too."

"So, when are they going to move on your replacement?" hinted Ron with a smile. Ron knew that Joe had repeatedly recommended him for a promotion based on his performance review and he eagerly anticipated Joe congratulating him on his promotion.

"That's just it, Ron," started Joe slowly. "They're not telling me. I've heard rumors that they want to use the regional job as a developmental position for someone else on the plan. They may rotate someone in from one of the other regions."

"What!" exclaimed Ron, his face starting to get red. "What do you mean, someone from the other regions? I'm the best there is, I know the territory, I deserve the promotion; you put me in as your replacement, right? Doesn't that count for anything?"

"Yes, I know. Of course, I put you on the plan—every year when they ask, I tell them you're ready to move up now, but they—"

"That's unacceptable!" charged Ron. "Who's making this decision?"

"Personnel, of course."

"You know, they have no clue what this job entails. Who are *they* to do this? What does Sam say?" Ron asked pointedly about Joe's boss, the VP of sales.

"I had it out with Sam, Ron, arguing for you to get the job; honest, I did. However, Sam hasn't been able to convince the selection committee. They're hung up on the sales figures as well as some of the other stuff."

"Listen, Joe, let me call your wife. I'll explain to her that your stress is—"

"Ron," interrupted Joe, "my wife didn't make the decision to retire; I did." Joe looked down and then up into Ron's eyes, saying, "Well, they made the decision for me. It's the best for all of us."

"I can't believe they forced you out after all these years."

"Times change, and I guess I have to, too. They're offering to pay for a program, as part of the deal, to help with my problem."

"You don't have any problem, Joe," said Ron.

"Thanks, Ron, but both you and I know I do," said Joe, lowering his voice. "I think they have my best interest at heart. Few people get this kind of support when they go. They really want me to straighten myself out."

The server arrived to take their order, and Ron picked out a special wine to celebrate Joe's retirement.

The rest of the afternoon was loud and raucous, like all the previous monthly lunch meetings between them. On the surface, Ron appeared happy for Joe and talked about visiting him and his wife up at the lake, fishing, and barbecuing. In his mind, however, he was planning his next move.

After lunch, they shook hands and exchanged a big bear hug. "I'll process these," said Joe, picking up the paperwork.

"Don't forget the package," reminded Ron, indicating the single-malt under the table.

"I won't be needing that anymore; I'm on a new path now. Thanks, though, you've always understood. I'll miss working with you."

Ron entered his corporate-paid apartment. "Damn," he swore, falling into the easy chair in the living room. He picked up his cell phone and began dialing. This would be a long night on the phone; time to call in some favors and get some dirt on his rivals for the promotion.

Jack got the promotion into the regional manager position, and was now Ron's boss. A methodical, focused, and detail-oriented person, Jack spent considerable time reviewing each salesperson's performance record and then planned to meet personally with each member of the sales team to establish objectives, meeting schedules, and new performance measures.

Ron had also done his homework: his friends in personnel gave him the lowdown on Jack's performance record (stellar); his friends in accounting gave him insight into Jack's spending habits (which paled against his own); and even his peers in Jack's old region gave him insights into his personal style and family details. As Jack moved through the region meeting individually with the salespeople, Ron followed up with calls to his colleagues to find out what Jack was saying. When Jack arrived for his meeting with him, Ron was ready.

While the others complied with the new procedures willingly, those who knew him waited to see how Ron would respond. Ron's reputation in the company as a "raconteur" had always been a cause of concern among the sales management committee. He had learned from his old boss Joe, an old-school "belly-to-belly" salesperson, how to gain customers and close deals using personal influence and personal charisma, but this style was growing less effective with the Internet's arrival, better-informed potential clients, and a new breed of sophisticated, hard-driving competitors. Sam, the VP, had inherited the Ron-and-Joe team a few years earlier. Knowing that Joe was close to retirement age, he tolerated his laissez-faire management style, but he never liked the fact that Joe protected Ron, covering for him when he missed targets and approving expenditures that exceeded corporate guidelines. With Joe gone, Ron's performance was fair game, and Jack was going to take care of the problem.

Jack and Ron met for a lunch meeting in Ron's territory. Ron started with the sweet approach, trying to butter Jack up with a congratulatory bottle of wine, small talk about Jack's kids' soccer games, and stacks of positive performance reviews written by Joe, miscellaneous charts, and letters of thanks from big customers (and long-term friends). Jack was not so easily swayed. When Jack began explaining how he wanted to manage the region and presented Ron with his new requirements, Ron started pushing back, eventually raising his voice enough to get the attention of other diners in the fine restaurant. He argued that he didn't need any more controls than those previously imposed by Joe, and promised to deliver whatever Jack needed to make him look good in the eyes of top management. Jack had heard that Ron would sometimes get loud in order to get his way, so he decided to hear him out, but then come back firmly. Ron's arguments eventually turned into veiled threats of turning the other salespeople against Jack, legal action, and possible damage to Jack's career.

This guy's nuts, thought Jack as Ron continued his arguments, almost ranting and raving. Sensing that Ron was about to end the meeting and walk out, Jack said, "Look, Ron, I appreciate all you have done, but the industry has changed. We're no longer in the cat-bird seat with our products, and this region—your region—is the weakest link."

"Then you—they—should have fired Joe years ago!" said Ron, finally. "I've been covering for him since I got here. Do you know what it's like working for . . ." Ron paused, and then continued, his voice cracking slightly, "someone who's never around when you need him to close a deal, can't get any advice worth listening to, forced to always cover for him? I've been all alone here, Jack, fighting for the company, and this is how they reward me—with more procedures, more demands, more grief!"

Although Joe's drinking problem had been an open secret in the region, others outside the region did not know, so Jack was taken aback by this revelation. His initial feeling was that this was an inappropriate topic for them to discuss, but Ron's persistence and obvious frustration began to get to him. He listened more carefully to Ron's difficulties in dealing with Joe, trying to apply some of the management techniques he had learned. He stroked Ron's ego and reflected his understanding of Ron's dilemma. By the end of the conversation—once Ron had calmed down—Jack promised to help Ron reorient his sales approach to what the company now needed, and take into consideration all that he had been through.

The conversation ended on a positive note and Jack felt he had accomplished his task. His objective for the meeting had been to turn Ron around or else take the necessary steps to get rid of him. Jack now felt that he could build a relationship with Ron and things would improve. They agreed to meet again in a month and parted with a handshake.

Ron entered his apartment and threw off his jacket and tie. Nestling in his sofa, he grabbed his cell phone and dialed. *This will be easy*, he thought, smiling to himself.

DISCUSSION QUESTIONS

- How did Ron manipulate his boss Joe?
- How did Ron manipulate his new boss, Jack?
- Was he or will he be successful?
- What psychopathic features did you observe in Ron?

A Kid in a Candy Store

Once the hiring process is complete, new hires undergo an orientation and socialization process that often includes training in job-related practices and procedures, exposure to key corporate messages, and indoctrination into cultural values of the company. This is a time of excitement and happiness for most new employees, as the chance to learn and grow in a new job is very motivating. It is also an exciting time for the individual with a psychopathic personality, but for different reasons altogether.

The psychopaths' simple one-to-one manipulative approach to life that governs many of their outside relationships is particularly effective in organizational settings (as seen in the case of Ron above).

Several characteristics of business life facilitate the application of these techniques. There is an assumption that new employees who have made it through the hiring process are honest people with personal integrity. Honesty and integrity are a "given," are rarely tested on any but the most superficial levels, and they color the perspective of coworkers who would never suspect that one of their own colleagues could have ulterior motives. This trusting environment may not rise to the level of that experienced in religious or other affinity groups, but certainly is sufficient for psychopathic manipulation to be successful in companies. As a result, the psychopath blends in well—a "good kid" like his or her peers.

Also, organizations actively seek out people who are able to get along with others and possess the traits that make them easy to get along with in return. Readers will easily recognize, based on their own work experience, that this makes good business sense, as agreeable people tend to be easier to work with in general; "getting along" makes work life a lot more enjoyable, and cooperation leads to greater productivity with minimal conflict. The psychological labels sometimes used for these personality traits include "need-affiliation," "agreeableness," and "socialization," among others. Many organizations look for these during their selection process, but even if not done through formal assessments, there is usually an attempt to glean information about these and similar characteristics during the interviewing process. On the surface, however, people with psychopathic personalities can and do easily come across as friendly and agreeable—they get along with the other "kids" at work or play. It is only beneath the surface, well hidden from view, that darker tendencies lie.

Most people join organizations because they *want* to work and make a living, a work ethic having been ingrained in them from their earliest years. While "work" can take on many different forms, the basic concept involves exchanging goal-oriented efforts for money or reward; essentially, an exchange takes place between employee and employer that satisfies the needs of both. There may be misunderstandings or disagreements about *amount* of effort expended on any given day, *how well* the goals were accomplished, and the appropriate *level* of reward received, but the basic model is pretty much part and parcel of any employment relationship. Having a sense of entitlement and being parasitic, however, psychopaths do not adhere to this fair-exchange model of work, wanting instead large rewards for mediocre effort or poor performance. Their "work ethic" is geared more to making themselves look good than to doing a decent job. Of course, they conceal this attitude (and related lack of performance) from their employers.

THE PSYCHOPATHIC FICTION

While masking one's true intentions may be easy in one-on-one social intercourse, it is a much harder task to establish and maintain the façade over the course of full-time employment, all the while interacting in close quarters with a large number of coworkers on a daily basis: There are just too many critical eyes around. So, once hired, how can psychopaths mask their self-centered, manipulative, and irresponsible traits? The answer lies in their ability to create what we call the *psychopathic fiction*, a story about themselves that fulfills the requirements and expectations of the company and its members. A company's expectations are not too difficult to discover. Many openly share descriptions of ideal behaviors, and encourage adherence to these descriptions through performance objectives, mission statements, standards of performance, codes of conduct, value statements, and other such communications. Companies also publicly reward those who are good corporate citizens with bonuses, promotions, "employee of the month" awards, and similar forms of recognition.

In actuality, the task is quite simple, as astute psychopaths are capable of *mimicking* the traits and characteristics of good performers and high potentials without actually being one. In this sense, the persona they adopt is more a reflection of the demands of the situation (for example, the corporate culture) than an indication of who they really are. The chameleon may mimic a leaf but does not turn into one. The resemblance is strictly on the surface and designed (instinctually in the lizard, cognitively in psychopaths) to offer protection while "hunting" and scanning for chances to take advantage of the situation.

. In the previous chapter, we suggested how easily those with many psychopathic features could enter organizations. Once employed, psychopaths revert to their natural three-phase behavior pattern—assessment, manipulation, and abandonment—to construct sometimes rather elaborate charades or psychopathic fictions that they ultimately weave into the organization's perception of them. This not only assures their ultimate manipulation of the organization but also fulfills the psychopath's needs for game-playing, thrill-seeking, and control; thus, it is doubly rewarding to someone so motivated.

We outline in the next sections how they create and maintain their fictional tale of the "ideal" employee and future leader.

Task 1: Assess the Organization and Its Members

Not surprisingly, the predatory manipulation used by psychopaths in public also applies to business settings. What may be surprising is how easily they can accomplish this. Corporate psychopaths use the early months of employment to study, understand, and ultimately penetrate organizational barriers by identifying key players, analyzing the personalities of potentially useful coworkers, and studying the interaction and communications patterns among them. They meet as many people as they can, spreading positive first impressions about themselves and collecting as much information about coworkers as possible. They quickly begin to understand and then integrate the culture of the organization into their outward style and approach, thus beginning to build a persona, a fiction that will be the basis for future manipulations.

ASSESS THE POWER BASE

When considering how people influence each other to get things done in organizations it is always important to consider the role of power. When people's value is based on where they fit into the organizational hierarchy it is referred to as *position power*, their technical abilities define their *expert power*, their access to information, *knowledge power*, and whether they control staff, money, and other assets, *resource power*. Another important type is *informal power*, which is the ability to influence what is going on without the official title to do so. Seasoned managers know who the informal leaders are in their organization, and will often engage them in their own efforts to manage the entire group. Almost instinctively, corporate psychopaths find these individuals and build strong relationships with them with the intent of using them to their advantage.

There are others with power and influence that are more formal. Individuals with position power are of significant interest to the psychopath, but getting close to those in power positions is not an easy task as they tend to be very busy, they may travel a lot, and they have many others surrounding them who also want their time and attention. An industrious psychopath manages these obstacles with ease, capitalizing on any opportunity, however contrived, to make contact and gain exposure.

The nature of organizational life actually *facilitates* the process of making contact with formal and informal leaders in the form of a typical "honeymoon period." This period, which can last up to a few months, is a time when new employees must learn about their jobs and the organization, and receive considerable leeway to do so. Being on the early part of the learning curve insulates new employees from organizational criticism as they move about freely, learning the ins and outs of the organization's culture. Relying on organizational naiveté during this period, a clever and motivated psychopath can approach individuals in power whom others with more seniority are too timid to approach or have learned to avoid, often for political or personal reasons.

Starting in the elevators and hallways, and landing eventually in their offices, psychopaths begin to introduce themselves to key managers and executives, brazenly disregarding the chain of command others respect. Recall Dave's appearance, unbeknownst to Frank, in the CEO's office—on day one! By the time the honeymoon period ends, they have established a strong, positive presence and identity in the minds of key players that will come in handy later on.

A talented corporate psychopath easily comes across to executives as an ambitious, enthusiastic player. To coworkers and peers, he comes across as a likable person, perhaps a bit narcissistic or manipulative, but friendly, open, and honest nonetheless. Whether one is an informal leader, a power holder, or a regular employee, it is quite refreshing to meet a charismatic new employee who expresses a desire to become an accepted member of the team or displays respect and admiration.

Psychopaths are not the only new employees who try to understand and make use of the sociopolitical structure of the company, of course; almost all new employees do. However, psychopaths do so with very little intent of actually delivering a work product to the company commensurate with the salary they receive. In addition, their emotional poverty does not support allegiance or loyalty to the company or their coworkers, although they can speak the necessary words to indicate intense loyalty to the firm. Their faked excitement might make them seem like a kid in a candy store.

IDENTIFY PAWNS AND PATRONS

If psychopaths are the writers, directors, and stars in the psychopathic fiction, then it is important that those around them fill supportive roles. The first goal in creating the psychopathic fiction is to identify potential "Pawns," or those individuals who have something the psychopath wants. There can be many pawns in an organization, all identified for the specific resources they can potentially provide, such as information, money, expertise, staffing, influence, contacts, and so forth.

Further down the road, when psychopaths need a resource, they will manipulate the pawns to get it or simply ask directly. Asking for favors of "friends" and never actually repaying is a surprisingly common technique used. Many pawns are so enamored by the psychopath's persona that they give him or her whatever is needed, however inappropriate or outrageous the request, as can be seen in Joe's approval of Ron's bogus expense account and call report.

Psychopaths also cultivate support from a small group of high-level individuals with only limited dealings with the psychopathic subordinate, but who accept the persona they perceive and the reputation they only heard about in the grapevine. Despite the limited exposure, the psychopath orchestrates each interaction so well, and fosters such positive impressions, that these higher-level supporters begin to advocate for the subordinate. Believing him or her to be loyal, competent, and extremely successful, they begin to accentuate the positive and eliminate the negative from their thinking.

This phenomenon was puzzling at first. Why would seemingly astute businesspeople take such a strong position in favor of a lower-level employee when they admittedly had only occasional interaction with him or her? We believe that the fictional "ideal employee and future leader" persona was so convincing that many members of the management team were readily charmed. Something out of the ordinary was going on here. For reasons only later to be uncovered, a group of high-level individuals began to act as "Patrons" of the psychopaths. Patrons are influential executives who take talented employees "under their wing" and help them progress through the organization. Once this patronage is established, it is difficult to overcome. With a patron on their side, psychopaths could do almost no wrong. Powerful organizational patrons (unwittingly) protect and defend psychopaths from the criticism of others. These individuals would eventually provide a strong voice in support of the psychopaths' career advancement vis-à-vis promotions and inclusion on corporate succession plans.

Psychopaths eventually establish large networks of personal and, when possible, intimate relationships, all supporting the fictional persona of the ideal coworker and future leader. During this phase, the psychopath identifies the pieces on the playing board as pawns (those the psychopath will manipulate) and as patrons (those who will unwittingly protect the psychopath).

We note that all talented and well-motivated employees attempt to make positive impressions on those around them. Only a small proportion deceives and manipulates to such an extent that they compromise the integrity of the organization. At this point in the process, however, it is exceedingly difficult, if not impossible, to tell the difference between normal impression management and predatory deception.

Although we have labeled this a distinct phase, assessment is in fact an ongoing process, occurring whenever psychopaths meet someone new. Many modern organizations experience continual change among staff members and potential new relationships emerge. This provides psychopaths with the continual opportunity to assess the pawn/patron potential of new players as they join the company or take on new roles. This constant change (often frustrating to the rest of us) adds interest, challenge, and new opportunities for psychopaths to perpetrate their fiction—a motivating factor not unlike that experienced by con men and women when dealing with people in open society. We will say much more about this in the next chapter.

Task 2: Manipulate Management and Coworkers

The Manipulation phase forms the great bulk of the daily organizational existence of psychopaths; they manipulate others toward their own end. The ultimate goal of their game is to set up a scam within the organization's structure that can fulfill their need for excitement, advancement, and power—all without concern about harmful outcomes to others. The fast-paced manipulation of coworkers (for example, Dorothy), executives (Frank and John), vendors, or customers satisfies the psychopath's thrill-seeking and game-playing needs. Winning almost always involves financial and power rewards, such as a steady paycheck for work rarely completed, and promotions into increasing levels of authority. It can also include derailing the careers of coworkers up to and including their unjust termination.

MANIPULATE HEARTS AND MINDS

Many psychopaths appear to be masters at understanding human psychology and at finding and exploiting the weaknesses and vulnerabilities of others. It is unclear whether this reflects an inherent talent or whether they simply work harder than the rest of us at searching for buttons to press. For example, Chuck was a very likable person with a stellar reputation as a solid citizen in the company; many described him as a straight arrow and a high-potential individual contributor. His integrity was unassailable and his work performance was above expectations; few challenged his decisions about his work (and sometimes that of others). Recognizing Chuck's potential, Dan, a psychopath, went to great lengths to build a bond with him. Eventually, this bond grew to the point where Chuck felt a special kinship toward Dan; what Chuck lacked in extroversion and leadership potential, he saw in Dan. Dan was the person he wished he could be. In fact, several coworkers referred to Chuck as Dan's "shadow" because they always seemed to hang out together. Others referred to him as Dan's "soul mate," a description we hear often in these cases. Chuck's association with Dan and his descriptions of him to his coworkers lent a lot of credence to Dan's persona as the competent, loyal, talented employee, much like Chuck.

On occasion, Chuck would explain away Dan's temper as an expression of his artistic, creative bent. What others saw as rudeness and hostility, Chuck saw as Dan standing up for what he believed in. In addition to defending him to the others, what made Chuck particularly useful to Dan was the fact that Chuck was an acknowledged expert at his own job (as well as the jobs of many others). As it turned out, Chuck was the key to Dan's success, working extra hours to help his "friend" do his job. No one realized that he was actually doing Dan's work for him while Dan was out politicking and manipulating others.

When trying to understand and explain their successful manipulation in organizations, we first thought that the psychopaths were merely ingratiating themselves with those at the top of the organization while abusing peers and subordinates at the lower levels. This is often a tactic of poor managers. However, the more we studied these individuals, the less we could explain our observations by simple ingratiation techniques—most executives and coworkers were too smart to fall for this approach for very long. The relationships between our subjects and their supporters turned out to be more complex than this.

We found that, by using a variety of influence tactics, the psychopaths manipulated their network of one-on-one personal bonds to gather information they could use to advance their own careers, derail the careers of rivals, or enlist technical support when the company made demands on them (to actually do their jobs). Specifically, their game plans involved *manipulating communication networks* to *enhance their own reputation*, to *disparage others*, and to *create conflicts and rivalries* among organization members, thereby keeping them from sharing information that might uncover the deceit. They also *spread disinformation* in the interest of protecting their scam and furthering their own careers. Being exceedingly clever, they were able to cloak their association with the disinformation, leading others to believe that they were innocent of manipulation.

Furthermore, they used a veil of secrecy to reinforce the bonds they built with others. Telling someone a secret, even if you know that it will be shared with others, implies a level of trust that cannot help but raise expectations of friendship and respect. Chuck admired Dan and wanted to emulate his outgoing, assertive nature, but would never want others to know this. Being his friend allowed him intimate access to Dan's behaviors and (apparently private) thoughts, and might, he reasoned, help some of these traits to rub off on him. Secretly helping Dan complete assignments was a small price to pay and not any different from sharing his homework with high school and fraternity brothers, years before. He also knew that Dan would never reveal his inner desires and would take care of him down the road, especially when Dan was selected to attend management seminars given by the company—a luxury Chuck could not experience. They were a natural fit, as Chuck never realized that he was de facto colluding with Dan.

Psychopaths identify and use *informal* leaders to support their quest for status and power. Consider Mary, a staff assistant for a major company. She was a delightful person, had a wealth of information about the organization, and as we learned from several others, was a major conduit of the office grapevine. Her cubicle was a regular stop for Doug on his daily rounds of the company. A simple "Hi, Mary! How was your weekend?" from Doug, followed by a leisurely discussion of life's events, would often lead to his sharing "secret" information with Mary about critical organizational issues, key managers, and potential changes. Enthralled with this amount of trust and attention from someone higher up, Mary in turn kept Doug informed of the behind-the-scenes information she had obtained from others.

Understanding that in every organizational rumor there is a kernel of truth, Doug was adept at singling out potentially useful information and storing it in his memory for future use. Given the right opportunity, Doug would "trade up" these bits of information by approaching key individuals and hinting that he was aware of key organizational issues and decisions. Believing that Doug was on the inside track, they felt comfortable about revealing additional pieces of information, which Doug mentally cataloged for future use.

Meanwhile, Mary spread positive, glowing stories about Doug throughout the organization, testifying to his integrity, sincerity, and generosity. "He's going places, I've heard, and I know," she volunteered to anyone who would listen. She would then tell tales of how Doug was being given important projects to work on, how he helped others with their jobs without taking any credit for himself, how some senior executives confided in him because they trusted him, and how he was on the inside track of what was going to happen in the future. She relayed these and other messages throughout the organization long before Doug's name made it to the corporate succession plan. Who was the original source of the stories? Doug, of course.

Although psychopaths manipulate coworkers into covering for them, some coworkers carry their workload in exchange for deep psychological satisfaction that is not readily apparent to observers. For example, all Chuck needed was a little attention and praise for his work, a need Dan managed to fulfill quite effectively. Mary needed a good source of reliable information, and Doug knew how to play her like a fiddle.

However, the strongest and perhaps most interesting challenges to the psychopath, no doubt, are individuals with strong personality traits such as narcissism, assertiveness, and dominance. These individuals are particularly important to psychopaths because they also tend to be in the higher levels of power in organizations.

Interestingly, those who believe they are smarter and more talented than others are the most surprised to learn that they have been psychologically manipulated. Narcissists tend to rise to management positions in organizations in disproportionately large numbers. Being particularly self-absorbed, they use (and sometimes abuse) their subordinates and play up to their superiors to assure their own personal career success. (See Chapter 3 for a detailed look at similarities and differences between narcissists and psychopaths.) We have spoken with a number of narcissistic managers who found themselves victimized by corporate psychopaths: it was not easy for them (executives, lawyers, physicians, politicians, or others) to admit that someone outclassed and outgunned them. Additionally, and this *really* plays into the hands of the psychopath, individuals with strong personalities, such as narcissists, are far less likely than most to seek assistance, guidance, or even personal feedback until it is too late, making them attractive long-term targets.

LOW-UTILITY OBSERVERS: THE EXTRAS

Not everyone whom psychopaths meet interests them. Many co-workers and managers have little to offer in the way of influence, assets, or potential support. By virtue of being ignored, these individuals are in a good position to see what is really going on. One group, the Extras, worked with or near the psychopaths and noticed inconsistencies, lies, and distortions of the truth. They were able, on some level, to see behind the mask; the psychopathic fiction failed to take them in. Unfortunately, few brought their concerns to the "victims" or to management; they did not speak up. Reasons for this silence most often included "I'm minding my own business," "No one would listen to me," and "It's not my place to intervene." In rare cases, some expressed the attitude that "if management is dumb enough to fall for this, they deserve what they get." Others stated that the individual was far too influential for them to cross; these observers preferred to stay out of the line of fire.

During confidential research interviews, we heard stories that helped us understand the psychopathic maneuvers that took place as members of the observer group volunteered numerous references to deceitful behaviors: "He's a liar and a manipulator. It's amazing he's so successful, but then, maybe not, considering how business is these days" was the conclusion of some. They often identified psychopathic workers as the source of departmental conflicts, in many cases purposely setting people up in conflict with each other. "She tells some people one story, and then a totally different story to others. Sometimes she'll tell one person that 'so-and-so said this about you' and then do the same thing with the other," said one exasperated peer. "It's so high school."

As we suspected, many in this group initially liked their manipulative coworkers, but learned to distrust them over time. "He's rude, selfish, unreliable, and irresponsible," said one coworker, "but there was a time, when he first started, that I liked him a lot." "I knew her stories were exaggerations," offered another coworker, "in fact, many times outright false, but I never wanted—I think *none* of us wanted—to call her on her lies. For a time she was entertaining. I can't laugh at her antics now; at best I think she's a sad case." After a pause, this coworker continued. "But that is giving her a lot more credit than she deserves—she's a snake."

ORGANIZATIONAL POLICE: THE ANTAGONISTS

Some individuals have policing roles in organizations, jobs designed to maintain order and control. They may work in security, auditing, and quality control, among other functions. They are necessary to the smooth running of any organization, but they pose a threat to corporate psychopaths, who try to avoid them as long as they can. Should someone in this role suspect that something is amiss, his or her job is to confront the person and/or expose the behavior to higher management. Many of these individuals have excellent critical thinking and investigative skills, with a special responsibility, typically fostered by professional and personal ethics and moral values.

Although they were few in number and rarely interacting on a daily basis with the psychopath, we found that these staff members were particularly astute when it came to their suspicions. "This guy is no good," said the auditor who reviewed expense reports. "I don't trust her; she's too good to be true," said the quality control supervisor. "Bad vibes," said the security manager. "I'm going to watch him for a while."

In corporate settings, people in these functions sometimes are called the "Organizational Police." While many may cringe when referred to by that name, their role, much like their municipal police counterparts, is to protect the organization and its members. We believe that by being on the lookout for deceitful and possibly illegal behavior, such as lying, cheating, bullying, and stealing, these individuals have the ability to uncover psychopathic manipulation early on. Unfortunately, in at least some of the cases we reviewed, the organizational police were unable to effect much improvement. Beyond making known their observations, collecting information on violations of company policy, and raising issues about "questionable" interpersonal behavior, some could not influence management decisions regarding the well-established fraudster. Without top management support, organizational police are often unable to uncover and handle the corporate psychopath's sub-criminal behavior.

RED FLAG: DISCREPANT VIEWS

The most striking thing about these and other cases was the mixed reactions of the corporate psychopath's coworkers. In every case, we found a strong discrepancy in the perceptions between those who viewed their actions in a very positive, favorable light and those who saw them in a negative light. We wondered how a fictional persona could continue to function in an environment that included negative perceptions and doubt. Eventually, it became obvious that the psychopaths were effectively balancing the discrepant views of their coworkers, and relying on consistent charm, occasional intimidation, the basic trusting nature of people, and frequent organizational changes to maintain their psychopathic fiction in the eyes of those who mattered most. On one side, the supporters (labeled Pawns and Patrons) felt that they were valuable contributors to the success of the organization; that is, team players and solid corporate citizens. On the other hand, detractors (labeled Extras and Organizational Police) reported all manner of underhanded, deceitful, manipulative behaviors by the same individuals.

It is common for individuals to be liked by some and disliked by others. This is as true at work as it is at home or school. However, in an organization, there usually is a majority point of view based on a specific, identifiable organizational issue, such as a turf battle, and a minority view based on a personal issue such as envy. Normal political battling rarely surfaces in so clear and intense a form as it does with a psychopath. Clearly, the detractors despised these individuals, and the supporters almost worshipped them. It was as if employees were describing two entirely different people to us. In a great number of these situations, it seemed that the psychopath could switch from warm and friendly to cold, distant, and almost hostile depending on with whom they were interacting.

Task 3: Abandon the No-Longer Useful—The Patsies

Because psychopaths no longer need to maintain the façade for individuals whose utility is spent, they generally will abandon them. Spouses and children left without support and the elderly who have given up their life savings are common examples in society. Abandonment does not always lead to the realization that one has been used or conned. For example, blindness to this reality might reflect the perceptions of an investor who still believes in the good intentions of an exposed scammer, despite having lost his life savings.

In organizations, the psychopath eventually abandons the pawn, in both the social sense—the psychopath no longer associates with them—and the psychological sense—the friendship generated as part of the psychopathic bond turns cold. Nevertheless, because the psychopath is working in an organization and cannot run away from the scene of the crime, abandonment becomes starkly obvious to those affected, as well as to those around them. This dramatic shift from friendly coworker to cold, dispassionate stranger affects victims in predictable ways: they frequently question their own behavior first, blaming themselves for the changes they are now sensing in the psychopath. "What did I do?" is a common self-doubt. Although victims may not yet understand what has happened, they begin to see glimmers of the true psychopathic personality—a realization that we understand is "chilling."

Eventually, pawns realize that they have been patsies all along. They feel cheated, defiled, and often incredulous that the person they liked and trusted betrayed that trust. Moreover, we found, it was not always over major things that the truth dawned on them. It was sometimes only a small incident that changed their perception enough so that the true nature of the "snake" in their midst became evident. However, embarrassment and shame often keep them from coming forward.

Organization members who were willing to discuss with us their interactions with their abusive, manipulating coworkers reported feeling abandoned when the latter moved their attention to others. They also reported experiencing the most common victim response: *silence* due to shame at being conned. Like so many other victims, they wanted to keep their shame secret. This response, of course, plays into the hands of the psychopath, protected by the tendency toward silence and secrecy. Interestingly, a few also felt disappointment when the psychopath in their company moved his or her attentions to others in the organization. They had lost something they valued—a close friend—when the psychopath stopped using them. We will say more about the impact of psychopathic manipulation on victims in Chapter 12.

Task 4: Confrontation

Over time, the constant need to manage the growing discrepancy in the views of them by a large number of fellow employees challenges the manipulation skills of psychopaths. We believe that a breakdown begins to occur when the psychopath's web of deceit and manipulation becomes unwieldy and too many people have had glimpses of his dark side. Eventually, *someone* tries to do something about it. Former pawns might challenge or confront the psychopath and perhaps even try to bring the situation to the attention of higher-ups. Unfortunately, by this time the psychopath has positioned himself so well through the influence networks already established with the power hierarchy that he turns the tables *on the complaining employees*: their credibility is "managed" and their attempt to reveal the psychopath preempted.

This has an intimidating effect on bystanders in two ways. Those working with the defeated employee see the demoralizing effects up close and conclude it is not worth fighting the psychopath. Others may assume that the company has selected the psychopath for future leadership roles and can do no wrong, and is therefore immune to attack. They have come to believe that this person cannot be challenged and is protected by upper management. Some might conclude that the management team is not as astute as once thought, and rather than signal to upper management that there is a deceitful person on board, they adopt a wait-and-see attitude. The increase in cautious inaction among coworkers is another subtle but powerful effect that psychopathic behavior has on the organization's culture. As the psychopath neutralizes rivals and detractors, he is free to continue operations unchallenged. By creating a niche safe from the attacks of rivals, the psychopath can maintain his or her operations for a lengthy amount of time.

Given the above scenario, one might predict that eventually the psychopaths would fail, that they would be uncovered, that they would offend the wrong person, and that the organization would remove them before they did great psychological and financial harm. This did not happen. Most of the ones we have studied over the years still enjoy successful careers in their original organizations. The few exceptions have left their companies for larger jobs in other companies—some of them competitors. Unfortunately, the companies reorganized many innocent victims out of their jobs, derailed their careers, or had them leave in disgust.

The natural manifestation of psychopathic manipulation—assessment, manipulation, and abandonment—is common among psychopaths in society. For the corporate psychopath we added an initial step to capture the process they use to gain entry into the organization, and now we will add a subsequent phase, which we label *Ascension*.

Task 5: Ascend

Corporate psychopaths are able to build careers that lead them to increasingly higher-level positions in the organization. This need not be the CEO's job, of course, but one position that often is immediately attractive is the one occupied by their patron.

The Ascension can take place once the psychopath's manipulation network has expanded to include the whole power structure of the organization and all key players are in his or her corner. Almost simultaneously, and seemingly overnight to the victim, the *entire* power structure shifts its support away from the patron and over to the psychopath, who moves up into the now deposed patron's position. The once high-power and high-status patron, who protected the psychopath from doubts and accusations, and who facilitated fast promotions, advanced assignments, and job rotations, finds him or herself betrayed. Sadly, the patron becomes a patsy, losing organizational status and often his or her job to the psychopath.

DISCUSSION QUESTIONS

- Consider the major roles in the psychopathic drama (Pawns, Patrons, Patsies, and Police): Have you ever observed someone with psychopathic features manipulate coworkers in these ways?
- Did you speak up and say something?

The Case of Dave

ACT III, Scene II

AN HONEST MISTAKE?

Frank got off the elevator on his floor of the hotel and pulled out his key card. He jammed the card into the lock twice before the hotel room door opened. He pushed his way in, dropped his suitcase near the door, and threw his computer case onto the bed. He quickly pulled his laptop out of the case and hit the start button as he opened the screen. It would be a few minutes before his system was up, so he fished some dollar bills out of his coat pocket, grabbed the ice bucket, and left the room, heading for the vending area. The humming sounds of the ice machine drew him down the hall and around the corner, where he found it. He knew he would be up late; caffeine was a necessity to combat the two martinis he had had with John earlier at the bar. Soon he had two sodas and a bucket of ice in his hands, and was on his way back to his room. *There better be an email from Dave*, he thought to himself, getting angrier and starting to walk more quickly.

Line after line of email scrolled up his screen. Most of it was junk. Finally, he saw it, an email from Dave. "Okay, let's see what this is," he muttered to himself as he opened Dave's email. There was an attachment, a positive sign—the first in several long hours. Frank read the message:

> Frank: I got your phone message; didn't understand what you were talking about. I left the thumb drive on your desk Friday afternoon. Anyway, I went to the office and found it on the floor in your office. Figured you ran out with the folder, but it must have fallen out. Here it is. I also sent a copy to John in case you didn't make it; you sounded upset.

"Left the drive in my office?" said Frank aloud. Like a person frantically trying to find a set of lost keys, Frank played back his steps from last Friday evening repeatedly in his mind. ". . . fell on the floor?" Frank was puzzled, but he had to stay focused. It was getting late and he still had to prepare for the next day's meeting. He clicked on the email attachment and it opened to the first slide of the presentation. He slowly clicked his way through the presentation, stopping here and there to read the text. At the first chart, he lingered for quite a while and studied the figures. Frank opened the original file that he had picked up in his office and searched for the same chart. Or, was it the same? No, the charts were different, very different. In fact, except for some introductory material and graphics, the entire presentation was different from the one he had picked up from his desk late Friday. Frank's mind was oscillating between attempts to answer the question *what the hell happened?* and focusing on what he was going to say during the meeting tomorrow.

Taking another gulp of soda, Frank continued to review the new presentation. He liked what he read. Eventually, a deep sense of calm overtook him. *This is good; this is really good*, Frank thought, smiling.

Having finished reviewing the presentation and writing notes for his talk, Frank packed up his computer and got ready for bed. *The committee is really going to like this*, he thought, getting under the covers and turning out the light. *Dave came through.*

The quiet in his mind did not last long. *But, how could I have left it in the office? I put everything I found in my briefcase.* Frank started doing the deep-breathing exercises he had learned in the stress management course. *No wonder John was pleased: this is really a creative, well-thought-out plan,* Frank sighed, smiling again, as he tried to refocus on the positives. *Good thing I ran into John in the lobby and he raved about it. I may not have learned about it until the morning— what a nightmare—if Dave hadn't found the thumb drive in my office.* Or had he?

Frank's eyes opened, paranoia starting to get the better of him.

DISCUSSION QUESTIONS

- What just happened here? Describe three possible explanations for these events.
- What does John think of Dave?
- What does Frank think of Dave?
- Was this an honest mistake?

Darkness and Chaos:
The Psychopath's Friends

Ginny sat in her office reviewing the interview schedule for the day. She pulled Al's material out of the stack and flipped through the folder. She sighed as she read the file. *Another one of these*, she thought, anticipating the boredom she would feel during the conversation. *But, maybe he'll surprise me.*

The receptionist rang Ginny and informed her that Al was in the waiting room. Ginny went to get him, files in hand, and led him back to her office through the maze of cubicles, copiers, and conference rooms. "Did you find the building okay?" she asked, smiling.

"Hard to miss, actually," Al said, with a slightly sarcastic tone as he looked around the department layout.

They got to Ginny's office and she gestured toward a chair for Al. He glanced around, obviously disappointed at the small size of the space, the stacks of paper and files, and the low-cost metal furniture.

Al hadn't seen anything like this in years; as VP of finance for Acme Tech, he had grown accustomed to oak, mahogany, and teak. "Nice office," he said, faking a smile.

Ginny reviewed the information Al had provided on the forms. As she worked her way through his employment history, she asked pointed questions about the responsibilities he had in various jobs, the types of things he could do, and his interactions with others. She also asked about his family and upbringing. "We were dirt poor," Al said proudly, "and I worked my way through college and supported my mom and younger sisters, as well. I had to become the man of the house very early because my father was a drunkard and left us high and dry." Ginny took careful notes as Al spoke, occasionally referring to her prepared set of questions.

"What kind of work are you doing now?" she inquired.

"I'm doing a bit of consulting, not much actually. I'm looking for the right fit."

"What kind of job would be the best fit for you, then?" she asked, checking a few boxes on her worksheet and writing in some comments.

"Vice President–Finance," Al started to say, but paused when he saw Ginny stop writing mid-word. "What? That's the job I had at Acme Tech—why should I settle for less? I have a lot of financial experience; I have a long record of accomplishment, as you can see on my résumé. A company would be very smart to hire someone with my experience. I just had a turn of bad luck; not really my fault, as you know reading my cover letter. There were some bad actors on the executive team at Acme; they put the blame on me because I had been tough on them. I was clearly the strongest leader the company had had in a long while, so they framed me."

Ginny continued making notes and asked a few more questions. "So you can be a tough boss?"

Al was ready for this question. It was his time to make his pitch: "You bet I can be tough—like getting my staff to work long hours and go the extra mile for the good of the company!" he said, beaming. "But, I'm not tough on everyone. Some people don't respond to tough love, you know—they need to be coddled. I do that too," he said, nodding. "A leader needs flexibility—I was nice to the big guys and, when it suited my agenda, hard on the little people. Little people like strong leaders; it makes them feel comfortable."

Ginny glanced at the clock on the wall over Al's head. Seeing this, Al continued, speaking very quickly, "I have the style, the smarts, and the looks to carry off any VP job. I worked hard my entire career and wasn't afraid to confront the competition. If you want to be successful, you have to be ambitious," Al said, leaning forward and gesturing, "and stab the competition in the back, right? I showed them I could run with the wolves and not falter if I met someone who stood in my way. I made hard decisions others didn't like, and then wasn't afraid to use their disagreements to uncover their disloyalty to the company." Al leaned back in his chair, paused, and said, "I always supported the company; I talked up company goals, objectives, mission, and vision and whatever the hell else they thought was important. I was always a team player, as well. I kept the important ones in the loop and proved my loyalty repeatedly. It paid off because I got the promotions, the big salary, the nice offices, cars, and all that stuff. It's hard for me to admit"—Al paused, dramatically—"but they were fooling me all along and I never knew it. I never realized they were really a bunch of crooks and they were using me—I was the fall guy."

Ginny interrupted Al and began to close the meeting. "Here is your copy of the consent form and a copy of the judgment. You're expected to pay restitution in regular installments. We'll work out the specific schedule during our next meeting. You'll need to look for a job and bring me a list of companies you've applied to, with phone numbers I can call to verify. We'll meet every week, here in my office, until you are settled, and then biweekly. I've signed you up for counseling and they will meet with you once we're through here. You'll meet with them weekly in a group setting, and take some course work on managing your finances and anger management, as well. They will report to me how you're doing. Do you have any questions?"

"No," Al said, feigning a humble smile. "I know what I have to do and, trust me, I'll pay everything back. My goal is to regain my integrity. Thank you for helping me and seeing my side of things."

Ginny rose as the counselor arrived at the appointed time. "Hello," he said to Al, "come with me. I'll introduce you to some of the others."

As Al left with the counselor, Ginny finished her notes. She added a few more observations, completed the assessment, and closed the file, placing it on top of one of the many piles surrounding her desk. *No surprise about his personality*, she thought.

As she walked to the break room to get another cup of coffee, she ran into a fellow probation officer. "How was your morning?" her colleague asked.

"You know, these white-collar guys are the worst," she said. "They get their hand slapped, never do time, brag about it, blame everyone but themselves, and then, once they land another job, do it all over again. What an attitude; give me a car thief any day over these guys—at least they're honest."

DISCUSSION QUESTIONS

- What psychopathic features did Al display in his interview with Ginny?
- How did he try to manipulate her?

Is Corporate Psychopathy on the Rise?

Not all psychopaths turn to a life of crime and only about 15 to 20 percent of incarcerated criminals have psychopathic personalities. Yet during the early part of the twenty-first century, it would seem that the number of economic crimes has soared as headlines revealed major corporate fraud across the nation and around the world. In addition, there are potentially many more, such as the case of Al, that did not rise to the level of a major headline. What are the reasons for this? Has the number of corporate psychopaths increased over the years?

One possible explanation is that we have become much better at identifying psychopathic features in individuals. Since its creation, investigators and clinicians have used the PCL-R and its derivatives in more than one thousand studies, yet as of this writing, only one focused on the corporate psychopath (see Chapter 9 for a detailed review of this research). Another, more systemic possibility is that the overall business environment has changed over the years such that psychopathic traits and behaviors have become more acceptable.

PSYCHOLOGICAL EMPLOYMENT CONTRACT

People join large organizations because of the many benefits they offer: the chance to build a career, access to financial and technical resources individuals rarely acquire on their own, and the opportunity for advancement. The "psychological contract" that defined employment in the 1940s–1970s included job security, health and pension benefits, and employment for life. The "gold watch" received upon retirement was one of the symbols awarded those who worked hard, did a quality job, and followed the rules. Loyalty and competence were the foundations of this contract and it afforded employees feelings of security, trust, and respect, and provided employers the well-trained and experienced workforce they needed to compete successfully.

Management theories popular at this time focused on maintaining the psychological contract by building and enhancing employees' self-esteem, listening and responding to their ideas, and capitalizing on basic human needs, such as security, social interaction, career advancement, and *self-actualization*, a term that captured the psychological need to achieve one's own potential in life. During the late 1970s, team-based models of management replaced traditional command-and-control hierarchies. Employees made their own decisions affecting their work, and organizations began to integrate systems and processes into their culture, such as quality circles and participative management that linked the most important elements of employee satisfaction to company profits.

Three to five percent turnover seemed normal, and was managed through recruitment, placement, and career development programs. Technological changes were relatively slow during this period, so it was possible to manage them effectively. Major business changes sometimes required replacing employees with those better educated in the latest technology, but given enough time and resources, it was possible to retrain many current employees to meet the challenges. Many organizations and most people were able to adapt quite well, and, though stretched, it was possible to maintain the psychological contract. Then the nature of change itself changed.

CHANGE IS A FACT OF LIFE

The rate of change in business—and many other aspects of life— accelerated dramatically during the 1980s and the 1990s. New technologies began to advance faster than many organizations' ability to keep pace. The changes came too quickly and there were too many of them at once. There seemed to be no calm between the storms, and little time to deal with today's frustration before another storm hit. The demand for better-quality and lower-cost products increased beyond the ability of many companies to cut costs and still meet quality and delivery demands. Government controls increased in many areas. Advances in computerization, in particular, led to dramatic social changes among the workforce as well.

Some of this change has had a positive effect. The Internet opened a completely new world of exploration and study. People no longer have to remember details of this or that, but can search the Internet while at dinner in a restaurant to resolve a discussion about some disputed fact. Commerce has advanced to the point where people can shop or do their banking at home at any time of night or day, and small entrepreneurial companies have grown in number as markets opened up, once thought out of reach. Education—on just about everything—is now available to a greater number of individuals around the globe.

There also have been negative effects of this accelerating rate of change. Large organizations had to reinvent themselves quickly in order to remain competitive. In a defensive maneuver, some corporations merged, acquired other companies, or moved operations offshore just to maintain their financial position. A large number of people lost their jobs, which dramatically altered the overall economy as well as society in general.

The operational impact of this period of instability was that there seemed to be little time to design and build new and more efficient policies, procedures, and systems before the next changes came about. In contrast to old-style bureaucratic organizations built on stability, consistency, and predictability, the new *transitional* organizations had to give up these "luxuries," and to become more fluid in the face of an unstable, inconsistent, and unpredictable future. In order to just survive, therefore, many bureaucratic processes were jettisoned because they were no longer effective (or efficient), and supporting them with time and energy could no longer be justified. Organizations got "flatter" as middle management positions were eliminated in an effort to streamline decision-making. Companies outsourced or moved entirely support services out of the region to save time and money. This degree of change did not allow leaders to maintain the same commitments to long-term employment as their predecessors. A dwindling workforce had to do more with less, or else join their colleagues who lost their jobs. At some point along the way, the psychological contract gave way to a world where the employee–employer relationship became a *transitory* one rather than a long-term partnership. People and their skills were now commodities whose value could vary with the prevailing demands of technology. This dramatically affected executives, managers, and employees emotionally, psychologically, and socially—causing even the most confident people to feel that they had lost control of their lives.

ARE WE THERE YET?

A state of chaos occurs when business or industry upheaval overtakes an organization's ability to respond effectively. Few of us are ready to handle chaotic change effectively, and evolution has not been very helpful, moving at its own slow pace. When thrust into chaotically changing situations, we, as employees and managers, experience intense feelings of frustration, stress, loss of control, and anxiety.

Now imagine that rapid change becomes the *rule* rather than the exception. Yesterday's change is changing today, and will change again tomorrow; there is seemingly no light at the end of the tunnel. Companies that once focused on determining the ideal "vision" of the future organization now find themselves in a constant state of transitioning. Furthermore, not everything changes at the same rate, and interrelated elements become unglued, adding confusion to an already unstable time. As a result, organizations in a constant state of transitioning are characterized by outdated, unenforceable, or nonexistent work rules and policies; inconsistent risk taking; greater tolerance for controversial, perhaps even abusive, behaviors; and antiquated measurement systems and communication networks. At best, the ideal future states of these organizations are fuzzy; at worst, it is chaos.

Who succeeds in this environment, in this new culture of change? Most management experts agree that in order to survive the chaos, employees, managers, and executives must adopt constant change as a work style and lifestyle—the management term for this is *embrace* change. They must become faster thinkers, more assertive and persuasive. They must become much more creative, capable of designing, developing, building, and selling new products and services to meet ever-changing demands in a world of fierce competition and highly selective buyers. They must learn to feel comfortable making faster decisions with less information, and recover from mistakes more quickly. They must be willing to live with the consequences, even if they risk failure. They must take control of their own careers by reassessing their talents and skills and then repackaging them for the new marketplace. While our parents and grandparents worked for one or two companies for their entire lives, we must be ready to move through six or seven.

Organizations that survive chaotic times are those whose employees not only grow comfortable with uncertainty, but also can build systems, processes, and structures capable of anticipating it and flexible enough to respond to it (that is, change again, as necessary). In order to do this, successfully transitioning companies need fewer *superfluous rules* (which hold back progress) and clearer *mission-critical rules* (which keep the business on track). They need a much more meaningful set of guiding principles that managers can use to make informed decisions when new problems and unique situations arise. Having clear, shared values and sticking to them unwaveringly is the key. So who succeeds in this tumultuous business environment? See S 7.1: *Opportunity Knocks.*

ENTER THE ENTREPRENEUR, STAGE RIGHT

At the top of our "success list" would be individuals with *entrepreneurial* spirit, those who enjoy change, the challenges it brings, and the opportunities it affords. Entrepreneurs, whether in business or science, seem to have very high tolerance for frustration. Contrary to popular belief, though, not all entrepreneurs start their own companies with their own or investor money. In fact, there is evidence that many entrepreneurial types can be very effective working within big companies, particularly those that are willing to make some accommodations for their needs. Entrepreneurial types require access to resources, a continuous stream of challenges to do new and exciting things, personal recognition for success, feedback about failures, and, most of all, freedom to act. While these accommodations are difficult for old-style bureaucracies to offer, the transitioning organization—forced to make changes to its business model, anyway—is in an ideal position to adopt these new approaches. By replacing the long-abandoned employment-for-life psychological contract with the new *entrepreneurial psychological contract*, transitioning organizations are better able to gain the flexibility needed to survive chaos. This requires treating employees as individual contributors, responsible for their own career advancement, and rewarding them with large salaries for innovative, fast-paced problem-solving—as well as the chance to work on new, exciting projects. The symbiosis of employees with entrepreneurial talents and the transitioning organization can lead to the constant reinventing, rebuilding, and reenergizing that both need for survival and growth. If well managed (using new management techniques, of course, not old ones), the results can be impressive.

Unfortunately, this business model is far easier to theorize about than to actually implement. There are several reasons for this, all of them very human. It is very difficult to convince current executives, managers, and employees that they should give up their need for safety and security—no longer part of the contract—in exchange for a model in which their skills and abilities may not be worth anything tomorrow, and the company feels no obligation to retain them. Therefore, it is difficult for a company to regain employee loyalty, especially once it has breached the employment-for-life psychological contract and substituted an entrepreneurial psychological contract. Management credibility, one of the foundations of employee loyalty, is also now open to question—"How come they let the company get into this situation?" and "Didn't they see this coming?" are recurring questions those in control must constantly face from the workforce if they expect to attract and retain talented entrepreneurs. Finally, those with power and authority rarely will give it up willingly, even in service of the greater good of the organization.

These individuals may feel threatened by the erosion of their own positions, and can sabotage the transition by virtue of their sense of entitlement. (President George Washington is one of the few great leaders who rejected "kingship" and refused to continue as president once he felt he had completed his job. Contrast this with dictators, would-be dictators, and ambitious politicians.) Organizations often look to much younger and less experienced new employees in order to find those with entrepreneurial spirit. This is easier and less expensive than converting those already on board because candidates from a younger generation bring with them a comfort level dealing with technological change, having dealt with it their entire lives. Understandably, current employees may not want to support the new entrepreneurial employees, who seem to be getting more attention than they ever got themselves. At the very least, this may create envy among the current staff, especially when asked to give up precious resources (such as plum projects, money, and staff) they may have fought long and hard to acquire. And then, all of this assumes that companies can find individuals who *truly* possess entrepreneurial talents in the marketplace, a task far more difficult than expected as competition for them is fierce and there are many young candidates who view themselves as entrepreneurial but lack the necessary experience and credentials.

ENTER THE PSYCHOPATH, STAGE LEFT

Here is where the corporate psychopath fits into the story. Would someone with a psychopathic personality, turned off by earning an honest living in general, even be interested in joining one of these transitioning companies? Unfortunately, the answer we found is yes, as organizations have become more psychopath-friendly in recent years. Rapid business growth, increased downsizing, frequent reorganizations, mergers, acquisitions, and joint ventures have inadvertently increased the number of attractive employment opportunities for individuals with psychopathic personalities—without the need for them to correct or change their psychopathic attitudes and behaviors.

What is it about the psychopath that makes these new organizations so attractive to them? To start with, their thrill-seeking nature
(research has shown it to be genetically determined) draws them to
situations where there is a lot of stimulus: a lot is happening and
happening quickly. Then, as consummate rule breakers they can
capitalize on the lessened reliance on firm rules and policies and
the increased need for free-form decision-making that characterize
organizations in a chaotic state. And, as seekers of power, they take
advantage of individuals psychologically and emotionally weakened
due to the chaos in ways that are not always obvious. In particular, the
opportunity to get a leadership or management position is extremely
attractive because these positions offer the psychopaths a chance to
exert control over people and resources, they tend not to require
involvement in the details, and they command larger-than-average
salaries. Because a leader's ability to get people to do things is often
of more importance than his or her technical capabilities to perform
work tasks, psychopaths lacking in real work expertise are not disad-
vantaged. Others often accept at face value their leadership talents
and their phony or exaggerated backgrounds.

Most importantly, they can hide amongst the chaos. While leadership may seem like an easy job to a psychopath, requiring little more than the application of his or her natural conning and
manipulation skills, in reality it involves much more talent, skill,
and experience. But the constantly changing state of the business,
the chaos, works in their favor, clouding the difference between
"good" and "bad" leadership, allowing them to move about the organization through rapid promotions and transfers faster than the
performance on their current jobs can be measured, evaluated, and
handled. Short-term results, or what *looks* like results, can be deceiving, especially if cleverly presented. This is especially true when the
performance measurement systems *themselves* are in a state of flux or
perhaps nonexistent, as they often are in transitioning organizations.
Furthermore, their irresponsible risk-taking and narcissistic, callous
decision-making contributes to the anxiety level of coworkers, leaving followers scrambling to figure out what to do next.

Psychopaths can enter, thrive on, and hide within the chaos of transitioning organizations easier than one would think. Would an organization in need of strong leadership hire a psychopath? Not willingly, of course, but because their presentation during the interviewing process, their persona, looks like an ideal leadership candidate to a company seeking entrepreneurial leadership they can slip in under the radar. Their psychopathic fiction takes the form of "savior" of the company.

Likewise, the corporate psychopath on staff, having already created a persona of the ideal employee in the minds of executives and employees alike, can easily morph into a high-energy, visionary, entrepreneurial leader. With this label, conning or bullying others can seem like an effective management style, especially when coworkers are paralyzed by the chaotic change surrounding them, caught in their personal frustrations, and unable or unwilling to accept the new business model. In contrast to the rest of the organization's members, the corporate psychopath looks like a knight on a white horse, cool, calm, and confident. Their self-serving bravado and the mystique that surrounds them cloud the fact that the efforts of psychopaths rarely result in long-term business improvements.

In conclusion, situations where there is stimulation and high drama and where the rules are lax or nonexistent are magnets for psychopaths. Add dramatic organizational change to the normal levels of organizational job insecurity, personality clashes, and political battling, and the resulting *chaotic milieu* provides both the necessary stimulation and sufficient cover for their entry and subsequent psychopathic game playing.

SECRECY: THE PSYCHOPATH'S FRIEND

There is another aspect of organizational life that facilitates the entry, manipulation, and deceit of the psychopath and it is secrecy. Secrecy is a part of organizational life. The need for secrecy is quite understandable and often is an integral part of the organization's procedures, as in the case of protecting trade secrets from competitors or keeping detailed financials confidential during premerger negotiations. Some secrecy is defensive in nature, as when a decision is made that will negatively affect some individuals, and the resulting action needs to take place before there is forewarning, as is often the case with terminations. Some secrecy is inadvertent, though, such as when events happen faster than the organization's communication mechanisms can respond. As a result, people are left in the dark and unable to do their jobs properly. In these cases, those in the know may not intend to keep secrets; they simply do not have the opportunity or time to share the information with others.

During times of chaotic change, when *more* information is better than less, secrecy will *increase* the vulnerability of organizations to psychopathic manipulation. Regardless of the appropriateness of the secrecy, the impact often is an *increase in the levels of distrust* among employees, a *reduction in the levels of management credibility or perceived trustworthiness* in the eyes of those kept in the dark, and an *increase in mistakes* made due to lack of timely, accurate information.

Secrecy is the psychopath's friend. The success of psychopathic manipulation, especially in large groups of people, depends on maintaining a cloak of secrecy about what is really going on. A *culture* of secrecy in an organization makes it much easier for psychopaths to hide and much harder for management to catch them in their lies, to accurately rate their performance, or to see the abuse they heap on coworkers. To the degree that transitioning organizations increase their level of secrecy, they run the risk of providing cover to corporate psychopaths who have entered their ranks.

DISCUSSION QUESTIONS

- What are the key differences between a true leader and a corporate psychopath masking as one?
- Have you worked for either?
- Have you ever worked for a company experiencing chaotic change?
- How did it affect you?

S 7.1
Opportunity Knocks

Many devastating events, from hurricanes to floods, fires, wars, terrorism, economic crises, volcanic eruptions, epidemics, and so forth, strike the world every year. Such events bring out the best and the worst in people. There is no shortage of common thugs, criminals, imposters, corrupt officials, and sundry predators ready to make a buck out of someone else's tragedy. Some of their depredations no doubt result from poverty, mob mentality, and understandable survival instincts. However, for many psychopaths—on the street and in the boardroom—their egregious acts stem from an opportunity too good to pass up.

Consider this exchange from Season 3, Episode 6 (2013), *The Game of Thrones:*

> **Lord Varys:** "Chaos? A gaping pit willing to swallow us all."
> **Petyr "Littlefinger" Baelish:** "Chaos isn't a pit. Chaos is a ladder."

Many viewers of the TV series have offered their interpretations of this exchange on the Internet. In general, the view is that Varys is Machiavellian and achieves his power and influence through scheming, patience, and the gathering of information for future use. Petyr, on the other hand, is more psychopathic and present-oriented. He sees chaos as a direct means to gain power, status, and influence. In a chaotic world, he is able to spot and use opportunities, to revise his loyalties to fit the situation, and to manipulate situations and people in order to further his own prestige, power, and self-interest.[1] Actually, most of the main characters in *Game of Thrones* are like Varys and Petyr, in one way or another, all given to scheming, violence, and brutality when it suits their self-serving goals. For example, "Cersei Lannister is a psychopath who sleeps with her brother. But admit it to yourself. You love her. We all do...perhaps it's because, on some level, we secretly admire her ruthlessness."[2]

The point here is that psychopaths are emotionally unaffected by the human physical and psychological carnage that accompanies chaotic disasters. They are, by nature, predisposed to take callous but pragmatic advantage of the turmoil and terror experienced by others.

The Case of Dave

LET'S DO LUNCH

Try as she might, Dorothy couldn't get the ringing out of her ear. Her eyes opened and she realized she was in her bed at home and the phone was ringing.

"Hello," she said sleepily, opening her eyes slightly to see the clock radio.

"Who is this? Dave? It's eight o'clock in the morning, Dave. And it's Sunday," she recalled, falling back on her pillows, the phone next to her ear. "What's going on?"

"Yes, you woke me up," she groaned. "I was out last night. I didn't get in until 2 A.M.

"Of course, I'm alone," she said, absentmindedly. "Jeez, Dave. Mind your own business.

"What?" she asked, not understanding what Dave was saying. "Can't this wait until tomorrow?"

Dave began his story.

"What does the off-site executive committee meeting have to do with me?" she questioned, sitting up. "Why should I—"

Dave cut her off. He explained that Frank was in a bind because he didn't have a presentation for the meeting. John, Frank's boss, was disappointed in his ideas for the upcoming year and wanted a whole new presentation by the next morning. Frank called Dave, desperately needing his help. Dave saw this as the perfect opportunity for Dorothy to get her material in front of those who counted.

As Dave's words slowly sank in, she got out of bed. "You want *what*?" she said, heading to the kitchen to put on some coffee. "Let me get this straight: John's pissed at Frank because Frank's new product idea sucks, and you want me to give you my stuff so you can give it to John? Am I getting this right, Dave?"

Dave continued.

"I'm not interested, Dave," interrupted Dorothy. "My boss hasn't even seen my project. Why should I give it to you for Frank or John or whoever?"

Dave explained his plan further.

"Oh, *sure* you're going to put my name on it," she said, rolling her eyes. "I wasn't born yesterday; I know how you operate." Dorothy watched the coffee drip as Dave persisted in telling her that this was her best chance to get her ideas in front of the executive committee and with both Frank's and John's support.

"I really don't relish the thought of you giving my presentation to the committee, no matter how 'opportune' the time," she said, getting a cup from the cupboard.

Dave explained further.

"You're not giving the presentation? Then, who is?"

"*Frank* is going to give my presentation—as his own?

"As *ours*, yours and, mine, then? Mm-hmm.

"Why would Frank want to present my project ideas—sight unseen, I might add—to his boss, just because you ask him to?"

Dave responded.

"It must be nice to be so trusted by your boss, Dave. I'm really not interested," she said, pouring her coffee and taking a sip.

"Yes, Dave, I'm your friend," she said, not believing Dave would be using this tactic. "And, you're my friend. And the *only* reason you called—not for Frank or John or the good of the company—is to help out your friend Dorothy."

Dave interrupted again, telling her that she could be the hero, and Frank would be indebted. Frank would never challenge any of her future ideas, and she might even get a promotion as a result of the exposure of her work to the executive committee.

Dorothy took another sip of coffee and thought. "How do I know I can trust you, Dave?" she asked, intrigued in spite of herself.

"Together? We'll put the presentation together—together, you and I. I get to put my name on it. You'll tell Frank the idea was mine."

Dave responded to each of her concerns, reassuring her at every step. Dave responded to her voice, but sang to her heart.

"Yes, of course I have my computer at home. Why, what are you thinking? You want to come here? Today? To work on . . . in your dreams, Dave," she said exasperatedly.

Dave continued. No, he wasn't going to hit on her. No, he wasn't going to tell everyone he had been to her apartment. Yes, he would bring lunch.

"Hmmmm," sighed Dorothy. "I'll tell you what, Dave. You can come over and we will work on this together. But, if I change my mind *anytime* while we're working, the deal's off. Got it?"

DISCUSSION QUESTIONS

- What is Dave really trying to do here?
- What is the real story behind his request of Dorothy?
- What lies is he telling her?
- What aspects of Dorothy's personality is Dave playing on?

8

I'm Not a Psychopath, I Just Talk and Act Like One

Smith charged down the hall toward his office. Marching past the staff without a glance, he reached the door and barked for his secretary to have Jones come to his office immediately. His face getting red, Smith threw the files onto the desk and dropped into his big chair with a huff.

Minutes later Jones arrived, half knowing what to expect, but not knowing why. There were stories about Smith's calling staff members into his office to read them the riot act after a senior management meeting, but since Jones's projects were not on the agenda, this couldn't be the reason for the summoning. So far, all her interactions with Smith had been cordial; there was no reason to suspect a change.

Smith's secretary greeted Jones and led the way to the office door. Smith motioned Jones to enter and the door closed behind them. The secretary went back to her desk and resumed typing. She glanced at the staff member sitting at the desk to her left and the staff member to her right and sighed. Everyone knew what was about to happen.

The "scoldings," as the support staff called them, occurred roughly once a week, usually on Friday afternoons after the morning senior management meeting. Smith was never happy after these meetings, but no one was sure why, as the minutes were kept quite secret. Obviously, someone was chewing him out at these meetings and he felt the need to take it out on members of his staff; how else could the staff explain it?

Jones was a very likable person. She was the newest addition to the staff and had come to the firm with outstanding references and portfolio. She was always nice to everyone, with a cheerful disposition and an even temperament. She had survived almost three months without being called to Smith's office—an unofficial record by all accounts.

The secretaries jumped in unison when the first binder hit the trash can. Throwing projects into the trash was one of the dramatic things Smith did to accentuate his disappointment, disapproval, and disgust with the work product. The effect is powerful at the time, especially with the professional staff, who take great pride in their binders and presentations. Soon the voices started to penetrate the air—loud voices: first Smith's and then Jones's, then back and forth, then a bit of quiet, then more loudness. It was always hard to hear the exact words through the walls, but occasionally one or two would slip through. Sometimes curse words, but not this time.

Smith had studied Jones long enough to know that foul language would not work on her; he was shrewd—he had to wear her down with intellect. He had to convince her that her work was less than optimal or even rather poor. He would threaten her with reassignment, demotion, or termination, but would leave the door open for her to redeem herself down the road. He *would* convince her, of course, of all these things, as no one left Smith's office until he was convinced. Jones could not pretend to be convinced—she would actually have to *be* convinced—and she would, eventually. Moreover, she would be *thankful* for Smith's help and guidance. Jones would fall into line as her coworkers and predecessors; Smith counted on it.

Smith prided himself on his ability to break people down and then build them up again—but not too far up, just enough to keep them on a leash. He needed to control people and couldn't stand it when someone had a thought, an idea, an insight that he, "the boss," should have had. He hated to be wrong, as well—and, of course, in his own mind, never was. At least this was the theory some of the staff members had developed about Smith. Others were more humorous: some hypothesized about his being dropped on his head by the doctor who delivered him, having been raised by wolves, left in a field by aliens, or bitten by a mad dog in his youth. Humor helped make the situation tolerable but did not always heal the psychological wounds. It was much harder for some than others to come to terms with Smith's behavior.

He did not confine his attacks to the office. Those on his staff—almost half of the company—were fair game just walking the halls, working in meetings, or sitting in their cubicles. When Smith entered a department, a veil of tension seemed to spread through the atmosphere; heads went down and people acted busier than they really were. It was even money that he would strike out with a rapid onset of rage, followed by an equally rapid return to calm and a grin. But, sometimes he just made the rounds of the offices smiling, wishing people well, asking about their kids' soccer practice, and just being nice. It was so disconcerting. The new staff always fell for this approach and often concluded that Smith was a warm, caring, easy-to-talk-to boss. No one dared warn them, however, about what lay behind the smiling exterior, for no one was sure who might be one of Smith's spies.

What really irked everyone was the fact that sometimes Smith was right. His ideas sometimes really were better than the staff's, and sometimes he did know more than they did. Nevertheless, all would agree, there were other, less venomous, ways to communicate that didn't involve the destruction of the egos of staff or morale of those trying to do a good job for the company.

Jones seemed to have a solid ego, not overly inflated like some or shrinking like others, quite healthy by most accounts, and she was definitely working her hardest to do a good job. The secretaries wondered how Jones would handle it.

Sounds of a few more crashes, yelling and shouting, and desk-pounding came through the wall. Then silence. The secretaries lowered their heads to their desks and computer screens as they heard the door open. Jones emerged, standing as tall as she could, but clearly taken aback by what had just transpired. She headed down the hall quickly, clasping her folders to her chest.

As if on cue, the secretaries rose in unison. They each, taking their handbags, headed down the hall toward the women's room. Smith's secretary indicated to the wide-eyed part-timer to watch the phones and handle any visitors. "It'll be okay," she said, realizing that the young person didn't really want to be left alone in the office.

At the door to the restroom, they stopped but did not go in. Jones was far senior to them, and their relationships were strictly professional. After a few knowing looks, the two junior secretaries returned to their desks. Today, Smith's secretary would stand guard and not let anyone interfere with Jones's privacy.

DISCUSSION QUESTIONS

- Have you ever witnessed bullying on the job?
- Have you ever been the target of workplace bullying?
- What psychopathic features might be at play here?

How Big Is this Problem?

Following training programs and talks, audience members frequently approach us. Because of what they just had learned about the traits and characteristics of psychopathy, they conclude that their boss, peer, or subordinate must be a psychopath. Although it is neither appropriate nor even possible for us to offer an opinion, we understand the audacious behaviors attributed to their coworkers by these individuals—and the similarities they exhibit to psychopathic behavior. Over the years, additional individuals have contacted us with similar concerns after having read about psychopaths in *Without Conscience, Snakes in Suits*, or in various popular books on psychopathy, newspapers, and business magazines. Some of the personal stories we hear most likely are descriptions of true psychopaths, but, of course, many are not. What is clear is that a large number of people believe that they do work for a boss, or with a coworker, from hell.

We estimate that about 1 percent of the population has a dose of psychopathic features heavy enough to warrant a designation of psychopathy. Perhaps another 10 percent or so fall into the gray zone, with sufficient psychopathic features to be of concern to others. Most people have very few or no psychopathic characteristics. What about the business world? (See Figure 9.1). There can be no simple answer to this question, for the philosophy and practices of organizations range from ethical and altruistic to callous and grasping, perhaps even "psychopathic." Presumably, the former would have fewer resident psychopaths than would the latter, although no doubt there are exceptions. For example, a religious or charitable organization—by its nature trusting and lacking in street smarts—might provide a comfortable niche for a smooth-talking, charismatic psychopath as illustrated in a case presented earlier.

Unfortunately, there is a dearth of scientific evidence concerning the number of psychopaths in business, for several reasons. First, few organizations will provide the sort of access to their staff and files required to do proper assessments with a standardized instrument, such as the PCL: SV. Second, psychopaths have a talent for hiding their true selves, so one could expect many to go unnoticed and un-counted, leading to an under-reporting of psychopathy in business. It may be only the patsies (former pawns) who see behind the masks of particularly successful psychopaths, Third, psychopathic-like traits and behaviors are also exhibited by some individuals who are not truly psychopathic, which could lead to over-reporting, that is, view-ing someone as a psychopath when he is not. Nonetheless, based on many anecdotal reports and on our own observations, it is likely that psychopathic individuals make up much more than 1 percent of business managers and executives.

Many people display what appear to be psychopathic charac-teristics; readers need only review themselves against the definitions and descriptions of psychopaths to see how this might be possible. However, we should be careful not to confuse the presence of a few psychopathic-like traits with the disorder itself. How many times have you been abusive at work, but are quite the opposite with your family or life partner? On the other hand, you may be charming and manipulative with business associates, but forthright with friends. You may not feel guilt or remorse while "cheating" on your taxes, but feel terribly guilty if you hurt your child in any way. You may have had to defend a difficult business decision that hurt coworkers but feel badly inside nonetheless. Judging oneself or others because of one or two traits or behaviors that appear to resemble those of psy-chopaths (but typically are much less severe) is common but not wise. Only a relatively few individuals, true psychopaths, demonstrate *most* of the expected traits and characteristics in a *consistent* manner across *all* aspects of their personal, professional, and social lives.

"BOSS FROM HELL"?

Your boss is cold, hard driving, and ruthless. Before concluding that he is a psychopath, you should carefully consider the possibilities that your judgment is at fault and that his behavior is more a reflection of a personal *leadership style* than of a psychopathic personality. Because management style is rooted in training and experience, there are as many styles of management as there are managers. It is not surprising, then, that the match between employee expectations of how a boss *should* act and the supervisory style actually *exhibited* by the boss is not often perfect, leading to disappointment, conflict, and misinterpretation.

How employees view management or leadership style and its impact on performance and effectiveness has long been the subject of study by organizational psychologists. One of the earliest investigations into the styles of supervisors took place from 1946 to 1956, but the findings still have relevance today.[1] Employees described their leaders' behaviors on the job, and leaders in turn described their own behaviors and attitudes. A large-scale mathematical analysis of the hundreds of descriptions attempted to categorize the responses into the smallest number of critical items. The results of these Ohio State studies showed that there are two large groups of behaviors, or "factors," that go into our evaluation of our boss's style. We labeled these factors as Consideration and Initiating Structure.

Consideration refers to those behaviors and attitudes that deal with the interpersonal interactions between employee and boss. Highly considerate bosses treat people with respect, consider the egos and self-esteem of others in their decisions, and build working relationships on mutual trust. Staff perceive bosses low on consideration as uncaring and inconsiderate of the feelings of employees; they seem to be distant and cold. It is easy to see that reports of bosses berating employees in front of others, ignoring them when common courtesy demands otherwise, and failing to build relationships based on mutual trust and respect might actually reflect a boss low on consideration, rather than a true psychopath.

Initiating structure, the second supervisory factor, means that a leader should decide on the work goals and tasks to be completed, flesh out the roles of the team members, and delineate the standards of performance or key success measures—in essence, "lead." Bosses high in this factor take an active part in determining what needs to be done and how to do it. Traditional boss roles, such as planning, organizing, communicating, setting expectations, and defining the "big picture," fit in the high end of this factor. A boss who dominates or who issues orders every step of the way may just be too high on initiating structure and not a true psychopath. Conversely, if the boss is rarely involved or even interested in the work you do, she may be very low in this factor—a "laissez-faire leader"—or may not be a leader at all.

Most people want a boss who is considerate and trusting and who builds rapport. Whether we also want our bosses to be high or low on initiating structure depends on whether we want someone to tell us what our job is and how to do it (most appropriate for new jobs or untrained employees) or we prefer to do our job with little interference from the boss (most preferred by seasoned workers). Both are equally valid styles and can be effective as long as there is a match between employees' needs and the boss's approach to management.

While this two-factor model of leader behavior is well founded and makes intuitive sense, subsequent research has shown that these two variables alone are not enough to predict who will be an *effective* leader. The boss–employee relationship is much more complex than this and involves other things, not the least of which is the work situation itself. Yet we all tend to refer to these factors (sometimes by other names) when asked to rate how "good" or "bad" our leaders are.

"COWORKERS FROM HELL"?

"Bad" bosses are not the only people we hear about. We have also heard a lot about coworkers and colleagues with negative attitudes, antisocial tendencies, manipulation, irresponsibility, poor performance, and a tendency to disrupt others who are trying to work. Clearly, these individuals are particularly difficult to work with, but there may be plausible explanations other than psychopathy for their behavior. To understand this we need to consider one of the factors people commonly use when evaluating colleagues and coworkers: industrial psychologists who study it refer to it as *conscientiousness*.

Individuals who are highly conscientious tend to focus on doing a good job; they like being accurate, timely, and thorough. They take pride in completing the jobs they start, are very responsible and detail oriented, and like to appear to others as competent. Low-conscientiousness coworkers can get sloppy about meeting deadlines, achieving goals, or finishing what they start. They can come across as irresponsible, unfocused, disruptive, and poor performers. Sometimes they rely on others to help them get their work done—or others may feel the need to "cover" for them so as not to hurt the team or department's overall performance. Clearly, most of us prefer to work next to individuals who are conscientious in their work. It seems fairer to us for others to carry their own weight on the job, especially if they are drawing a salary similar to the one we receive.

A lot of research has shown that conscientiousness is a primary dimension of personality, rather than just a style or personal preference. People vary on this trait as much as they do on other personality traits—we all have various degrees of conscientiousness in our makeup. However, being at the extremely low end or extremely high end of the scale, while disconcerting to some of our coworkers, is not necessarily a bad thing. Your effectiveness at work depends, once again, on the match between your degree of conscientiousness and the specific job you do. Examples of jobs requiring moderate levels of conscientiousness typically include artists, creative research scientists, or visionary leaders because of the need to step out of the box or take risks when creating new works of art, pursuing new knowledge, or leading in uncertain times. Jobs like design engineer and nuclear power plant operator tend to require high degrees of conscientiousness because they manage many important details critical to their success.

While the "fit" between levels in conscientiousness and job requirements may not be perfect in real-life situations, there is no reason to conclude that coworkers low (or high) in conscientiousness (alone) are psychopaths.

Psychopath or Difficult Person: The Assessment Challenge

Individual differences in consideration, structuring, and conscientiousness are normal parts of human behavior in any organization. However, some clusters of psychopathic traits *do* manifest themselves on the consideration, structuring, and conscientiousness scales. Specifically, many psychopaths would clearly rate *very low* on consideration (rude, arrogant, and self-centered, among other things), at the *extreme* for structuring jobs (either uncaring or overbearing), and *very low* on conscientiousness (irresponsible, impulsive, arrogant, self-centered, and seemingly unwilling to accept responsibility). As we stated before, these factors alone do not indicate psychopathy, but they certainly are warning flags. What else does one need to look for?

In general, psychopaths are all egotistical, having a sense of entitlement and the assertiveness to demand it, which often makes them appear selfish in relationships. They all have a grandiose sense of who they are and *insist* that others give them the respect due them. They are not as goal oriented as the rest of us when it comes to actual diligence and hard work. Nonetheless, they frequently tell others how ambitious they are and weave a (phony) hard-luck story about how they overcame immense odds growing up poor or underprivileged or from an abusive home. Yet they are all irresponsible when it comes to attending to appropriate behaviors (for example, not doing the job they were assigned or making promises they do not keep), both on and off the job. They rarely, if ever, experience guilt or remorse for any of their transgressions, even the most outrageous and hurtful.

However, some psychopaths are different from others. Some

come across as more impulsive or erratic than others do. The more impulsive psychopaths require immediate gratification and use short-term predatory strategies to get what they want. The less impulsive types tend to appear less predatory in their pursuit of gratification, instead relying on opportunities coming to them. This difference is possibly due to different physiological factors, but the exact mechanism is unclear at this time. Some psychopaths (arguably the less intelligent ones) seek to satisfy the most basic instinctual needs, such as food and sex, while others seek higher-level satisfaction in power, control, or fame. Some are more subtle or clever in their manipulations of others, using charm and linguistic skills to get others to obey and conform. Others are blunter, attempting to con in clumsy ways, and then resorting to abusive demands when their "charm" does not work. This latter type acts out their aggressions in violent, vindictive, ruthless ways, while the former are less reactive—perhaps more in control of their inner drives—relying on suggestions, intimidation, and "passive aggression" to get their way.

Cons, Bullies, and the Puppetmaster

When we analyzed the anecdotes and stories from readers and program participants as well as others we have worked with, and then added in our own research, we discovered three distinctive styles of corporate psychopath that seem to fit well into the subtype model.

Some psychopaths, the *Corporate Cons*, are adept at using others in pursuit of fame, fortune, power, and control. They are deceitful, egotistical, superficial, manipulating, and prone to lying. They do not care about the consequences of their own behavior, rarely thinking about what the future might hold. They never take responsibility, despite promises to deliver on goals, objectives, and personal favors. When confronted, they will blame others for the problem at hand, not accepting responsibility for their actions. They are rude and callous to individuals who have nothing to offer them, feeling superior and entitled. They never think about the harm they inflict on people or institutions, often coming across in interactions as totally devoid of human emotions, especially empathy. To apologize for something they did is foreign to them, as they do not experience remorse or guilt.

Yet, despite all this, the cons can be surprisingly successful in dealing with others, relying primarily on their excellent ability to charm and weave a believable story to influence others. They are adept at reading situations and people, and then modifying their approach to best influence those around them. They can turn on the charm when it suits them and turn it off when they want. Because of their chameleon-like ability to hide their dark side, they can quickly and easily build trusting relationships with others and then take advantage of them or betray them in some way. Manipulators seem to experience a game-like fascination in fooling people, getting into other people's heads and getting them to do things for them. This ability to win psychological games with people seems to give them a sense of personal satisfaction.

While they may come across as ambitious—a trait they will play up—they actually have few long-range goals of any consequence, relying more on their innate ability to seize an opportunity that interests them at any given moment and then weave it into the story they tell others. Should something else more exciting come along they will move quickly toward the new opportunity, a tendency that can make them look impulsive and irresponsible to observers. While they may blow up at coworkers, flying into a rage and then calming down just as quickly (as if nothing has happened), they can also control their anger if it is in their best interest to do so—saving their vindictiveness for a later time.

Another group of psychopaths is much more aggressive: the *Corporate Bullies*. Corporate bullies are not as sophisticated, charming, or smooth as the conning type, as they rely on coercion, abuse, humiliation, harassment, aggression, and fear to get their way. They are callous to almost everyone, intentionally finding reasons to engage in conflict, to blame others for things that go wrong, to attack others unfairly (in private and in public), and to be generally antagonistic. They routinely disregard the rights and feelings of others and frequently violate traditional norms of appropriate social behavior. If they do not get their way, they become vindictive, maintaining a grudge for a considerable amount of time, and take every opportunity to "get even." They frequently select and relentlessly attack relatively powerless targets.

Bullies react aggressively in response to provocation or perceived insults or slights. It is unclear whether their acts of bullying give them pleasure or are just the most effective way they have learned to get what they want from others. Similar to the cons, however, psychopathic Bullies do not feel remorse, guilt, or empathy. They lack any insight into their own behavior, and seem unwilling or unable to moderate it, even when it is to their own advantage. Not being able to understand the harm they do to themselves (let alone their victims), psychopathic Bullies are particularly dangerous.

Of course, not all bullies are psychopathic, though this may be of little concern to the victims. Bullies come in many psychological and physical sizes and shapes. In some cases, "garden-variety" bullies have deep-seated psychological problems, including feelings of inferiority or inadequacy and difficulty in relating to others. Some may simply have learned at an early age that their size, strength, or verbal talent was the only effective tool they had for social behavior. Some of these individuals may be context-specific bullies, behaving badly at work but more or less normally in other contexts. Nevertheless, the psychopathic Bully is what he is: a callous, vindictive, controlling individual with little empathy or concern for the rights and feelings of the victim, no matter what the context.

In addition to these two specific types—the Con and the Bully—we have seen a handful of cases that are even worse. *Corporate Puppetmasters*, as we labeled them, seem to combine the features of con and bully in a sophisticated way. They are adept at manipulating people—pulling the strings—from a distance, in order to *get those directly under their control* to abuse or bully those lower down in the organization. In essence, they use both strategies—conning and bullying—much like historical figures such as Stalin and Hitler, individuals who surrounded themselves with obedient followers and through them controlled much of their countries' populations. Any sign of disobedience (often accentuated by a paranoid temperament) led them to attack their direct supporters as well. To the puppetmaster, both the intermediary (the "puppet") and the ultimate victim are expendable since he considers neither as a real, individual person. We believe that Corporate Puppetmasters are examples of the much more dangerous classic psychopath. See S 8.1: *The Puppetmaster.*

Our research has shown that conning psychopaths would do well in business, politics, and other professions because of their ability to convince people they are honest and ethical and have talent, experience, and a flair for leadership. In management positions, bullying psychopaths keep rivals and subordinates at a distance, allowing them to use their power to get what they want. Furthermore, members of top management, not close to the day-to-day action, may hear rumors of such bullying behavior, but discount them as exaggerations due to envy and rivalry, or even accept the behavior as indications of the person's strong management style. To the degree that bullying psychopaths have bolstered their reputations as major contributors to the successful running of the business, they are immune to criticism or might receive a token "slap on the wrist" occasionally. The puppetmasters are immune to organizational discipline because they themselves are in control of a greater number of employees, as well as systems, processes, and procedures designed to protect the organization and its members.

In our original research working with 203 high-potential executives (see Chapter 9 for a full accounting of this research), we found about 3.9 percent who fit the profile of the psychopath as measured on the PCL-R. While this may not seem like a large percentage, it is considerably higher than that found in the general population (1 percent), and perhaps more than most businesses would want to have on their payrolls, especially as these individuals were on the road to becoming leaders in their organizations. Of these individuals, we found that all had the traits of the conning, manipulative psychopath: superficial, grandiose, deceitful, impulsive, irresponsible, not taking responsibility for their own actions, and lacking goals, remorse, and empathy. Of these individuals, two exhibited bullying, as well. From the cases we have reviewed from others in the field, as well as from readers, this level of incidence seems correct.

Variations on a Theme

It is interesting that the preceding observations bear some resemblance to the results of recent empirical research on "varieties" of psychopathic and other offenders.

We note that this is not merely a statistical exercise but rather a way to identify individuals with things in common, in this case, patterns of psychopathic traits. Most research involves a *variable-oriented* approach, which looks at correlations and associations among variables. A *person-oriented* approach, described here, allows us to identify people with various patterns of behavioral and personality traits, and helps us to make predictions about how an individual with a particular pattern will act. In the next chapter, we relate this research to the Babiak, Neumann, and Hare[2] study of corporate psychopathy.

The four-factor model of psychopathy allows us to plot an individual's profile as a score on each factor. Statistical programs (latent profile analyses) sort these profiles into clusters or subtypes according to their similarity to one another. Mokros and colleagues[3] analyzed the profiles of offenders with very high PCL-R scores (30 or higher). As Figure 8.1 shows, two profiles or behavioral styles emerged from this analysis.

- The *Classic* or *Aggressive* profile consisted of individuals with a high score on each of the psychopathy dimensions:

interpersonal, affective, lifestyle, and antisocial. They exhibited virtually *all* the features that define psychopathy.

- The *Manipulative* profile consisted of those with a high score on all but the antisocial factor. They manipulate, deceive, and charm, but are less antisocial than are those in the previous profile. They are more talk-oriented than action-oriented.

We considered these clusters to be *variations on the central theme of psychopathy*. We present them here because some psychopathic executives may have the same two profiles, as depicted in Chapter 9.

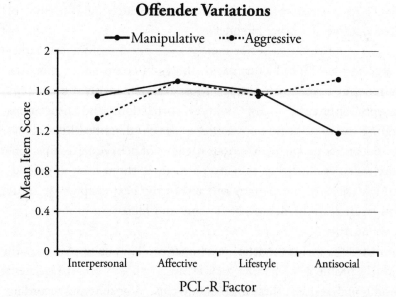

Figure 8.1. Factor profiles of offenders with a PCL-R score of 30 or higher.

Good Leader or Corporate Psychopath: How Can You Tell?

Early research suggested that the behaviors of most psychopaths were too dysfunctional to make long-term survival in organizations possible and that they might be better suited to work on their own or in some other career. However, based on our own research and that of others, we now know that some organizations *actively seek out* and recruit individuals with at least a moderate dose of psychopathic features. Some executives have said to us, "Many of the traits you describe to us seem to be valued by our company. Why shouldn't companies hire psychopaths to fill some jobs?" A proper, scientific answer is that more research is needed to determine the impact of various doses of psychopathic characteristics on the performance of different types of jobs (see Chapter 10 for a more detailed discussion of corporate research using the B-Scan assessment instrument). The "optimal" number and severity of such characteristics presumably is higher for some jobs (such as stock promoters, politicians, law enforcement, used-car salespeople, mercenaries, and lawyers) than for others (such as social workers, teachers, nurses, and ministers). Until such research becomes available, we can safely say that those who believe that "psychopathy is good" clearly have not had much exposure to the real thing . . . and certainly have never worked for one.

For an organization, one psychopath, unchecked, can do considerable harm to staff morale, productivity, and teamwork. The problem is that *you cannot choose* which psychopathic traits you want and ignore the others; psychopathy is a syndrome, that is, a package of related traits and behaviors that form the personality of the individual. Unfortunately, for business the "good" traits often conceal the existence of the "bad" when it comes to a psychopath. However, there are cases in which some individuals fake or simulate bad traits and behaviors in order to "fit in." See S 8.2: *Emulating the Psychopathic Lifestyle.*

A true corporate psychopath can easily feign leadership and management traits sought after by executives when making hiring, promotion, and succession planning decisions. A charming demeanor and grandiose talk can be mistaken for *charismatic leadership* and *self-confidence*. Furthermore, because of its critical importance to effective leadership, charisma observed in a candidate can lead to a "halo" effect—that is, a tendency for interviewers and decision makers to generalize from a single trait to the entire personality. The halo effect acts to "fill in the blanks" in the absence of other information about the person and can overshadow more critical judgments. As mentioned earlier, even seasoned researchers—who *know* they are dealing with a psychopath—often accept things at face value.

The ability to *influence* events and decisions and to *persuade* peers and subordinates to support your point of view are critical executive management skills. Not everyone has these skills at the level required by general management jobs. Organizations constantly seek people with these skills and invest significant sums of money in training, coaching, and development of staff to improve them. To find someone who seems to have a natural talent for influence and persuasion is rare. When found, it is hard for decision makers to look past it. We know that psychopaths are masters of conning and manipulation—especially with their deceitful veneer of charm—leading to the perception that they have strong persuasion and leadership skills.

Visionary thinking, the ability to conceptualize the future of the organization, is a complex skill requiring a broad perspective, the ability to integrate multiple points of view, and a talent for looking into the future—that is, to *think strategically*. Psychopaths are not good at establishing and working toward long-term, strategic objectives; they are much more opportunistic. Yet they can weave compelling stories about situations and events of which they know very little into surprisingly believable visions of the future. Because visioning is so difficult for the average person to understand, it is little wonder that the vague but convincing, illogical but believable, rambling but captivating, and compelling but lie-filled discourses of the psychopath can look like brilliant insight into what the organization should do. This is especially true in times of chaos, when few can make these lofty predictions and many are looking for leadership—a savior or knight in shining armor—to fill the vacuum.

History offers some good examples of leaders who embody and are able to apply the complex mix of high-level executive skills necessary to handle difficult situations. In the last and most decisive battle for Gaul, the enemy was mercilessly overpowering Julius Caesar's army. His troops were significantly outnumbered and they were surrounded; the end seemed near for Caesar and his long campaign to take Gaul. However, seeing that all would be lost, he put on his armor and his bright crimson cloak—so the enemy easily could see him—and led his reserve troops into the middle of the battle. Still outnumbered, his troops rallied, and the enemy soldiers, realizing *Caesar himself* led the charge, faltered. History records Caesar's victory, his valor, and his fighting acumen. We know that he was charismatic, a strong orator, influential, and persuasive, and a visionary leader whose strategies military schools teach to this day. Was Caesar a great leader, or did he succeed because of psychopathic impulsivity and extreme risk-taking traits?

It is important to note that psychopaths—like great leaders—*are* risk takers, often putting themselves and others (in Caesar's case, his own life and that of his army; in the case of business, the entire company) in harm's way. Risk-taking, often difficult to quantify or differentiate from foolhardiness, is a trait that closely lines up with what we expect of leaders in times of crisis. How much risk is appropriate? How much risk will be effective in saving the day or, in more mundane business settings, achieving objectives? Another psychopathic trait, *impulsivity*, accentuates risk-taking behavior, leading to acting without sufficient planning and forethought. *Thrill-seeking* often involves taking dangerous risks just to see what will happen. Elements of extreme impulsivity and thrill-seeking can also be mistaken for *high energy, action orientation, courage,* and the ability to *multitask,* all important management traits.

Despite the risks to his own life, Caesar's risk-taking behavior in this last battle for Gaul was far from psychopathic. He was a *prudent* risk taker, sizing up the realities he faced, the resources he (and the enemy) had, the probabilities that would influence the outcome, and the risk to his legion posed by *not* taking a risk. He was also not a thrill seeker, at least not to the degree exhibited by psychopaths. He and the Roman legion he commanded were a disciplined machine, hardly the image of a rampant leader and his band of psychopaths fighting for the thrill of it.

Psychopaths' emotional poverty—that is, their inability to feel normal human emotions and their lack of conscience—can be mistaken for three other executive skills, specifically the ability to *make hard decisions,* to *keep their emotions in check,* and to *remain cool under fire.* Making hard decisions is one of those management tasks that executives have to do on almost a daily basis. Whether it is to choose one marketing plan over another, litigate or settle a lawsuit, or close a manufacturing plant, major decisions have emotional components that influence decision-making. Most executives often must suspend their own emotional reaction to events in order to be effective. They have feelings, but the constraints of their jobs often preclude them from sharing them with others, except family members or close confidants. Of particular importance, as dictated by some business realities, is appearing cool and calm in the midst of turmoil. One can imagine Caesar calmly putting on his red robe as he contemplated the possibility of his own death. Certainly, New York City mayor Rudolph Giuliani and US president George W. Bush displayed amazing calm and did so for an extended period in the aftermath of the World Trade Center attacks. They received credit for keeping the city, as well as the country, under control as they analyzed and dealt with the problem.

In addition to temperament and intelligence, leadership often requires experience and wisdom, especially when faced with situations never before encountered. On January 15, 2009, Captain Chesley "Sully" Sullenberger had just taken off from New York's LaGuardia Airport when a flock of Canada geese flew into his path, disabling the plane's engines. With no time to spare, as his multi-ton aircraft was instantaneously turned into a falling glider over one of the most populated cities in the country, Captain Sullenberger made the decision to land on the Hudson River—declining the clearance air traffic control had given him to try to turn around, glide over the city, and land at the airport. He had never attempted this before; few commercial pilots have. In what the newspapers of the day referred to as "the Miracle on the Hudson," he landed his aircraft and oversaw the evacuation. All 155 aboard survived. Subsequent investigation and analysis showed that he made the correct decision in those few minutes.

It is easy for someone to confuse behavior that is psychopathically motivated with expressions of genuine leadership, especially when carefully packaged as leadership. In such a case, with the phony *persona* so tightly bound up in business expectations, the psychopathic fiction "I am the ideal leader" works well. It often takes good results and a solid track record to differentiate between the two.

DISCUSSION QUESTIONS

- Have you ever worked for a Con, a Bully, or a Puppetmaster?
- Was he or she effective as a leader?
- Think of the "best boss" you ever had: What traits or behaviors endeared him or her to you?

S 8.1
The Puppetmaster

In describing his role in the murder of his friend's father and the attempted murder of his friend's mother and sister, an offender had this to say:

"A friend of mine came in and we started talking, getting to know each other. Well, I started to get to know *him* better. Because the more he told me about himself, the more leverage I had. The more I know about the guy, the more I know what buttons to push. So, I started pushing those buttons. He had a lot of unresolved issues from his childhood, so I tried to get to the root of the problem and started to get him to feel very angry, very hostile toward his family. I said, they have money. Why don't you take some? I'll help you spend it because I'm your friend. We got together, and it escalated and I encouraged the escalation. I don't know if in the back of my mind I truly believed what the capabilities were, but I didn't care. So, it started to become a plan. I just keep fueling the fire; the more fuel I added to the fire the bigger the payoff for me. And, plus that sense of control, power. I was the *puppetmaster* pulling the strings." The first two murder attempts failed, but the third did not. The offender watched while the quiet, introverted person he was manipulating killed the mother of the third offender with a baseball bat. They then set the house on fire.

For his actions, the offender received a sentence of twenty-five years before the possibility of parole. He married in prison and has a daughter. In the outtakes from a TV documentary provided to Hare, the offender explained his behavior in many curious ways, including blaming his father for the abuse inflicted on him. At the end of the session the interviewer asked, "So if you could go back and change things, where would you start?" The offender replied, "I have often pondered if I could go back, *but then all that I have learnt would be lost*... I don't want to dwell on the negative aspects of it. I want to reemerge into society and make a life for myself and for my family now. Be a husband to my wife, be a father to my daughter, be a son once more to my mother. That is what I look forward to." He now is on parole, ten years before his eligibility date.

S 8.2
Emulating the Psychopathic Style

The attitudes and behaviors of individuals with many psycho-pathic features are systemic, a natural and pervasive syndrome defining their general lifestyle. However, there are others whose nature is less psychopathic than pragmatic and adaptive. They *adopt or feign* some of the trappings of a "psychopathic life-style" in order to succeed, "fit in," or excel in a profession or organization that rewards such behaviors. Some may succeed in this personal makeover by becoming sycophants, opportunistic acolytes, and free riders who model their behaviors after those of their psychopathic superiors, a process common during war, in cults, and in terrorist and criminal organizations. In other cases, special circumstances at hand, as in war, may require individuals to engage in behaviors that otherwise would be alien to them. In the fictional television series, *Black Sails* (Season 4, Episode 3), pirates and the Royal Navy are vying for control of early 18th-century Nassau, in the Bahamas. The Military Commander of Nassau tells the Governor, "Good men is not what the moment requires. Right now, the time calls for dark men to do dark things."

Of course, the more psychopathic one is to start with, the easier it is to follow a road map of personal preservation and corporate predation! Many pop-psych and self-help books promote or justify a philosophy of aggressive greed, self-entitlement, and the importance of "number one." Some pundits write about "the good psychopath" (an oxymoron?), whereas others tell us how to use our dormant psychopathic tendencies to achieve success, fame, and fortune.

This could present a problem for those (e.g., Human Resources personnel) who monitor and evaluate these faux psychopaths, and who must separate them from the real thing. For this reason, it is essential to conduct evaluations about a given individual using much more than just work-place behavior and "gut feel."

The Case of Dave

ACT IV

DOUBTS DANCE AWAY

Frank waved to the security guard as he parked his car near the building. He grabbed his briefcase and went directly through the entrance to the cafeteria for his coffee. It was Tuesday, gourmet pastry day, so he went straight for the good stuff. He always liked getting in early after a business trip so he could get a head start on the work he knew had piled up on his desk during his absence. Waving to a few staff members as he left, he went to his office, turned on the light, stopped, and stared. His office looked the same as it did when he left Friday night, except for the wastebasket that he had put near the door and that Marissa, the cleaning supervisor, had emptied and returned to its spot behind his desk.

"Hmmmm," he muttered as he walked over to the credenza, placed his briefcase down, and opened it. He turned, and as he placed his coffee on the coaster on his desk, he saw a bright yellow thumb drive on the pile of papers he had left.

"I hear the meeting went very well," said Dave from the doorway.

"Yes, it did. They liked the material," said Frank, picking up the drive.

"That was a close one, wasn't it," said Dave, laughingly.

"Dave, come in. Let's talk," said Frank, deciding to take a firm approach with Dave; he wanted to get to the bottom of what had happened over the weekend. Dave took a seat across the desk and crossed his legs. Frank continued, holding the drive in his hand and waving it. "Dave, what happened on Sunday? I tried to reach you after I looked at the material you left for me. I was—"

"I was away that morning," interrupted Dave. "When I got your message, I realized that something terrible had happened. I rushed to the office, hoping that this was just a simple mistake—that maybe you had dropped the thumb drive on your way out—and found it here," Dave turned slightly and indicated the center of the carpet, "so I immediately realized what had happened. I knew you were already on the plane, so I decided to email it to you and John just in case you didn't have your computer with you."

Dave paused, and Frank turned the yellow thumb drive over in his hand, asking, "This is what you left me for the meeting?"

"Yes, Frank, why?" Dave looked puzzled. "Didn't I do the right thing getting the file over to the meeting?"

Frank turned to his briefcase and pulled out the blue thumb drive he had found in the package from Dave on Friday. "Then what is this?" he asked.

"That's my draft material. Blue is for drafts, yellow for final product," said Dave matter-of-factly.

"Dave, there was nothing in the folder to indicate that there was a final product file, yellow or otherwise. Why did you give me the draft drive, when I . . ."

"Frank," said Dave, getting serious, "I gave you both—it's not my fault you dropped one on the way out. I did what I could to help you. It was a mistake, I understand, but I didn't tell John about you leaving the file. I covered it up and things worked out, didn't they?"

"Dave . . ." started Frank.

"Frank, I don't know what you are implying here, but I gave you the draft material as well because I know you are a stickler for details and like to check everyone's work. I figured you might want to see the background material, too."

"Your draft came from a magazine!" said Frank, raising his voice slightly, and toughening up his tone.

"I know that," dismissed Dave. "Don't you remember pointing that article out to me as an example of an excellent presentation? I scanned it in and used it as a template for your presentation to the committee. I thought it was what you would want. Wasn't it as good as the article you admired?"

Frank was perplexed. Dave's story made sense. Yes, he had praised the story about the competitor and showed it to Dave.

"And the numbers and charts?"

"They were just placeholders until I got the data I was collecting. The final is the same format, but with our numbers, graphics, and pictures." Dave paused, a serious expression crossing his face. "I wasn't doing anything devious here, Frank, and I'm a bit disappointed that you're suggesting I did."

"I'm not suggesting that, Dave; I'm just trying to understand what happened."

"Well, you said it yourself: you dropped the file on the way out. A simple mistake; nothing to make a federal case over. I was hoping to get a pat on the back for both a great presentation and saving the day. But . . ."

"The presentation was terrific, Dave. You did a great job, thanks. I really mean it. Everyone was impressed," said Frank.

"I appreciate it, Frank, thanks. Do we have the go-ahead?"

"Yes, full steam ahead," said Frank smiling. "Put together your recommendations for the team, and let's meet tomorrow to discuss timing."

"Yes, boss!" said Dave, giving a mock salute, but smiling broadly. Frank rose and extended his hand to Dave; they shook firmly and Dave left the office.

Frank worked all day and into the evening. At about 7:30 P.M., Frank called his wife to say he was on his way home. He sometimes felt that he had to make up the time he spent out of the office, but his wife knew that he just missed the excitement and enjoyed working late.

As he hung up, Pete, the cleaning person, entered the doorway. "Excuse me, Mr. Frank," he said backing out into the hall.

"Oh, that's okay, Pete, I'm just leaving. You can come in." Frank packed his briefcase, grabbed his jacket from the back of the office door, and waved to Pete. He paused, thought a moment, and asked, "Is Marissa around tonight?"

"Yes," said Pete. "She's down the hall to the left."

"Thanks, have a good evening," said Frank as he headed down the hallway.

DISCUSSION QUESTIONS

- Is Dave telling the truth?
- How did Dave defuse Frank's anger and cause him to question his own analysis of the situation?
- Who really wrote the final presentation?

A Unique Empirical Study of Corporate Psychopathy[1]

NOT ALL PSYCHOPATHS ARE IN PRISON. SOME ARE IN THE BOARDROOM.

The above statement was a casual response by Hare to a question asked at the end of a 2002 address to the Canadian Police Association meeting in St. John's, Newfoundland and Labrador. The questioner turned out to be a journalist, and over the next few days, the international media picked up his newspaper article, treating the statement as somewhat of a revelation. The media reports clearly reflected both the popular view that psychopathy equates to criminality and violence, and the public and media fascination with murder and mayhem, typically attributed to "psychopaths" or "sociopaths." Media headlines and popular television crime shows are often the only exposure the public gets to the concept of psychopathy, resulting in considerable misinformation and misunderstanding. Most people see only entertainment that often portrays psychopaths as somewhat heroic individuals who are not bound by ordinary social conventions. However, most of the public would react in horror if they actually experienced or watched the callous acts portrayed on TV or in the movies. This is also the case with business professionals, who see little relevance of such portrayals to their daily interactions with coworkers.

Unfortunately, empirically sound studies of corporate psychopathy are uncommon. Most studies (including several by the authors of this book) rely on self-report personality inventories and measures of various dark personalities. These include *The Dark Triad* (psychopathy, narcissism, and Machiavellianism), and, with the inclusion of sadism, *The Dark Tetrad*. This is problematic, given that self-descriptions of one's personality in a corporate context likely involve presenting oneself in a good light, especially by those with a natural tendency to manipulate and deceive others. Many of these studies do not involve people in their actual workplaces. Instead, they often use university students or recruit people through Internet crowdsourcing marketplaces such as *Amazon Mechanical Turk*. Moreover, much of this research takes place in a laboratory-like setting, using tasks designed to simulate the real world of business. It is difficult to know how much these *proxy* simulation studies, and their interpretations by the researchers, inform us about the role played by psychopathy and personality in the real world of business. Unfortunately, many media reports of these studies take their findings at face value.

This is not to say that self-report inventories are not useful in the study of personality in the public and corporate worlds. They provide general insights into how personality traits relate to behaviors in different contexts, provide the basis for developing theories relevant to a particular context (e.g., types and patterns of corporate misbehavior), and make it easy to conduct large-scale studies.

For their part, organizations often are reluctant to use measures of psychopathology except under special circumstances, such as the hiring of critical public safety staff (e.g., police, firefighters, nuclear power plant operators).[2] The fear of violating privacy laws and the risk of lawsuits inhibit research in this area. As a result, we know relatively little about the association between psychopathy and, for example, corporate status and performance.

Although psychopathy, broadly speaking, reflects a fundamental antisociality,[3] some psychopathic features (e.g., callousness, grandiosity, manipulativeness) may relate to the ability to make persuasive arguments and ruthless decisions, while others (e.g., impulsivity, irresponsibility, poor behavioral controls) relate to poor decision-making and performance. Furthermore, while a particular mix of psychopathic features might be compatible with good performance in some executive positions in some corporate milieus, it is likely that the confluence of many psychopathic features generally relates more to appearance than to good job performance.

Exacerbating the problem is that much of what we know about psychopathy comes from clinical and empirical research with offender and forensic psychiatric populations (where the base-rate for psychopathy is high and the information needed for reliable assessments is readily available). In addition, most of the research on corporate personalities makes use of various self-report instruments with limited validity when used to evaluate sophisticated job applicants and candidates for promotion.

Until recently, we had few small-sample studies, anecdotes, and speculations about corporate psychopathy and its implications. In large part, this is because of the difficulty in obtaining the active cooperation of business organizations and their personnel for research purposes. At the same time, there is considerable public and media interest in learning more about the types of person who violate their positions of influence and trust, defraud customers, investors, friends, and family, successfully elude regulators, and appear indifferent to the financial chaos and personal suffering they create.

In the face of large-scale Ponzi schemes, embezzlement, insider trading, mortgage fraud, and Internet frauds and schemes, it was inevitable that psychopathy would be invoked as one explanation for such callous and socially devastating behavior. However, there is a dearth of empirical data on the role of psychopathy in fraud, corruption, malfeasance, and other egregious violations of the public trust. We need research in this area, but we also need investigations of a related and equally important issue: *the prevalence, strategies, and consequences of psychopathy in the corporate world.* The information gained from such investigations would provide valuable clues about corporate psychopathy in general and would establish an empirical base for conducting and evaluating research on the more high-profile miscreants who have wreaked financial and emotional havoc in the lives of so many people. While the latter recently have received enormous amounts of media and regulatory attention, we also should be concerned with the less spectacular, but more common, in-house fraud and corruption experienced by many corporations as well as small companies worldwide. We know little about these individuals or about the ways in which they often manage to avoid prosecution, termination, or formal censure, sometimes with the help of organizations that strive to keep problems in-house. See S 9.1: *Economic and Corporate Fraud.*

An Empirical Corporate Study Using the PCL-R

We mentioned a seminal study very briefly in the previous chapter but want to offer the interested reader an in-depth analysis of what we found. This study arose from an unusual set of circumstances. Over a period of several years, the senior author (P.B.) had consulted with seven companies in the US to evaluate 203 high-level corporate personnel (77.8 percent males; 22.2 percent females) selected to participate in management development programs. He completed the PCL-R (see Table 2.1) for each participant using comprehensive field notes from face-to-face meetings, observations of social and work–team interactions, as well as meetings with participants' supervisors, peers, and subordinates. He reviewed some scores with the second author of this book (R.H.). We needed to omit two items as being inapplicable as they are focused on criminal subjects (Revocation of conditional release; Criminal versatility) and prorated the remaining eighteen items to a twenty-item scale, using the standard procedure as outlined in the PCL-R manual.[4] With this information, we were in a position to determine the prevalence, distribution, and structure of psychopathic features in the sample. Importantly, we had access to *independent* key performance and management development measures provided by the corporations, thus allowing us to determine the extent and manner in which psychopathy was related to these variables. For an example of how *not* to use the PCL-R as the basis for research in the business world, see S 9.2: *The Mismeasure of Corporate Psychopathy*.

COMPETENCY DOMAINS

Although they differed somewhat in the format and wording of some items, the assessment instruments used across the companies shared the same outcome variables, which was typical at the time for defining "leadership." These assessment items reflected six broad management competency areas or domains:

1. **Communication Skills:** making presentations; report/letter-writing; representing the company to others publicly; training others;
2. **Creativity/Innovation:** ability to generate new and different ideas (Creativity) and/or bring them to market (Innovation);
3. **Strategic Thinking:** seeing the big picture; visioning; setting long-range objectives;

4. **Leadership Skills:** decision-making; problem-solving; resolving issues without direction; integrity;
5. **Management Style:** ability to use people effectively to get things done; resolve personnel issues; sensitivity to others, including diversity issues; delegation; building a team; and
6. **Team Player:** ability to get along on a team with co-workers as well as on interdisciplinary teams; collaborates; shares information and credit with team; keeps others in the loop; works toward consensus.

For each of the six assessment variables, participants received an average score categorized as High (that is, a strength), Medium (indicating some improvement needed), or Low (indicating a weakness area requiring training or executive coaching). We coded these as 3, 2, and 1 respectively.

Most large organizations use formal, annual performance evaluations, which often lead to recommendations for training and development. Most companies use a five-point scale for the Performance Appraisal, ranging from five (far exceeds expectations) to one (far below expectations). An exploratory factor analysis of the six management competency items plus the performance appraisal item revealed two clear factors, or composites:

1. **Charisma/Presentation Style.** This composite consisted of the first three competency areas listed above: Communication Skill, Creativity/Innovation, and Strategic Thinking.
2. **Responsibility/Performance.** This composite consisted of the second three competency areas: Management Style, Being a Team Player, and Leadership, as well as Performance Appraisal.

The main reason for the study was to answer the question: To what extent do these composites relate to psychopathy? In light of what we know about psychopathy, we expected that those with high PCL-R scores would score high on Charisma/Presentation Style and low on Responsibility/Performance. That is, they would look good but perform poorly.

PSYCHOPATHY SCORES

The executive PCL-R scores varied from 0 to 34, with a group mean of 3.6. That is, the level of psychopathy in this sample was very low. "However, nine of the participants (4.4%) had a score of 25 or higher, eight (3.9%) had a score of 30 or higher (the common research threshold for psychopathy), two had a score of 33, and one had a score of 34. By way of comparison, the mean score for incarcerated male offenders is approximately 22, with about 15% of the scores being 30 or higher" (p. 183).[5] Babiak and colleagues noted that interestingly, "of the nine participants with a PCL-R score of 25 or higher, two were vice-presidents, two were directors, two were managers or supervisors, and one held some other management position; thus, they had already achieved considerable rank and status within their respective organizations" (p. 185). Statistical analyses indicated that the PCL-R scores identified the same four factors or dimensions as those found with the PCL-R and PCL: SV: Interpersonal, Affective, Lifestyle, and Antisocial.

COMPARISON WITH COMMUNITY SAMPLES

Because there were no large community PCL-R samples for comparison with the corporate distribution of scores, we converted the PCL-R scores to "PCL: SV equivalents" by multiplying each PCL-R score by 12/20 (the PCL: SV has twelve items and the PCL-R has twenty items). This allowed us to compare the distribution of PCL: SV scores in the corporate sample with a large community sample,[6] part of a large study to identify predictors of inpatient violence. The comparison tells us something about the prevalence of psychopathic features in a community and a corporate sample.

The two distributions displayed in Figure 9.1 are very similar to one another, with most of those in each sample having very low scores. The mean score for the community sample was 2.7, whereas the mean score for the corporate sample was slightly lower at 2.2. However, ten (0.2 percent) of those in the community sample and six (3 percent) of those in the corporate sample had a PCL: SV equivalent score of 18 or higher (the research threshold for psychopathy). Interestingly, 5.9 percent of the corporate (versus 1.2 percent in the community sample) had a PCL: SV score of 13 or higher, considered by some researchers to indicate "potential" or "possible" psychopathy.[7] As we indicated above, individuals with a score this high may pose many serious problems for those around them and for the public.

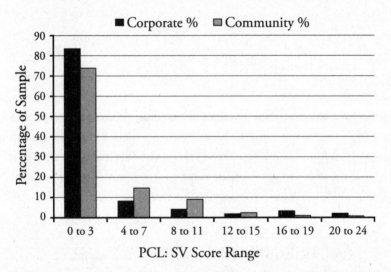

Figure 9.1. Distributions of Community PCL: SV Scores and Corporate PCL: SV "Equivalents." Community from Neumann and Hare (2007). Corporate from Babiak et al. (2010).

TALKING THE WALK

The title of the article described in this chapter is "Corporate Psychopathy: Talking the Walk." We based the title on the results, which were quite dramatic.

First, consider ratings on the variables in the *Charisma/Presentation Style* composite. As Babiak et al. (p. 196) put it, "as the PCL-R cut score increased there was a slight increase in the perception that a participant had good communication skills, and was creative and innovative."[8] Note that at a moderate or high PCL-R threshold, most of the ratings were between "meets expectations" and "above expectations." In sharp contrast, as Figure 9.2 shows, as the PCL-R threshold *increased*, there was a strong *decrease* in ratings of the participant's management style, role as a team player and leader, and performance appraisals. Indeed, the competency variables that had ratings of "Medium" or "High" at low PCL-R thresholds dropped sharply to "Low" at the upper thresholds. Similarly, their overall performance evaluations dropped from "exceeds expectations" at the lower PCL-R thresholds (that is, low psychopathy) to "below expectations" or "far below expectations" at the upper thresholds (high psychopathy).

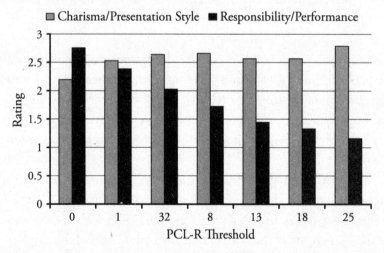

Figure 9.2. Mean ratings of Charisma/Presentation Style and of Responsibility/ Performance as a function of different PCL-R thresholds. From Babiak et al. (2010).

Recall that nine of those in the sample had a PCL-R score of 25 or above. This group, that is, those in the psychopathy range, had the *highest* communications ratings and the *lowest* performance ratings.

Does this explain how they were able to maintain their jobs as well as their inclusion in the management development and succession planning programs of their respective companies? We believe so.

On the surface, psychopathic executives showed great promise for promotion. They talked a good line and put on an impressive show. However, they failed to live up to expectations, some miserably. In several cases, their performance and leadership ratings were low enough to warrant dismissal or transfer. In fact, two such individuals received disciplinary action and were placed on probationary review. Yet, at the time of the study, they were still with the company. Not surprisingly, these executives had initiated legal action against their respective companies!

CORPORATE VARIATIONS ON A THEME

In Chapter 8, we described the construction of individual profiles based on the PCL-R factor scores. Here, we applied the same procedure to the sample of 203 executives discussed in this chapter. Statistical analyses revealed much the same profiles among corporate executives as among offenders, although the numbers in the former were very small (Figure 9.1). That is, in each case there were two variants of psychopathy, manipulative and aggressive. As expected, these variants were far less common in the corporate sample than among offenders.

Nonetheless, they stood out dramatically from the rest of the sample in terms of their performance ratings. Each of these variants had performance ratings that were less than half as high as the ratings for the 91 percent of the sample that scored low on all four psychopathy factors. These two variants of corporate psychopathy included vice presidents and directors. The aggressive variant scored high on the *Poor Behavioral Controls* and the *Early Behavioral Problems* items of the PCL-R (see Table 2.1). We might assume that they are more heavily involved than others in serious and harmful behavior to employees and the company, including harassment, bullying, and intimidation. We might also assume that the manipulative psychopath would be involved in serious malfeasance, including fraud and embezzlement. In either case, the distress, frustration, and hopelessness inflicted on other employees must be difficult to bear. Yet, these and other destructive executives manage to survive and even flourish in their organizations.

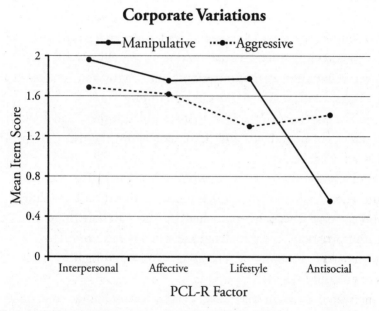

Corporate Variations

Figure 9.3. Factor profiles of executives with a PCL-R score of 30 or higher.

WHAT DOES IT MEAN?

As summarized by Babiak et al. (pp. 190–181),[9] and as we pointed out earlier in this book, the persona of the high-potential or "ideal leader" is an often amorphous and hard-to-define concept, and executives tend to rely on "gut feel" to judge such a complex attribute. Unfortunately, once decision makers believe that an individual has "future leader" potential, even bad performance reviews or evaluations from subordinates and peers do not seem to be able to shake their belief. The bottom line is that it is very easy to mistake psycho-pathic traits for specific leadership traits. The corporate psychopaths' "talk" overshadows their actual "walk."

The results of this study validated our observations noted in the previous chapters, but bear summarizing here because of their importance to understanding how true corporate psychopaths can so easily manipulate organizations:

- Their charm and grandiosity can be mistaken for self-confidence or a charismatic leadership style, thus overshadowing their actual performance; likewise, good presentation, communications, and impression management skills reinforce the same picture.
- The psychopath's ability to manipulate others can look like good influence and persuasion skills, the mark of an effective leader.
- Lack of realistic life goals, while a clearly negative trait that often leads the psychopath toward a downward-spiraling personal life, when couched by the psychopath in the appropriate business language can be misinterpreted as strategic thinking or "visioning," a rare and highly valued executive talent.
- Even those traits that reflect a severe lack of human feelings or emotional poverty (lack of remorse, guilt, empathy) can be put into service by corporate psychopaths, where being "tough" or "strong" (making hard, unpopular decisions) or "cool under fire" (not displaying emotions in the face of unpleasant circumstances) can work in their favor.
- Executives with high scores on the PCL-R factors present a particularly serious problem to their organizations and employees.

For an outline of how the media misreported and misinterpreted the study just described, see S 9.3: *The Wall Street "Ten Percenters."*

DISCUSSION QUESTIONS

- Have you ever worked for or with an executive who exhibited the corporate psychopath profile outlined above?
- Were they successful or were they eventually uncovered and removed from their position?

S 9.1
Economic and Corporate Fraud

In its 2018 *Global Economic Crime and Fraud Survey*,[10] PricewaterhouseCoopers (PwC) reported that 49 percent of 7,200 organizations in 123 countries were the victims of economic crime, up from 36 percent in 2016. The most frequently reported frauds were asset misappropriation, consumer fraud, and cybercrime. Internal "fraud actors" committed 52 percent of the crimes, up from 46 percent in 2016. Senior managers, with a sophisticated understanding of the company's internal controls and risk management procedures, committed 24 percent of the internal frauds. PwC noted that the opportunity to commit fraud is a key element in internal economic crime. The extent to which psychopathy is part of economic crime is unknown but likely to be significant. The *B-Scan 360* offers some promise for empirical investigation of this issue.

External actors committed 40 percent of frauds; two-thirds of these were "frenemies of the organization—agents, vendors, shared service providers and customers" (p. 9). PwC provided extensive methods for preventing organizational crime. The advice they gave in the 2003 Global Survey is valid today. PwC suggested that corporations should be on the watch for the executive who:

- Engages in activities indicative of a lack of integrity
- Is prone to engage in speculative ventures or accept unusually high business risks

- Displays a poor attitude toward compliance with regulatory or legislative obligations
- Is evasive, uncooperative, or abusive of the audit team
- Lacks a proven track record

S 9.2
The Mismeasure of Corporate Psychopathy

In a series of articles, Boddy and his colleagues[11,12] have described and used what they refer to as a new tool for identifying corporate psychopaths. Boddy et al. (p. 134)[13] stated, "A management research tool, the Psychopathy Measure—Management Research version (PM-MRV) . . . now exists. This is based on the world's most commonly used psychological instrument for identifying psychopaths [the PCL-R] and relies on the reporting of fellow employees. This research tool can be used to identify when psychopathy is present in corporate management."

The basis for this "management research tool" was a quiz ("Is your boss a psychopath?") published in *Fast Company* magazine.[14] The quiz consisted of a simple listing of the titles of the eight items that form the Interpersonal and Affective dimensions (Factor 1) of the PCL-R. Deutschman (p. 48) stated that Hare's PCL-R evaluates twenty personality traits and that a subset of eight traits (i.e., Factor 1) defines what Hare calls the "corporate psychopath." The latter part of this statement is incorrect. Neither Factor 1 nor Factor 2 alone is sufficient to define psychopathy. In discussions between Boddy and the publisher of the PCL-R, Boddy admitted that he has never actually seen a full clinical version of the PCL-R instrument and has read that it mostly involves extensive interviewing into twenty separate areas of behavior (personal communication to Hare from Claudia Roy, Multi-Health Systems, October 7, 2010).

The procedures used by Boddy are well outside the psychometric and professional standards for test development. Moreover, the PM-MRV not only misspecifies the construct of psychopathy, but also fails to differentiate psychopathy from other dark personalities: Machiavellianism, narcissism, and sadism[15,16] (see Supplemental S 2.3). "Disentangling psychopathy, narcissism, Machiavellianism, and other dark personalities is critical to advancing research on corporate harm. The PM-MRV may assess only features common to these dark personalities (Factor 1 traits) and therefore cannot provide essential information about how they differ with respect to their nature, the strategies they use, and their dispositions toward corporate misbehavior. As a research tool, the PM-MRV is not specific with respect to psychopathy and provides misleading information about the role of the PCL-R psychopathy construct in the business world. The real danger is that executives or human resources personnel will use it to make decisions about individual employees" (p. 585).[17]

S 9.3
The Wall Street "Ten Percenters"

The article on corporate psychopathy by Babiak et al.,[18] described above, generated many newspaper articles, blogs, and other Internet postings, most based on some variation of an incorrect statement by Sherree DeCovny in the *CFA Institute Magazine* (March/April 2012, Volume 23, Issue 2).

In the article, titled "The Financial Psychopath Next Door," DeCovny stated: "Studies conducted by Canadian forensic psychologist Robert Hare indicate that about 1 percent of the general population can be categorized as psychopathic, but the prevalence rate in the financial services industry is 10 percent" (p. 34).

Alexander Eichler picked up DeCovny's statement, and wrote an article in the May 19, 2012, edition of *The Huffington Post* titled "One Out Of Every Ten Wall Street Employees Is a Psychopath, Say Researchers."

Neither DeCovny nor Eichler contacted me (Hare) to determine if this information was correct. The first to do so was Dr. John Grohol, who wrote, "I've searched PsycINFO for a study that backs this claim, and came across your 2010 study on 'corporate psychopathy,' where, if one adds up the numbers, you can get to 8.9% in the studied population, if you include the category of 'potential' or 'probable' psychopathy as well. But this study was not on the financial services industry specifically."[19]

Grohol posted my response, along with his views on reporters who do not bother to check their facts.[20] Not everyone read Grohol's web page or my comments.

In an article for the May 13, 2012, edition of *The New York Times*, William Deresiewicz wrote the following under the headline of "Capitalists and Other Psychopaths": "There is an ongoing debate in this country about the rich: who they are, what their social role may be, whether they are good or bad. Well, consider the following. A recent study found that 10% of people who work on Wall Street are 'clinical psychopaths,' exhibiting a lack of interest in and empathy for others and an 'unparalleled capacity for lying, fabrication and manipulation.' (The proportion at large is 1%)."

On May 15, 2012, the deputy editor of the op-ed page for *The New York Times* wrote to me, "I'm afraid that an essay by William Deresiewicz this past Sunday, about ethics and capitalism, incorrectly described your research. We are trying to get it right now . . . Although we fact-check every opinion essay, this slipped past us. We really want to set the record straight."

We exchanged emails and the deputy editor arranged for *The New York Times* to issue a correction, which was as follows:

"This article [Capitalists and Other Psychopaths] has been revised to reflect the following correction.

"An opinion essay on May 13 about ethics and capitalism misstated the findings of a 2010 study on psychopathy in corporations. The study found that 3.9% of a sample of 203 corporate professionals met a clinical threshold for being described as psychopaths, not that 10 percent of people who work on Wall Street are clinical psychopaths. In addition, the study, in the journal Behavioral Sciences and the Law, was not based on a representative sample; the authors of the study say that the 4 percent figure cannot be generalized to the larger population of corporate managers and executives" (May 20, 2012).

On June 23, 2012, *The Huffington Post* stated, "An article that appeared on *The Huffington Post* on February 28, 2012, 'One Out Of Every Ten Wall Street Employees Is a Psychopath, Say Researchers,' was incorrect and has been removed." Further, "CFA Magazine did not respond to repeated requests for comment. *The Huffington Post* regrets the inaccuracy."

Why did these exchanges concern me? An empirical study on a specific sample of executives turned into false media reports about psychopathy on Wall Street. Scientists conduct research because they wish to understand a particular problem or phenomenon, not to have their work used for political comments about "the rich" on Wall Street.

10

The B-Scan: A Measure of Corporate Psychopathy

Ever wonder what leads a lavishly compensated C.E.O. to cheat, steal, and lie? Perhaps he's a psychopath, and now there is a test, the B-Scan 360, that can help make that determination. The B-Scan was conceived by Paul Babiak, an industrial psychologist, and Robert Hare, the creator of the standard tool for diagnosing psychopathic features in prison inmates. The B-Scan is the first formalized attempt to uncover similar tendencies in captains of industry, and it speaks to a growing suspicion that psychopaths may be especially adept at scaling the corporate ladder. (M. Stein-berger, New York Times Magazine, *December 12, 2004)*

This quote appeared in the *New York Times* fourth *Annual Year in Ideas* issue as one of the top new concepts presented during the previous twelve months.[1]

The PCL-R and its derivatives are rating scales scored by qualified professionals using interview and file/collateral information. Self-report measures of personality and psychopathy are popular for large-scale research projects but have limitations for assessments of individuals. In particular, they are prone to positive impression management by sophisticated and psychopathic individuals.[2,3] Our intention was to construct an instrument that measured psychopathy through the subtle and often covert behaviors, judgments, and attitudes of corporate psychopaths who escape the notice of management. Part of our motivation was not only to advance the field of corporate psychopathy research, but also to offer organizations insight into the unseen, truly problematic behaviors that can lead to damage to their organizations and their employees.

Origins of the Business-Scan 360 (B-Scan 360)

Based on his early work with industrial psychopaths, Babiak described the next steps:

> Following the realization that I had uncovered a psychopath working in industry, which we reported in Chapter 5, I published a scientific paper of my findings including some theoretical observations.[4] Now with my antennae up and with more knowledge about psychopathy, I felt better prepared to look for additional examples that may reside in other organizations. With caution and with Bob Hare's advice I kept my eyes open as I continued my career as an executive and organizational development consultant, which brought me in contact with hundreds of executives. I was careful to avoid the common pitfall of those new to the field, that is, to find psychopaths everywhere! As it turns out, it took over ten years to amass and analyze the data reported in Chapter 9.
>
> Along the way I realized that many of the problematic

behaviors were already known to these companies and being ad-dressed through various management development programs and succession planning processes (for example, through management training, job rotation, and executive coaching). Thankfully, the small number of individuals available for the research possessed enough traits and characteristics ("red flags") to warrant inclu-sion in the corporate psychopathy group reported above. The rest were usually untrained in management skills, or had other attitudinal or personality issues.

I wanted to continue this line of research (as yet unexplored empirically), but how could I accurately tell the difference be-tween a corporate psychopath and a just plain "bad boss" in a user-friendly, less time-intensive way that was acceptable to organizations wishing to participate in the research? We needed a new instrument, one that was purpose-built for the business world. The result was the B-Scan (Business-Scan).

BUILDING THE B-SCAN

We developed items for the B-Scan from a content analysis of cor-porate Succession Plans and Individual Development Plans from eight US companies. Direct supervisors (as well as some coworkers) with firsthand knowledge of the employees' workplace behaviors, attitudes, business judgments, and developmental needs made these assessments. Often, they were in free form, allowing considerable variability in content as well as expression. We pruned the large number of items to approximately two hundred unique character-istics and then reworded each (as needed) into standard business language, while eliminating any potentially illegal verbiage (from a human resources perspective). We then presented this seed list of items to a group of psychopathy experts asked to rate how "relevant" or useful each item was to an evaluation of psychopathy or some feature of psychopathy. Separately, we had a group of operations and HR executives (who were not aware of each item's potential regarding psychopathy) to rate the "criticality" of each item to the running of their business. We defined criticality as how much concern each trait or behavior would generate if observed in an employee, and the actions that followed. We selected items rated *both* as *highly relevant* to the assessment of psychopathy and as indicative of *problematic business behaviors*, to form two research versions of the B-Scan, the B-Scan Self-Report (consisting of 126 items for rating oneself) and the B-Scan 360 (consisting of 113 items to be completed by supervisors or others familiar with the person being assessed. *Note*: 360-degree feedback is a common technique used in management and executive development to assure that various, multiple observers "around the employee," such as boss, subordinates, and peers, contribute to the overall, combined assessment).

An important part of the validation process (evidence that the instrument actually measures what it purports to measure) was to assess how *accurately* the B-Scan reflects the traditional construct of psychopathy, as measured by the PCL-R. This process involved several stages. The first step was to determine if the structure of the B-Scan parallels the Hare Four-Factor Model of Psychopathy. A series of statistical analyses reduced the item pool to twenty, and showed that the four-factor model of the B-Scan is consistent with the four-factor model of the PCL-R.[5] The factor labels for the B-Scan are as follows, with the corresponding labels for the PCL-R factors in brackets:

1. *Manipulative/Unethical* (Interpersonal)
2. *Callous/Insensitive* (Affective)
3. *Unreliable/Unfocused* (Lifestyle)
4. *Intimidating/Aggressive* (Antisocial)

We conducted the second test of validity in the field with employees in various public, private, non-profit, public service, and other areas. We also included community samples such as those sourced through Amazon's MTurk online data collection service. The purpose of these studies was to a) statistically confirm the placement of the items within their theoretical facets and b) shorten the list to only those items that contribute the most information; that is, we only wanted items that captured the most relevant behaviors, attitudes, and judgments related to psychopathy.

The results led to the creation of four versions of the B-Scan: the B-Scan Self Short-Form and the B-Scan 360 Short-Form (for use by researchers), and the B-Scan Self Long-Form and the B-Scan 360 Long-Form (for potential use by human resource and business consulting professionals, perhaps as part of their selection, promotional, and executive development programs).

The third test has to do with whether corporate psychopathy, as measured by the B-Scan, accurately measures or predicts known or suspected relationships with other variables associated with psychopathy in general. Does the B-Scan offer us any insights into corporate psychopathy beyond what we can glean from other measurement methods? Our research findings suggest that it does.

THE B-SCAN SELF

The B-Scan Self (Self-Report version) correlates strongly with a self-report scale based on the PCL-R, the Self-Report Psychopathy Scale-III (SRP-III).[6] Like other measures of psychopathy, the B-Scan Self is strongly associated with narcissism and Machiavellianism. As for normal personality traits, the B-Scan Self and the SRP-III are associated with low levels of *Agreeableness* (trusting, honest, altruistic, compliant, modest, tender-minded) and *Conscientiousness* (competent, orderly, dutiful, achievement-oriented, disciplined, plans ahead). In a validation study[7] we found that the B-Scan and the SRP-III presented the same pattern of associations with normal personality traits, while narcissism and Machiavellianism were associated with different normal personality traits. This indicates that although the B-Scan is for use in the workplace, it still represents psychopathy, and its structure follows the same four-factor structure as the PCL-R.

What We Know So Far About Corporate Psychopathy Using the B-Scan

The list of research studies being published using the B-Scan has grown over the years since the *New York Times* article cited above. It is beyond the scope of this book to delve into detail about all studies that used the B-Scan. However, they, along with our work with executives in a variety of organizations over the years, have informed our revision to this book. There are several findings worth noting here. (Also, see a recent review that discusses the role of the B-Scan and the Dark Triad in the workplace.)[8]

CORPORATE PSYCHOPATHY AND GENDER

Most of the research on psychopathy has been with men. In the general population, the prevalence of psychopathy is significantly higher in men, meaning there are more men than women who score high enough on psychopathy measures to "qualify" as psychopathic.[9,10,11] For incarcerated offenders, the same pattern seems to be present[12] (see S 2.4: *Gender, Ethnicity, Culture* for a brief discussion of race, gender, and ethnic/cultural differences in psychopathy and its measurement).

Using the B-Scan Self and the Self-Report Psychopathy scale (SRP-III; Paulhus et al., 2016), we found that men scored *significantly higher* than did women on both measures.[13] This indicates that gender differences for psychopathy exist in the workplace. Furthermore, in a sample of 425 employees from a public organization, we found that female supervisors scored significantly lower than did male supervisors on all four factors of the B-Scan 360 and on the B-Scan 360 total score.[14]

These are very interesting results, as they introduce a new angle to the study of psychopathy in women. Not only do women score lower on psychopathy than do men, but those who work for them also perceive them as less psychopathic than men. Considering the negative impact perceived psychopathic traits in managers can have in the workplace, these results give new meaning to the quote by media mogul Peter Gruber, "The best man for the job is often a woman."

HARASSMENT ON THE JOB

Harassment in the workplace has received a lot of media attention after the #MeToo movement following media coverage of high-profile cases of harassment and sexual misconduct in a work context. Many efforts encourage victims to come forward. Research on the negative impacts of workplace harassment has been prolific, including, for example, lowered organizational commitment, job satisfaction, and life satisfaction, and higher levels of turnover intentions, anxiety, depression, and physical symptoms.[15] We know less, though, about the personality traits of such individuals. In general, we know that perpetrators of workplace harassment tend to be rebellious,[16] and have low levels of the personality trait called Agreeableness.[17] They also exhibit attitudes toward revenge,[18] have low honesty/humility,[19] are concerned about "being a man,"[20] and tend to hold management positions.[21]

As the reader can see, all of the traits identifying workplace harassment perpetrators are also traits similarly displayed by psychopathic individuals. We therefore wanted to explore whether one of the underlying factors associated with workplace harassment is psychopathy.

Mathieu and Babiak[22] conducted a study in a public organization using the B-Scan 360 where employees rated the individual who perpetrated harassment against them on psychopathy as well as other personality traits. We found that psychopathy was the *strongest* predictor of workplace harassment (beyond the influence of the other personality traits usually considered when hiring employees). This underscores the importance of having sound psychometric instruments, such as the B-Scan 360, to assess some of the dark personality traits responsible for harassment in the workplace.

EMPLOYEES DON'T LEAVE THEIR JOBS; THEY LEAVE THEIR (PSYCHOPATHIC) BOSS

In a study on the impact of leadership on employees' job satisfaction, organizational commitment, and intention to quit their job, a team of industrial-organizational (I-O) psychologists[23] found that their managers' lack of interpersonal skills affected employees more than their lack of technical skills. What this means is that, to have a positive influence on employees, leaders need to possess good interpersonal skills such as listening, empathy, and being able to encourage and motivate employees, manage conflicts, provide support, and demonstrate integrity, to name only a few. While task-oriented leaders may fall short on these interpersonal skills, there are dangerous types of leaders who not only lack interpersonal/human skills, but who also use callous manipulation and violence to get what they want and where they want to be.

Mathieu, Neumann, Babiak, and Hare[24] assessed the influence of psychopathy traits in managers on employees' work-family conflict, psychological distress, and job satisfaction. We found that employees who scored their managers higher on the B-Scan 360 (psychopathy) also reported *higher* levels of psychological distress and work–family conflict and *lower* levels of satisfaction in their job. In a subsequent study, we found that psychopathy in supervisors predicted employees' lower levels of job satisfaction that, in turn, predicted employees' intention to quit their job and leave their company.

In a highly competitive world, organizations cannot afford to have employees who are unsatisfied and suffering from psychological distress. Unsatisfied and unhappy employees are not productive, and unproductive employees have a direct impact on the company's financial performance. Retention of talented employees is the key to organizational success and we now know that at least one factor influences employee retention, and that is the direct supervisor's core personality.

PSYCHOPATHY AND LEADERSHIP STYLE

What makes a good leader? Leadership is the most studied subject in business literature. Many leadership theories have been developed and tested over the years. I-O psychologists Avolio and Bass[25] developed one of the most influential leadership models, the Full Range Model of leadership. The Full Range Model comprises three leadership styles: Laissez-Faire Leadership, Transactional Leadership, and Transformational Leadership.

Laissez-Faire Leadership refers to leaders who are absent, who avoid interactions and dealing with problems, and who are not there when their employees need them. Laissez-Faire Leadership is associated with employees' lower levels of job satisfaction and lower satisfaction with one's supervisor.[26]

Transactional Leadership is concerned with task-oriented and goal-oriented behavior, that is, leaders who reward these behaviors, monitor mistakes, and set standards. Leaders overly high on this leadership style focus on mistakes and use disciplinary threats to get employees to reach organizational goals.

Transformational Leadership is the most positive of the three leadership styles composing the Full Range Model of leadership. It has four factors: individualized consideration (giving employees personal attention); intellectual stimulation (encouraging employees to think outside the box); inspirational motivation (influencing employees through confidence and dynamic presence); and idealized influence (displaying role model behaviors through personal achievements and character). Transformational leadership style is associated with stress reduction in employees,[27] increased organizational commitment,[28] enhanced team performance,[29] and employees' positive psychological well-being.[30]

We were interested in understanding which of these leadership styles, if any, is associated with psychopathy. Mathieu and Babiak[31] asked employees from two different types of companies (one was a public sector organization and the other was a large financial company) to assess their immediate supervisor on the Full Range Model of Leadership and on psychopathy (using the B-Scan 360). We found that supervisors who scored high on psychopathy scored significantly *lower* on both positive leadership measures (that is, Transactional and Transformational Leadership). We also found that supervisors who scored high on psychopathy scored *high* on Laissez-Faire Leadership. These results indicate that not only are psychopathic individuals not likely to be very effective at people management, they are not likely to be effective at task management either. In fact, once they obtain a leadership position, they are highly likely to be unreliable leaders who are not there when employees need them and who do not support their employees.

These results support what we found using the PCL-R: psychopathic leaders excel at "talking the walk." Their charisma helps to get them hired as leaders, but they are not able to succeed as good leaders over the long haul.

PSYCHOPATHY AND ABUSIVE LEADERSHIP

Management consultant Bennett Tepper[32] described abusive supervision as *"the sustained display of hostile verbal and nonverbal behaviors, excluding physical contact"* (p. 178). It is associated with relatively low job and life satisfaction, low commitment to the organization, high work–family conflict, and overall psychological distress. The estimated cost to US-based organizations is $23.8 billion annually in productivity losses, absenteeism, and health care costs.[33] During development of the B-Scan, it struck us quite clearly that the PCL-R Antisocial Factor (which includes the items for poor behavioral controls, early behavior problems, juvenile delinquency, revocation of conditional release, and criminal versatility) manifested in the B-Scan as Intimidation and Bullying.

Therefore, we were not surprised when, in a study conducted within a non-profit organization of ninety-five employees, we found that psychopathy as measured with the B-Scan 360 is *strongly asso-*

ciated with abusive leadership, which, in turn, leads to decreases in employees' job satisfaction and increases in their intentions to quit their job.[34]

Why hire these managers in the first place, and how did they manage to stay in their jobs? We have outlined in this book our answers to these questions; we believe that many bosses are good people, well trained and positively motivated; others simply are "bad bosses"; and still others are corporate psychopaths, the ones discussed in the previous chapters.

The fact that psychopathy predicts abusive leadership behavior is perhaps not a big surprise. However, these results indicate that it is possible to identify psychopathic traits using a psychometric instrument (in this case the B-Scan 360). Organizations and HR professionals should hire leaders not solely based on their task-oriented skills; they also should take into account interpersonal skills associated with positive leadership styles. Such interpersonal skills include listening to employees, empathy, ethical behavior, team-building, being able to motivate and support employees, honesty, and humility. Psychopathic individuals typically score low on such skills.

The field of study is still young, so it will take several more years of research before organizations take the situation seriously enough to implement stronger selection, placement, and promotional processes that take into account the negative aspects of people with dark personalities. The reality is that organizations do not create abusive leaders. Rather, the organizations hire and promote them.[35]

11

Enemy at the Gates

Carla hurried down the corridor, with coffee in hand and file folders under her arm. She hated to be late for these meetings, but she had just received some new information that might help with the decision-making today.

10:02 glared the large clock at the head of the room.

"Sorry I'm late," said Carla, putting down her folders onto the conference table at her place. Pulling her wallet from her purse, she retrieved two dollars and placed them in the center of the table. Despite all the changes the company had undergone during the past year, it maintained this one ceremony—a dollar a minute for lateness. Some time-management consultants had recommended it years ago to the executive committee as a means of disciplining themselves, and it stuck. They just loved it; now every meeting involving directors and above is run by this rule. The pot, when the fine was a quarter a minute, used to come up to enough after a year to buy pizza for the entire company staff. Now, with inflation, the fine was up to a buck, but the resulting improvements in timeliness led to fewer pizzas overall.

"Glad we're all here. Thank you," said Johnson, the CEO. "You all interviewed Morgan and Tom for the new director of communications job and this meeting is to share our impressions, review what information we got from references, et cetera, and make a decision. Are we all on board with that?" he asked, looking around the room at the members of the selection team assembled in the conference room.

Heads nodded around the table.

Carla handed out two candidate packets to each member of the team. These contained the results of their interviews, reference checks, background checks, and assessments from the executive recruitment firm. "The cover sheet gives the summary of all that we have. I'll give you a minute to read through it," she said, as they perused the page while she took out some other notes from her pile.

"It's pretty obvious that they're in a dead heat according to the competency list. They both got high marks from their references on understanding the business, building external relationships, oral communication style, written communication, and business acumen. Morgan did a bit better in problem-solving and decision-making overall, but one reference said he tended to take on too much of the detail work himself and did not delegate enough. Tom got the opposite review; he tended to delegate too much, sometimes handing off details his last boss thought he should have handled himself."

"I got the same impression during my interviews," said Nate, the hiring manager. "Tom told me he liked to develop his people, and delegation was a means to that end. Morgan did not seem to think doing it all himself was a problem; actually, he was quite proud of the fact. But then he didn't have the same staff level as Tom."

The conversation continued with a detailed review of the remaining competency areas. At the end of this topic, the two candidates were about even in their attractiveness to the group.

"Any developmental areas mentioned?" asked Johnson, paging through the reports.

"Yes, on the next page you'll see them listed. Tom has not had much exposure to the rest of the business side; he has primarily been in communications. Morgan, on the other hand, came to communications from a marketing background," answered Carla, "so he's had more exposure."

"I like that about Morgan," added Nate. "While Tom did have an appreciation for the business based on his MBA, Morgan could really talk to the day-to-day issues. I'd have to score him higher on that one."

"How about Morgan; did he have any developmental areas?" asked Johnson.

"Yes, he had very little supervisory experience in his career. He started as a market analyst and then moved up into a senior-level position, still as an individual contributor. He made a lateral switch to communications because they had an opening and he had always liked journalism," responded Nate. "Morgan moved up twice in three years, but it was only in his last job that he got to supervise people."

"So delegation would be one of his developmental areas," added Carla, making a note on her file. "I did get some feedback on Tom's style from one source, who suggested Tom was pretty tough on his people. No real information about Morgan's management style from his references."

"I spoke with Morgan at length about his supervisory style, and although he doesn't have much hands-on experience, he said all the right things," added Nate.

"I got the same impression," said Carla. "Morgan came across with a lot of management theory, but he really didn't have the experience."

"Well, I think we can take care of that with some training," added Nate.

The group continued to discuss the strengths and weaknesses of each candidate, sharing their personal impressions as well as the data from the references.

"How about their abilities to handle the media issues we're facing. What are your thoughts?" Johnson asked, looking toward Nate.

"Regarding Tom," Nate started, "I liked the fact that he had quite a bit of media exposure and personally represented his company during one of their product crises. Morgan has had almost no face time with the media. He did, though, create a sophisticated communications plan, which I circulated to you about a week ago."

"What did the tests show?" asked Johnson, referring to the battery of psychological tests that every top-level candidate takes as part of the hiring process.

"Tom was more outgoing and assertive, almost too much so," reported Carla, "and Morgan came out reserved, maybe not assertive enough. However, overall, the results were interesting."

"Interesting?" asked Johnson, smiling. "That's a new one. What do you mean by 'interesting'?"

"Both came out well on conscientiousness, openness to ideas, intelligence, and socialization," continued Carla, "but, surprisingly, Tom's scores were the highest the consultant has ever seen in a businessperson."

"Say more about that," said Nate, moving forward in his seat.

"There are certain ranges we look for, specific to each open position. Morgan did well, high enough on all scales to be a good fit. However, Tom got *perfect* scores on all the scales. I'm not really sure what that means, but I do wonder how he could have done so well."

"Maybe he's a perfect fit for us?" asked Nate.

Johnson looked at his watch and told the group that he had another appointment to prepare for. Getting up from his seat, he suggested they continue the meeting without him and asked them to let him know of their decision by the end of the day.

DISCUSSION QUESTIONS

- To whom would you offer a job?
- What additional information would you want to have before you decided?
- Do you notice any "red flags" regarding either candidate?

Hiring and Selection: The First Line of Defense

This section will focus on how the company can forestall the hiring and promotion of corporate psychopaths. While no procedure is a guarantee against infiltration, vigilance based on greater understanding can improve one's defenses.

We start by briefly summarizing the typical personnel procedures used by businesses to hire and promote employees. We invite the reader to look for potential weak spots or loopholes in these processes where a psychopath might be able to slip through or operate unnoticed, and we will also offer suggestions for closing some of these entry points.

Managing the human assets of an organization is one of the most challenging functions of the executive, and the ability to identify and handle problematic individuals is critical. The human resources department is responsible for finding and hiring new employees, administering compensation and benefits programs, managing employee and (where applicable) union relationships, developing and providing employee orientation and training programs, and administering the performance appraisal and talent development processes. Some larger HR departments also provide coaching and guidance to executives on change management issues, executive development, and succession or replacement planning.

The most value-adding HR management function centers on finding, attracting, and retaining talented staff. The *hiring manager* with a vacancy to fill, and coworkers who are working overtime to fill the gap in the interim, sometimes wonder why it seems to take a long time to hire someone. The answer lies in the screens or hurdles through which the candidate must pass before receiving an offer of a job.

In general, the hiring manager first reviews the work required and possibly redefines some of the requirements contained in the job description. This can be a tedious process, but it is critical to making a good hire. The next step is to advertise the open position on a company job-posting board and on the Internet. If the job is at a sufficiently high level or requires very specific expertise, the company may retain a professional recruitment firm to prescreen candidates. The next steps are critical to protecting the organization from hiring a possible psychopath.

SCREEN RÉSUMÉS CAREFULLY

Before the advent of the Internet, companies might receive perhaps ten résumés for any given opening and then have to review them manually. Today, Internet advertisements could lead to stacks of résumés from candidates, but algorithms automatically screen them, looking for key words that match criteria for the job description. The major weakness in using a résumé as a screening device is, of course, the tendency for applicants to overstate or falsify their qualifications, and computer algorithms are not sophisticated enough to tell the difference between truth and lies. Certainly, applicants will tailor details on their résumés for a specific company to reflect a better match between their own knowledge, skills, and abilities and those described in the company's advertisement. This is actually a smart approach to take, as it highlights what is important to the hiring company and often includes key words for which the algorithm is screening. This may get the candidate through the first hurdle. However, tailoring a résumé assumes that one *truly* has the qualifications and experience required.

Psychopaths, notorious liars, often will cross the line between good marketing and outright lying. In our work with psychopaths, we have seen résumés that contain jobs the applicant *never held*, companies that *never existed*, promotions that *never happened*, professional memberships that *do not exist*, awards and commendations *never received*, letters of recommendation written by applicants *themselves*, even *fake* education, degrees, and professional credentials, among other things. To uncover possible psychopathic deceit, it is essential to verify *every* piece of information contained on the résumé *before* starting the interview process. This is time-intensive but worth the effort. Typically, however, verification of résumé data starts *after* the interview phase. This puts the hiring manager at a disadvantage during the interview, because she has only the résumé data to go on and the psychopath is so good at justifying what she has written.

At the very least, education should be checked before the initial interview by contacting the registrar's office at the university cited. Sometimes applicants misrepresent their actual degree by substituting something that sounds more impressive (for example, engineering is a more difficult field of study than engineering technology). Also, because advanced degrees often require the writing of theses or dissertations, and experienced technical professionals sometimes write articles and scientific papers, cautious companies may find it worthwhile to get a copy of these documents and let their technical staff read and assess them. Google Scholar is a good resource for this purpose. Professional credentials and licenses, especially those granted by the government to protect the public, such as in the fields of medicine, psychology, engineering, and others, can be checked through the appropriate authorities. Online databases can be searched quite easily. Google can also be very helpful in obtaining information about candidates, some of whom will have their own web page.

Unfortunately, other than uncovering the most outrageous lies, it is difficult to assure the accuracy of this initial screen. In general, an impressive résumé requires deeper digging to assure that your impressions are accurate.

TELEPHONE SCREENING INTERVIEW

An initial telephone (or Skype, Zoom, or FaceTime) screening interview saves considerable time and expense and allows for consideration of a larger pool of candidates. It is an ideal way to get to know the candidate on a more personal level and to collect more details about his or her work experience. Typically, it is possible to explore a candidate's motivations and personal interest in the job by asking open-ended questions like, "Tell me more about . . ." and "What got you interested in applying for this job?" Well-informed candidates will catch glimmers of what interviewers are looking for, and strategically offer examples of work experience that respond to their often unspoken concerns; those with good communication skills can advance their candidacy. Psychopaths, of course, are quite astute at noticing what others need to hear and will begin their verbal manipulation during this interview; however, it is nearly impossible to differentiate them from legitimate applicants at this time. Even having the benefit of nonverbal cues during video calls cannot guarantee that the interviewer will accurately spot lies and distortions.

Ideally, a company may wish to record these interviews (with the applicants' permission) and allow other staff to review them. They can then prepare lists of follow-up questions to ask during subsequent, face-to-face interviews. The conversational and manipulative skills of psychopaths can fool even seasoned psychopathy researchers, who then find during subsequent review of the tapes that the candidate's banter contains excessive use of *flowery phrases*, *inconsistencies*, *lies*, *distortions*, *discrepancies*, and *bad logic*. Moreover, these researchers have the advantage of collateral information (such as criminal records and psychological assessments) about the psychopaths, which the company might not have. On the other hand, interviewers must be careful not to place too much credence on subtle discrepancies gleaned during these interviews. Despite the ubiquity of telephones, many people are not at all skilled in speaking over them, especially when stress takes over good judgment and smooth conversation, as is often the case during a job interview. Certainly younger candidates prefer texting to virtually any other mode of communication, which puts them at a disadvantage during telephone calls and face-to-face meetings. At the very least, though, the interviewer should take detailed notes about any inconsistencies, and should use them to address concerns in follow-up interviews.

FACE-TO-FACE SCREENING INTERVIEW

Candidates who pass the initial phone screen receive invitations for face-to-face interviews with HR staff, the hiring manager, and, in many cases, a technical person from the department with the vacancy. The perspective of each is different, but they share the common goal of finding out as much about the candidate as they can in a limited amount of time in order to make an informed hiring decision.

The HR staff often thinks that it has the best chance of determining the "people skills" and "fit" of the applicant. Some hiring managers also expect the HR staff to determine the mental health (a generic term, often misused) of the applicant. This is clearly an unreasonable expectation as, short of a psychological assessment, formal evaluations of mental health are not possible by untrained interviewers—and perhaps not even relevant to a given job. Keep in mind that psychopathy is *not* a mental illness.

Surprisingly, many managers make two critical mistakes when approaching the employment interview, and both play directly into the hands of a psychopathic candidate. Some do not prepare the right questions for the interview; some do not prepare any at all! Good candidates have a clear and legitimate agenda: they want the job, they want to advance their career, and they want to work for a particular company. To candidates, the interview is the chance to impress the company with their ability and motivation to do the job. They will have rehearsed their presentation and answers to potential questions, and they will have read books on interviewing techniques and have ready answers for the most common questions, including the challenging ones, such as "Tell me your greatest weakness"; "How would you handle it if . . ."; and "If you could do something differently in your career, what would it be?"

Psychopathic candidates also have a *hidden* agenda: they want to play "head games" with the interviewer, and their goal is to get money and power because they feel entitled to it—not in exchange for real work. The employment interview is the ideal setting for the psychopathic candidate to shine. Therefore, it is well worth the time and effort for the hiring manager to prepare questions carefully designed to elicit the *specific* information needed to make the right choice and to force the candidate to go beyond pat or rehearsed responses.

The second mistake some managers make is not attending a training program on interviewing techniques, believing they do not need it because their social skills and experience will suffice. Some interviewers use a free-flowing, unstructured approach to the interview and rely on "gut feel" or personal impressions, a style that goes against most of what we know about good interviewing techniques and, unfortunately, leaves the average interviewer open to manipulation and sophisticated impression management by a psychopathic applicant.

Many training programs on interviewing techniques are available, and best practices suggest a format similar to this:

The Opening. Handshakes, offer of a beverage, inquiry about travel to the interview site, and talk of the weather are common icebreakers that help break the tension of a face-to-face meeting and pave the way for the real work.

Initial Exploration. General questions about the candidate's background, experience, expertise, education, and interest in the job, typically following the résumé format.

Detailed Questioning. Probing for specific aspects of the applicant's background that seem to be relevant to the open position.

The three levels of responses for which a trained interviewer listens: *overt answers* to questions; the *impression* the candidate makes on the interviewer; and the *underlying* competencies, motivations, and values the answers reflect.

First, *overt answers* address questions and/or concerns about issues like:

- What did the candidate really do in this job?
- What role did he or she play in the organization—was it supportive or leading?
- How much influence did the candidate exert on the outcomes of projects?
- How did the candidate handle problems that came up?
- Did the candidate grow in his or her career and take on more responsibilities over time?

Second, as the candidate speaks, the interviewer develops *impressions* that can include:

- How does this candidate come across? Did first impressions change over the course of the interview?
- What is his or her body language saying?
- How serious (and realistic) is the candidate about his or her career and this job?
- Is he or she likable, bright, and engaging?
- Did the candidate seem prepared for this interview with knowledge about the job and the company?
- Is the candidate being forthright with information; does he or she come across as honest?

Third, gleaning *underlying* competencies, motivations, and values.

- Can this person communicate well in a somewhat stressful face-to-face conversation?

- Does the candidate show interest in and stay focused on the question asked, or ramble along?
- Did the candidate exhibit good judgment in the career moves made?
- Did the candidate demonstrate leadership, integrity, effective communications, teamwork, and persuasion skills?

One common mistake interviewers make is to concentrate only on the overt answers and their own impressions and *not* to consider underlying, and transferable, competencies, motivations, and work values. It takes a lot of work to construct probing questions that will elicit this information and a lot of interviewing experience to be able to interpret responses correctly. Good listening and note-taking skills are critical, as is a keen ear for the inconsistent, exaggerated responses offered up by psychopathic candidates.

PROVIDING INFORMATION ABOUT THE JOB AND THE COMPANY

The more candidates know about the day-to-day ins and outs of a job, the better able they are to decide for themselves whether there is a good match between their aspirations, competencies, and what the job has to offer. A candidate who opts out of a job because of information learned during an interview saves both parties additional time and energy. A common mistake made by interviewers, though, is to spend so much time in describing the job and their department that the interview time flies by without asking important probing questions. Candidates are naturally reluctant to interrupt, and psychopathic candidates will use this time to feed the interviewer's ego.

FOLLOW-UP ON CONCERNS

If the candidate reveals only bits of information, glosses over details, or makes comments that just do not sit right with the interviewer, then this is the time to circle back and probe more deeply. For example, when a candidate states, "My team won the company award for bringing the project in under budget and ahead of schedule," the interviewer may wonder:

- Was the candidate the leader of the team, or an active though non-leader participant?
- Did the candidate use this team experience to demonstrate leadership, despite not having the actual title?
- Did the company recognize the candidate's performance by assigning a subsequent project with increased responsibility?

The follow-up-on-concerns phase is the time to pursue these and other details that do not jibe or that conflict. Inconsistencies and discrepancies may be the result of hasty answering or the result of purposeful distortion, exaggeration, or outright invention. The interviewer drills down in order to get a good read on actual skills and true motivations. A typical question asked during this phase of the interview might be, "I'd like to go back to your description of the project team you were on. What was the *specific* role you were assigned?" (The candidate answers.) "What was your relationship like with . . ." and so forth. This line of questioning is sometimes difficult for less experienced interviewers to execute, yet pointed questions may be the only way to satisfy concerns, and perfectly clear answers should be the only way for the candidate to maintain his or her candidacy. Again, analyze answers on many levels, thus providing more information about competencies, motivations, and values.

THE CLOSE

Candidates will want to know what the next steps are in the hiring process, and the interviewer should have an answer that is appropriate to the situation. And the company must honor commitments regarding follow-up.

Following are suggestions for hiring managers to improve the effectiveness of their interviewing process, based on our experience working with corporate psychopaths (and the companies who have unwittingly hired them):

Retain Control of the Interview!

Psychopaths perform exceedingly well during an interview primarily by avoiding answering direct questions, instead introducing topics into the conversation that they believe are interesting to the interviewer in the hopes of building rapport. This is an easy trap to fall into; before you know it, the *candidate is interviewing you* and has derailed your plan. Recall that the first step on our corporate psychopath's agenda is to convince the hiring manager/team to make a job offer even if the candidate lacks the necessary knowledge, skills, or experience. Psychopaths quickly ascertain whether the interviewer will respond better to a soft sell or a hard sell, and they experience little social anxiety and discomfort during conversations that most would find daunting. This allows them to weave convincing tales of professional experience, integrity, and competence, and to use an array of technical terms and jargon with such confidence and panache that even some experts are fooled, although an astute interviewer might be able to determine whether or not these tales reflect more than a superficial knowledge of the topic. Even so, the task will not be an easy one.

When challenged on any detail during an interview, the psychopath will simply shift gears, subtly change the topic, and generally weave an altered tale so believable that even an interviewer who *knows* the individual is lying might have doubts. The psychopath's goal is to convince the hiring staff that he has the ideal background, experience, and motivation to fill the job, and the personal attributes to fit right in on day one. The psychopathic fiction, "I am the ideal employee," can be very seductive.

ASK FOR WORK EXAMPLES

It is customary in the arts and entertainment field for job candidates to show up with examples of their work in the form of a portfolio, filled with photos for models, movies for visual media professionals, and articles for journalists. This allows the hiring manager to judge the candidates' quality, style, and appropriateness to the open position. In the case of business job candidates, the hiring manager should ask to see examples of actual reports written, presentations made, and projects completed. These, of course, should have any identifying or confidential information blanked out, but the manager can read and judge the great bulk of the work, giving the hiring company a good indication of the type of work output to expect from each candidate.

While we would not be surprised if an enterprising psychopath created a phony report or found one on the Internet just to satisfy a potential hiring company, the effort may be more than most psychopaths are willing to invest. If you suspect that the candidate has falsified or plagiarized the portfolio, the only option may be to drill into details behind the actual report. However, this approach assumes that the hiring manager has the technical expertise to do so, and, if not, knows to call on a staff technical interviewer.

FOCUS ON ACTION AND BEHAVIOR

Some interviewees speak vaguely about their past without providing sufficient detail about what they really *did*. Others exaggerate their contributions, giving themselves the appearance of being more important to the outcome than they actually were. A full answer should include a statement about achieving some goal or solving a problem, followed by a review of the actual things the candidates did, whether directly or tangentially, to address the goal or issue, and, finally, the outcome of their efforts, including what impact their efforts had on the results.

CLARIFY DETAILS

As noted above, when faced with responses that do not provide sufficient details, the interviewer must go back during follow-up questioning to flesh out the complete picture. The interview should redirect candidates to specific areas of interest as much as possible. "Who, what, when, where, and why" types of follow-up questions can help get to the truth behind the experience being described.

Supporting roles are quite important, and the job being filled may require this sort of background and experience, but supporting roles are very different from supervisory and management roles. It should be easy for the interviewer to clarify the level of authority the candidate claimed by pressing for details. Psychopaths pay little attention to detail and in fact, due to their tendency to be easily bored, they will not respond well to detail-focused questioning. There can be many reasons for the candidate to continue to provide vague and rambling answers, including nervousness and forgetfulness, so the interviewer should keep this in mind while pressing for details in search of the truth.

LOOK FOR APPROPRIATE FEELINGS

One of the hallmarks of a psychopath is the inability to express a full range of normal emotions. For example, when telling a story that would normally elicit visible emotional reactions in most people, psychopaths may come across as cool and shallow, or as B-grade actors. Psychopaths do not understand what others mean by their "feelings," yet they will attempt to mimic them on demand. This often leads to superficial expressions or even exaggerations of emotion inappropriate to the event they describe.

Book and colleagues (p. 91)[1] found that, with careful observation of others and with practice, those with the interpersonal and affective traits of psychopathy (PCL-R Factor 1; Table 2.1) may have an "ability to accurately mimic emotional expression (fear and remorse) leading others to perceive emotional genuineness." Elsewhere, Book noted, "It's difficult to spot a psychopath; in fact, they can look actually like they're more genuine than other people. Part of it is that most people do not have to fake emotions all the time, so they do not have any practice at it. But someone who doesn't feel these emotions will have practice at faking them, so they will probably be better at it."[2] See S 11.1: *Does Practice Make Perfect?*

Recent research on the use by psychopaths of verbal and nonverbal behaviors is shedding some light on how they are able to provide convincing accounts of themselves and their achievements, and to manipulate others so well. For example, they may be animated speakers, use many hand movements (perhaps as a distraction from what they are saying), express what appear to be genuine smiles, and use aggressive language to gain dominance over others. For a review of this research, see S 11.2: *Politics and Poker: A License to Lie.*

Displays of emotion commonly expressed by psychopaths during an interview might include indignation, anger, or exhilaration, as, for example, when describing being passed over for a promotion, the termination of a close coworker, or passion for one's work, respectively. Expect some display of emotion during these expositions. However, excessive, or over-the-top, emotions might raise questions about the candidate's emotional control and judgment regardless of the reason—psychological or otherwise. Sometimes the absence of an emotional component to an answer may also raise questions. The key is to look for emotions appropriate to the story line and to be sensitive to how realistic (as opposed to superficial) these emotional expressions appear. This is the one time when "gut feel" and the interviewer's "emotional antenna" have a valuable place in the interviewing process.

TAKE NOTES

It is easier to recall impressions and feelings about the candidate than facts, so it is the best practice to make detailed notes during the interview on the résumé itself or the list of questions provided by human resources. These notes should be clear enough that others reading the document could decipher them. It is also useful to review these notes prior to the follow-up-on-concerns phase. Simply telling the candidate that you need a moment to review your notes is a reasonable request, often welcomed by a candidate, who may wish to take a break.

DO NOT DECIDE ALONE

A well-structured hiring process will include a meeting of interviewers—a selection committee—to discuss the qualifications and relative merits of the candidates. This is a best practice because different interviewers see different strengths and weaknesses in any single candidate, which they should compare and discuss. Nevertheless, it is an *invaluable* requirement in the case of screening out a potential corporate psychopath. Recall that psychopaths attempt to build private one-on-one relationships with those who have utility to them. This now would include all interviewers and decision makers involved in the hiring process. As astute students of human psychology, psychopaths will easily ascertain the specific psychological needs and wants of each interviewer and then customize their approach to best advantage. On the surface, each interviewer will come away with a positive impression, and, to the degree that decision-making relies on this good feeling, they will all agree that the psychopath is the ideal candidate, almost "too good to be true."

Now, by increasing the number and varying the *types* of interviewers (beyond the human resource professional and hiring manager), the chances of finding discrepancies that lie behind the "ideal employee" façade increase. Therefore, expanding the interview schedule with a technical expert, a future peer and/or subordinate, the current job holder (if still on staff), a member of upper management, and even the department staff assistant, can provide different perspectives that might uncover important information;

we know that psychopaths treat individuals differently depending on their perceived utility and *status*. Psychopathic responses to "low-status" interviewers may include condescension, flirting, disparaging side comments, and displays of entitlement, among other things. "High-status" interviewers may provoke discussion of overly ambitious career aspirations and expectations, bravado and deceitful boasting, and even the disparagement of a "lower-status" interviewer. By getting *all* of the interviewers in a room together for a discussion of the candidates, the selection committee can flush out these discrepancies and critical inconsistencies, and possibly deceitful claims can be uncovered. A good meeting facilitator will get each person to share his or her impressions, feelings, and facts about each candidate. They then list the positive and negative aspects of the slate of candidates, and make the final selection.

Certainly, adding interviewers to the schedule is time-consuming, expensive, and logistically challenging, and is not always feasible when the open position is an entry-level one. For example, with candidates just out of college the interviewer may have little to go on, save their academic performance, coursework, and college extracurricular experiences. However, such individuals, if they are truly (or potential) corporate psychopaths, could cause many problems down the road if they slip past the company's defenses because they were not evaluated sufficiently.

KNOW THYSELF

The objectives of psychopaths are to ingratiate themselves with their targets, establish trust, talk their way through any inconsistencies, build strong relationships with those in power, and then take parasitic advantage of everyone. During employment interviews, psychopaths will quickly assess the interviewer's value system, personal needs, and psychological makeup, and then tailor their speech and behaviors to make a good impression. A worst case would be for the interviewer to be so gullible that he does not challenge the data contained on candidates' résumés, or does not push back very hard on vague reports of their performance on the job. A perceptive interviewer will push past subtle attempts at influence, stick to the interview agenda, and avoid making the decision alone. A team of interviewers sharing information is the best defense.

However, only by having a clear understanding of one's *own* strengths, weaknesses, biases, and idiosyncrasies can the interviewer hope to maintain the course of the interview and not fall prey to ingratiation. This is not an easy task, as it requires personal insight, which we will discuss in a subsequent chapter.

EXECUTIVE HIRING AND PROMOTION

When trying to fill technical positions, such as chemists, engineers, computer programmers, and financial analysts, there are clear requirements of what they have to know and specific experiences that they had at various points in their careers. The selection of a senior manager is significantly more difficult, as the nature of the executive's job is so amorphous or so tailored to the individual that it is difficult to ascertain exactly what is required. It should be obvious to the reader by now that a good job description is critical to understanding the qualifications sought in new hires and promotional candidates. Unfortunately, many executives we have met just do not have adequate job descriptions with which to work.

In addition, as we have pointed out, there is some overlap between things psychopaths do and good executives do, at least on the surface. A complete understanding of the differences is important because one can be mistaken for the other, and the amount of damage a high-level bad hire can do to the organization can be significant.

Succession Planning

Succession plans provide orderly continuity of leadership, and they are the most effective means of identifying and grooming leadership talent. Formal succession planning can be cumbersome, but if well designed, it can minimize the chance of a corporate psychopath slipping through. Like the hiring process, succession planning is composed of several screens or hurdles through which potential future leaders must pass. In many companies, the person in charge of succession planning solicits recommendations from key managers about subordinates who have the potential for higher levels of responsibility, or more generally, the "right stuff." They base the initial evaluations on information gleaned from performance appraisals, record of accomplishments, and personal interactions with the manager making the preliminary recommendation.

A succession planner will have access to formal assessments of the candidate, often including a "*360-degree*" rating, a report on *assessment center* performance, and psychological evaluations. A 360-degree rating involves confidential surveys about the candidate's performance, attitudes, and competencies completed by peers, current and former bosses, and subordinates. Assessment centers are formal training events designed to evaluate many candidates simultaneously during a simulated work setting. Company personnel and business experts ask the participants to "run a company" and to solve several business issues. At the conclusion of the exercise, they provide feedback to the participants concerning their performance, as well as suggestions for improvement. The company also receives a summary report on the candidates' performance. Then, a management committee charged with running the succession plan reviews the information to determine each candidate's *potential* for having a successful management career, and for rising up the management ranks. The committee also evaluates the candidate's *readiness level*—how long before a candidate will be ready to assume greater responsibility and authority.

Those with sufficient potential and acceptable readiness levels are assigned a personal *mentor* or *patron* who is responsible for overseeing the company's investment in this person. Together, they create an *individual development plan* that outlines the growth and improvement needs of the candidates based on the ratings, as well as personal information, such as aspirations and any career constraints, including geographic preferences and family commitments. Recommendations for improvement often include training programs, rotational assignments, special projects, and regular meetings with a professional coach.

Those with high-level potential receive job rotations through a variety of departments, such as finance, sales, marketing, research, human resources, and manufacturing, in order to provide them with a broader understanding of the business. Many companies also require the completion of international assignments, which will give the candidates exposure to different cultures, languages, and sets of business problems.

As the reader can appreciate, formal succession planning provides multiple assessments from a variety of sources across a lengthy period of time in a variety of job functions, thus assuring that almost every aspect of the future leader's behavior has been reviewed and cross-checked. If the reader feels that the process is quite bureaucratic, this is in fact the case. Succession planning systems originated during the period when bureaucracy was the organization model in vogue. Succession planning was an attempt to improve the chances of making the right promotional choices while removing cronyism, nepotism, and other "old boy network" influences from the process. Formal succession planning is one of the few bureaucratic processes that *transitional* companies can benefit from and should retain.

However, and this is a big however, we would argue that there are still some risks involved, as the very nature of the process can be taken advantage of by manipulative employees. One problem is that corporate psychopaths already on staff have had a significant amount of time to establish a cadre of supporters, an *influence network*, some of them patrons who advocate for the psychopaths' candidacy, others pawns who do their work for them. The second problem is the disinformation spread by the psychopaths, with the express purpose of disparaging rivals and enhancing themselves in the eyes of management.

Companies can do several things to counter these problems. First, the management committee should take every opportunity to interact with management development and succession planning candidates personally, and (this is critical) solicit *confidential* and *anonymous* information from those who are in the best position to provide it, including supervisors, peers, and subordinates. It is always possible that some misinformation will be included even in well-prepared plans, but by increasing the number of sources and balancing their perceptions, any perceived discrepancies should raise any red flags and prompt further review and validation.

Second, companies should avoid identifying only one person per position for grooming. This approach, called the "crown prince/princess approach" by experts, almost guarantees that once identified, a candidate, psychopathic or not, will obtain the higher-level job without the added security of internal comparison. To avoid this, management should identify *several* candidates for *each* important position, creating a *talent pool* in which no one person is certain of obtaining the promotion.

A third approach would be to include additional psychological assessments, such as interviews and written tests designed to measure personality traits. It is important that the psychological assessment be considered just one source of data in the list of criteria used to make its promotional decision as, in the end, it is the performance and observed behavior of the candidates that should be the deciding factors.

Finally, it is critical to review carefully and challenge repeatedly all data to ascertain their validity: were goals actually attained, projects completed on time and within budget, increase in sales and revenues reported correctly? Following this, it is important to evaluate the human cost. Did the candidate leave a trail of bodies in his or her wake, or, instead, inspire others to take on a challenge and come through with success? When considering management and executive candidates, verify the record of accomplishment in important competency areas.

HANDLING CHALLENGES TO ORGANIZATIONAL RESPONSIBILITY AND EFFECTIVENESS

Executives face challenges every day as a routine part of their job. Their ability to meet these challenges goes beyond whether they are good at specific technical competencies. Broadly speaking, executives must make organizationally responsible choices, and be judged by how effective these choices are in advancing the aims of the corporation. Over time, a pattern of responses will define the "true" person. While individual lapses in judgment may garner attention in many cases, the ability of psychopaths to cover or explain away their individual decisions makes evidence of these lapses difficult to obtain. Rather, it is the long-term impact of their behaviors in a variety of situations and their dealings with a variety of people that can shed more light on who they really are. The *choices made in response to organizational challenges* provide a clear picture of the person as a future executive.

Some "Red Flags" to Consider

The following list gives the reader a sense of some of the long-term consequences of psychopathic features that might occur in a business setting. While no single consequence is necessarily indicative of psychopathy, all of them are problematic if not addressed in training and coaching sessions. At the very least, evidence of these outcomes should send up the "red flag" and warrant further investigation and evaluation.

INABILITY TO FORM A TEAM

The most debilitating characteristic of even the most well-behaved psychopath is an inability to form a workable team. This occurs in narcissistic and Machiavellian businesspeople as well as in psychopaths. The inability to form a team is a critical factor in career derailment, a reflection of an unwillingness and inability to collaborate with others, especially with those whom they see as adversaries. Being highly competitive, and in the name of the "good fight," they withhold or distort information to the detriment of the team and ultimately the company. They will often exhibit disruptive tactics and behaviors designed to either take over the team themselves or disturb the working of others.

As they prefer to manipulate others in private one-on-one meetings, psychopaths will attempt to derail a team before the first meeting by challenging the need for the team itself, offering typical organizational rationales (for example, "meetings are a waste of time") to buttress their disruption—but crafted to sound as if they have the company's best interest at heart. Alternatively, they may participate in a halfhearted manner, showing up late and making a dramatic entrance, or perhaps even leaving in the middle of the meeting to do tasks that are "more important." They are highly competitive and unwilling to listen to the directives of anyone whom they cannot value (i.e., those who do not have high utility for their career). They berate members of the team, disrupt the team's progress by distracting it from its purpose, and openly criticize the team, its objectives, and individual teammates. Recall that psychopaths believe they possess higher status than do others and will treat coworkers like pawns in their drama. The best sources of information about these disruptions are the other team members, themselves.

Of course, when teamwork is in their *own* interest (for example, as a platform for bravado and grandstanding) they will attempt to dominate others. Predictably, they attack other team members and sabotage the leader, lacing their complaints with examples of such poor leadership that they had to take over and save the project. In doing so, they often come across as bullying. The psychopath will tell you he is a real "team player"—but there really is only one member of his team!

With a dysfunctional executive or psychopath in charge, others will see decreases in morale, productivity, and cohesion. Some team members will transfer off the team and in rare cases resign. Confidential conversations by senior executives of each member of a dysfunctional team will often uncover the source of the problem.

INABILITY TO SHARE

Living peacefully in a civilized society requires the citizenry to share a variety of life-sustaining resources. Likewise, corporate citizens need to share resources in the interest of the greater good, reflected in higher profits, job security, or a stress-free workplace. Because they do not see others as equals or as having any legitimate claim to resources, psychopaths (as well as some narcissists and Machiavellians) see no need to share; they see sharing anything as giving up too much power. In fact, their parasitic, competitive nature drives them to siphon off resources from others, often for their own personal use.

Not sharing *information* is a common offense, in particular, and is often justified by a "need to know" rationale. While certain governmental agencies charged with national security can operate in this mode, keeping secrets from one's boss or a subordinate in most organizations is not justified. "The right hand not knowing what the left hand is doing" is a common embarrassment in organizations under the best of circumstances. Purposefully creating such dilemmas is contrary to organizational success and leads to dysfunction.

Psychopaths who keep others "out of the loop" use the power this gives them to their own personal advantage. Keeping others in the dark makes them look stupid and is a form of neutralization. For example, "They wouldn't understand" was the condescending rationale used by one psychopath we met; another claimed to be protecting the department from the disruptions of a coworker, stating, "She would only get upset and then we'd have a bigger problem," a statement designed to bolster the psychopath's superiority and plant the seeds of distrust of the "emotional" coworker. Clearly, comments that discount the value of others, especially their ability to think and reason as equals, are consistent with the elevated (grandiose) self-perceptions psychopaths have of themselves. They are too self-centered to see the danger of this approach, let alone its unfairness or unethical nature.

An extension of the inability to share information is the inability to share *credit* with others (unless there is some benefit to the psychopath). Credit sharing can be difficult to measure, as upper management does not have easy access to the truth about the relative contributions of employees. Complaints from coworkers, who feel they are contributing to the outcome but not getting proper credit, may be the only hint that something is amiss. Supervisors and human resources staff should pay attention to complaints of this kind, some of which may turn out to be groundless. Others may uncover serious managerial and morale problems.

DISPARATE TREATMENT OF STAFF

Because psychopaths see people playing different roles in their psychopathic drama (that is, Pawns, Patrons, Patsies, and Police), they will treat some better than others. The individuals involved may be alone in knowing about this disparate, and often subtle, treatment. In addition, for reasons explained in the next chapter, victims may never come forward to report their feelings. As a result, it may take a very long time for coworkers and management to figure out what is really going on, if they do so at all.

Unfortunately, the corporate psychopath readily explains away and justifies even the most egregious treatment. For example, one psychopathic manager promoted a junior staff member as a reward for her good work, even though another person in the department had more experience and was more deserving of the promotion. The psychopath considered the one passed over as a rival because she had received some positive attention from others in the company. The promotion of the inexperienced staffer was an attempt to block the potential rival's career and to guarantee continued support from an obedient, indebted junior person.

In a similar case, an individual who had been in a supervisory position for only three years was nominated as a high potential with an eye toward taking a position as vice president within the next two years. Although there were more qualified people in the organization than the individual, the psychopathic nominator was able to persuade the succession committee to select his choice. In this case, he spent a considerable amount of money, from a limited fund, on developmental activities over the objections of others on the committee. At the end of two years, the "high-potential" candidate was no more ready to assume the responsibilities of a vice president's job than he was at the time of his nomination. When not promoted he left in disgust, having been promised a great career by his psychopathic boss.

In a third case, a truly high-potential secretary worked for a boss who was well connected politically, but completely incompetent. Realizing the talent of his secretary, he promoted her into an assistant position and began giving her increasingly larger projects to complete. On the surface, this looked like good management practice and the employee was highly motivated, worked toward an MBA at night at a well-respected school, and completed each assignment perfectly. Over time, it became clear to the assistant that her boss really did not know what he was doing and was giving her work that *he* should be doing. She persevered, though, thinking that management would eventually recognize her achievements. However, with the increase in responsibility came badgering, abuse, and, ultimately, bullying. Wanting to do a good job, and still learning to be more confident in her own abilities, the assistant took the abuse, convincing herself that she had to pay her dues; meanwhile her psychopathic boss was taking all of the credit. She eventually learned that her boss had been complaining about her so much and so often—blaming her for failures on projects not assigned to her—that she would never be a candidate for promotion. In fact, she had come close to *termination* on more than one occasion. The human resources staff member she complained to was surprised that she had no knowledge of her "poor performance record." All she had ever heard was that there was more for her to learn; all HR heard was that she was an incompetent secretary put into a role over her head.

INABILITY TO TELL THE TRUTH

Pathological lying is a hallmark of psychopaths, as the reader knows. They cross back and forth easily between lying and honesty during conversations because they do not have the guilty feelings the rest of us have when we try to tell a lie. They weave their lies with a thread of truth, and, if questioned, they indignantly mount a convincing defense. Honesty is one of the most important traits in a manager. Yet, we have almost never seen an executive's file in which the ratings of honest and ethical behavior were less than perfect.

The problem is twofold. First, it is unpleasant and not socially acceptable to accuse someone of dishonest or unethical behavior. Second, just how do you measure honesty? Psychopaths can easily slip through the fog by appearing honest and ethical on the surface, yet doing things that many would agree are dishonest and unethical if they knew about them. On the other hand, an organization can forgive mistakes if the perceived intention was honest and motivated by the best interest of the company. However, psychopaths often use this excuse to get themselves out of a lie, making it difficult to separate the honest employee from the dishonest.

INABILITY TO BE MODEST

Not everyone is modest, although it is an admirable trait where it exists. Modest people do not brag about their accomplishments, but typically enjoy doing a good job for its own sake or accept only an occasional pat on the back as a reward. Many who are modest shun the spotlight, preferring to let the record speak for itself. Both narcissists and Machiavellians tend to be *immodest*, but it is the psychopath's immodesty, coupled with *arrogance*, that stands out so clearly to coworkers. Unfortunately, when dealing with higher-ups, the ability of psychopaths to manage and promote their arrogant self-perceptions, and to package themselves as self-confident and strong leaders, effectively hides their true nature. Genuine modesty among psychopaths is almost nonexistent. Its absence in an executive, while not an indication of psychopathy directly, can help to corroborate other suspicions.

INABILITY TO ACCEPT BLAME

Taking responsibility for one's own mistakes and not blaming others is highly valued in corporations, as well as in society. Psychopaths rarely, if ever, take responsibility for their actions, even if they clearly made mistakes or their actions and decisions led to failures. However, they go a few steps farther; they will routinely *blame* others and create "evidence" that others are to blame. Clearly, this is a form of lying and quite different from the shifting of blame or pointing fingers that most of us sometimes engage in. This is active, instrumental aggression. Because it is hard to uncover covert blaming, it often takes a series of failed projects under the functional control of the psychopath to produce any significant evidence of incompetence or wrongdoing.

INABILITY TO ACT CONSISTENTLY
AND PREDICTABLY

We are all more comfortable with people who are somewhat predictable. Businesses need to know that those working for them will show up at work, perform their jobs according to accepted safety and quality standards, get along with others, and not disrupt the work of others. Even creative types, who may surprise us with their idiosyncrasies, may appear predictable once we understand their day-to-day work habits. What a business cannot afford are "loose cannons," individuals who wreak havoc on the normal flow of business and social intercourse amongst other employees. They disrupt meetings, embarrass others and the company, make erratic decisions, change course seemingly without reason, and surprise even the most seasoned. Few executives like surprises, often priding themselves on being aware of the goings-on in their business. Loose cannons can be an executive's worst nightmare.

Unless one truly understands the machinations of corporate psychopaths, it is almost impossible to predict what they will do. Rarely are others privy to the inner workings of their mind, making them potentially dangerous employees to have on staff.

INABILITY TO REACT CALMLY

The ability to remain calm during a crisis is the hallmark of good leadership, and psychopaths are quite adept at maintaining their cool when in situations observed by those in power. Yet when out of view, they can overreact in socially inappropriate ways, and many who observe this phenomenon will describe them as being dramatic. Although occasional outbursts by supervisors, such as when responding to a dangerous safety violation, are acceptable and even expected, psychopaths tend to overreact in response to perceived personal insults or when insufficient respect is given them. This harms the work group, and ultimately the company, because it puts everyone on notice they must treat the psychopath with kid gloves. Groups subjected to dramatic bosses often lose their cohesion and team spirit, falling back on an "every man for himself" mentality.

Because psychopaths are able to moderate this behavior while in the presence of authority they respect, it can go unnoticed for considerable amounts of time—until they move on and the stories start to emerge. Unfortunately, the only evidence available before a psychopath's departure is rumors and tension in the department. Insightful HR organizations can learn more about what is really going on if they follow up on such information.

INABILITY TO ACT WITHOUT AGGRESSION

Bullying, coercion, and intimidation have no place in business; they disrupt work, hurt people, and are unfair to those who cannot defend themselves. However, learning about this type of behavior is often difficult unless targets and victims come forward. Because of the legal ramifications of such behavior, many companies institute no-bullying policies and create confidential mechanisms for affected employees to report this behavior. Formalized Codes of Conduct often have provisions concerning bullying and intimidation. In some European countries, it is also against the law. To be effective, though, it is important to communicate to all the policy and the procedure for reporting violations. In particular, supervisors and managers need to learn how to recognize bullying, coercion, and intimidation, and how to deal effectively with them.

DISCUSSION QUESTIONS

- Have you ever interviewed job candidates?
- Did you follow any of the suggested best practices (or did you wing it)?
- Have you ever hired the wrong person for a job? What did you miss?
- Have you ever observed "red flags" as described above?

§ 11.1
Does Practice Make Perfect?

Hare consulted with Nicole Kidman on the movie *Malice*. She wanted to let the audience know, early in the film, that she was not the sweet, warm person she appeared to be. He gave her the following scene: "You're walking down the street and come across an accident at the corner. A young child, struck by a car, is lying in a pool of blood. You walk up to the accident site, look briefly at the child, and then focus on the grief-stricken mother. After a few minutes of careful scrutiny, you walk back to your apartment, go into the bathroom, stand in front of the mirror, and practice mimicking the facial expressions and body language of the mother."

Of course, this scenario is not unique in suggesting that psychopaths learn to mimic emotions they themselves do not fully experience. As Cleckley (p. 374)[3] put it, the psychopath "can learn to use ordinary words . . . [and] will also learn to reproduce appropriately all the pantomime of feeling, but the feeling itself does not come to pass."

In Bill Watterson's comic strip *Calvin and Hobbes*, Susie tells Calvin that he is lying and that it's written all over his face. Calvin rushes home and practices his facial expressions before the mirror.

In a scene in the 1956 film *The Bad Seed*, eight-year-old Rhoda Penmark poses in front of a mirror, ostensibly learning to mimic the expressions of those watching her. Similarly, in the 2018 remake of *The Bad Seed*, when Rhoda (renamed Emma Grossman) is asked by her father, "What would you give me for a basket of hugs?" She replies, "A basket of kisses." She practices saying "Basket of kisses! Basket of kisses! Basket of kisses!" in front of a mirror while trying on different smiles. The result is a poor attempt at a genuine (Duchenne) smile (see S 12.1: *Psychopathic Interviews*). For a psychopath, practice may help, but some observers will see through the simulations of emotions.

S 11.2
Politics and Poker: A License to Lie

In poker, a *tell* is verbal or body language that conveys information about the hand another player holds. Good poker players
spend a lot of time learning to detect the tells of their opponents.

Do psychopaths emit tells that provide others with useful information about themselves? It appears that some do. In *Without Conscience*, Hare described many examples in which some
people feel uncomfortable in the presence of psychopaths, whom
he described as social predators. Although they may be unable to
"put their finger" on what bothered them, many commented that
it was a predatory stare and empty eyes that made them feel as if
they were lunch. This is a common theme in accounts of psychopathic interactions in true crime books.

Other nonverbal behaviors include the tendency of psychopaths to intrude into and dominate our personal space, mimic
emotions, use excessive hand gestures during emotional speech,
and generally put on a good show.[4] Can such behaviors function
as tells?

Leanne ten Brinke and colleagues[5] examined the emotional
facial expressions, body language, and verbal content of the
video clips of offenders with PCL-R scores. One of their main
interests was the use of *Duchenne smiles* (upturned lip corners
with cheek raiser activation, which creates crow's-feet around
the eyes). Most people view a Duchenne smile as an authentic,
genuine, and trustworthy expression of happiness or delight.[6]
However, compared with other offenders, those with high psychopathy scores exhibited *more* Duchenne smiles, more hand
gestures, and more angry emotional language.

Were the psychopathic offenders happier than were other
offenders? Apparently not. With practice, Duchenne smiles are
easy to fake (see S 11.1: *Does Practice Make Perfect?*). Further,
psychopathic offenders used Duchenne smiles *while using angry emotional language*. Naive observers noticed this *behavioral
incongruence* and were quite successful in identifying the psy-

chopathic offenders. As ten Brinke and colleagues (p. 273)[7] commented, "Interestingly, such impression management tactics may result in a behavioral profile marked by inconsistency—wherein one aspect of more psychopathic individuals' behavior reveals their true nature (e.g., the use of negative, or angry words), which is contradicted by their attempts at behavioral control (e.g., the expression of charming happiness, to appear friendly and be disarming)." The definition that ten Brinke and colleagues gave to the naive observers was "Factor 1—People high in Factor 1 psychopathy tend to have an inflated sense of self-importance, to be 'smooth talkers' and to lie and manipulate others without feeling guilty. They lack empathy for other people, and rarely accept responsibility for the things they do wrong."

The Case of Dave

ACT V, Scene I

CIRCLE THE WAGONS

"Do you have a minute?" asked Frank, peering into John's office.

"Yes, sure, what's up?" asked John, the vice president, putting down his pen.

"I need to talk to you about Dave," started Frank, entering the office, closing the door, and taking a seat. "I've been hearing a lot of bad reports about him the past couple of months, and one of my best analysts just asked to be transferred off Dave's project team."

"Transfer? That's not good. You think Dave's the issue?"

"Well, I know he is," said Frank, exasperatedly. "One of my guys came to me two nights back, after hours, to tell me what has been going on." John leaned forward, interested in what Frank had to report. "He said that since the project started, over six months ago, things have been getting steadily worse. Dave has been disrupting and dominating the team to the point that many don't want to work with him anymore. He apparently doesn't come prepared, often comes to the meeting late, leaving a whole room full of people idle, yells at folks, cuts people off while they're making their status reports, and embarrasses them if they make a suggestion. People are afraid to speak up, and they're losing interest in the project because they feel they can't do anything right by Dave."

"That's really odd, Frank. Dave has always come across as a good leader, and I thought he was well liked. Have you spoken to him about this?"

"Yes, the first time was about three months ago, when I read his interim report. It was a mess: a hodgepodge of material he seemed to cobble together because I asked. There was no organization, no synthesis, and no accurate timeline. He couldn't—or wouldn't—even answer some basic questions about the details and figures. I told him I expected more of a status report, complete with his personal analysis and recommendations, and more details about dates, costs, and so forth."

"How did he respond?" asked Frank.

"Well, at first he went ballistic on me, ranting about how we have too many meetings at this company, I should trust him, and on and on. I had to close the door because he was disrupting the floor. After he calmed down, we spoke and I outlined my expectations. He seemed to understand and said he would improve."

"Did he?" asked John.

"Yes, actually he did—dramatically, I'd say. His next two reports were outstanding. I didn't agree completely with the timeline, and some of the material was overly self-serving, but most of it was what you would expect. So I was surprised when I heard things had gotten worse on the people side of the equation; I was under the impression that the team was working well together. Plus, some other things have come up."

"Could it just be a personality clash between Dave and your guy on the team?" interrupted John. "Maybe Dave's style is getting in the way."

"No, I don't think so. This was the second transfer request this week, and my secretary has heard other rumblings through the department. He tried to give one of the temps something to type last week and she told him that he had to get it approved first. Well, he made a big scene and got her crying before she finally agreed. Plus—"

"Frank," started John, slowly, "I have to tell you that Dave came to me about three or so months ago. He complained that you were getting on his case."

"He went to you about me?" said Frank, at first surprised, and then getting annoyed.

"Yes, well, we're on the softball team, you know, so over a beer I asked him how things were going, you know, the usual chitchat, and he started in on you. He seems to have a very short fuse."

"What did he say?" asked Frank.

"Basically, it boiled down to your being too demanding, too detail oriented, stuff like that. I told him that's why you make the big bucks." They both laughed halfheartedly. "I also told him that getting things done on time and in budget is what makes success here, and that he should focus more on pleasing you."

"So maybe it was your pep talk that got to him, not mine," suggested Frank.

"Neither here nor there, Frank. If he's hurting the team and disrupting others, then that's a problem. You should meet with him again," said John. "Did you say you saw him yesterday?"

"No," Frank said. "I wanted to touch base with you first, put together a strategy."

"I think you can meet with him, tell him you've heard things, and see where it takes you," offered John.

"There's more, John," said Frank seriously.

"Oh." John paused. "What?"

Frank continued. "I've heard that Dave hasn't been writing the reports himself or meeting with the other departments to coordinate the different phases. Even some of the other department heads are wondering why Dave is not meeting with them himself. Some say he's not doing any of the work he's supposed to. Apparently, Dorothy is doing most of the heavy work for him."

"There's nothing wrong with delegation, Frank. Maybe he's developing her, or she just wants to be helpful." John paused and thought. "Dorothy? She's not one of yours, is she?" he asked.

"No, she's from Jerry's area. Dave insisted we put her on the team because she's very motivated and can help with the artwork. I really had no problem with it and neither did Jerry," added Frank.

"Hmmm, that's odd. Dave was complaining about some female on the team—I don't think he gave me her name—who wasn't carrying her own weight. He was blaming her for some of the delays; he had to spend all his time tutoring her and fixing her mistakes. I suggested he move her off the team, but he said you wouldn't allow it; you had made a deal with Jerry to give one of his hotshots some exposure to the product development process and couldn't back down."

"Well, no. Putting Dorothy on the team was Dave's idea, and, interestingly enough, Dave never complained to me about her. Jerry does think highly of her, yes, but she needs more experience. I never heard that she wasn't doing well at all; in fact, Dave praises her all the time. He thinks that *Jerry* is holding her back." Frank and John looked at each other.

After a pause, Frank continued. "We've—I've—got a problem, John. There are too many contradictions here. I need to deal with it."

"You're right, we need to find out what is really going on. Look, I have a meeting in a few minutes. Why don't you come back late this afternoon? Bring Dave's file and whatever else you can dig up. Let's review everything first, and then decide what to do."

"Okay," said Frank, getting up and heading toward the door. "I hope this is just a big misunderstanding." He sighed.

"Doubtful, Frank," said John.

DISCUSSION QUESTIONS

- What advice would you offer Frank about how to handle Dave and the project team?
- Have you ever had this happen to you, either as a manager or a member of a team?
- How broad do you think Dave's influence network really is?

12

Personal Self-Defense

Nancy loved being a traveling nurse. Like many travelers, Nancy had put in her time at a major city hospital, got the experience she needed, and then, at age thirty-two, decided to make a career change. Travelers, she found, get more money, and a bit more respect from the medical staff, than the regulars do.

As a young nurse, Nancy was appalled by the egocentricity of the surgeons she worked with; she had been surprised, actually, that they were entirely different than she had fantasized about in school. She used to wonder why some of them did not require psychotherapy, or at least an anger management course. A wise old nursing instructor explained to her, following a public dressing-down she received from a doctor, that they act this way—rude, crude, and lewd—because of the intense pressure they face every time they cut into a human body.

"They really do feel for their patients deep down inside," assured the instructor, "but years of making life-and-death decisions hardens them, and their only outlet is to act out in the OR." Nancy accepted this explanation for a while, and it helped her deal with her frustration, but then she learned about traveling nurses and saw an opportunity to work at her craft knowing that she would be back on the road in a few months. She knew she could not change who the doctors were, but it appealed to her that she could change the working relationship between her and them, so she made the switch.

Then one day she met Marshall. They happened to sit next to each other on a plane as Nancy was moving to a new job in the Midwest and they struck up a conversation. As often happens when we find ourselves locked into a seat next to a stranger for a few hours, Nancy started to talk about herself to Marshall. Normally not very talkative, Nancy found herself captivated by a handsome man in a dark gray suit who seemed to take an interest in her. When she found out that he was a physician, she got nervous. *Oh, jeez, not a doctor*, she thought, but his calm demeanor and friendly smile eased her concerns.

"My career choice came late in life," he admitted. "It was difficult juggling my schedule to attend classes, particularly the labs, but my boss at the time understood, probably because he was a veteran, too."

"You were in the war?" asked Nancy, beginning to wonder whether Marshall was much older than she had surmised.

"Well, for a short while, but then I got shot down."

"Oh, my God," she said, gasping.

"Yes, well, that's the nature of war—it truly is hell. I couldn't just leave my guys there; I had to save them," he added casually.

"My dad got a Purple Heart in Vietnam; did you get one?" Nancy interrupted excitedly.

Marshall turned toward her, smiled briefly, and then stared coldly. "Medal of Honor," he said so seriously that Nancy feared that she might have offended him.

"Oh, that's really impressive," she said meekly, worrying even more that she had blown the opportunity to finally meet a decent man. "Tell me what happened," she added quickly, hoping to repair the conversation; then, just as quickly, she remembered that her father would never talk about his combat experience. It was just too painful for him. Nancy felt that the conversation was heading into a death spiral, and she did not know how to save herself.

Marshall, leaning back, closed his eyes briefly and then proceeded to tell her about his war experiences. Nancy listened intently. The valor Marshall showed that day impressed her; she felt pride for him and, in a moment of reverie, her late father.

"After I got out, I got a job as a private pilot and made good money, but I then decided I wanted to help sick people more than ferry rich ones to and from exotic vacation spots," he said, rolling his eyes. "I guess having the medics sew me back together," Marshall paused, looked away and then back, "I guess I was grateful, and it was then that I decided that I should help others."

Nancy was touched, and toward the end of the flight, when Marshall asked for her phone number, she eagerly obliged.

Marshall and Nancy dated for about four months. While her crazy schedule kept her close to home, Marshall, who lived and worked eighty miles away, made the trek whenever he could steal enough time to stay with her. He always arrived at her place with flowers, candy, a small piece of jewelry, expensive champagne, and sometimes a naughty negligee. Nancy loved all the attention. They dined at fancy restaurants, and being proud of her ability to support herself as a traveling nurse, she often offered to pay.

Their conversations were different from any she had ever had with a man—serious, humorous, lighthearted, and deep. Marshall surprised her with what he knew about the world, about people, and about medicine.

At times, she would fantasize about their spending their lives together, but she would catch herself before being too carried away. Her girlfriends—most of them nurses, as well—repeatedly warned her about *doctors*, but she knew they were envious of her catch and would have fallen for Marshall if they had met him. She never told him about her dreams, for fear of scaring him off. Yet day by day, she felt her commitment to him increasing, and judging by his words, she felt he was growing more attached to her as well.

When he told her he was going to borrow some money to start his own private practice—he was tired of the long hours his hospital job required—she got excited and then very nervous. While his current job was hectic, at least he could get time off occasionally. She knew that once he started his own business it would consume him. Entrepreneurs often worked very long hours trying to build their new businesses, and she feared that their visits would diminish.

Maybe I could work in his office as his nurse, she fantasized. *Maybe I could be his business partner!* She had loaned him some cash once to pay a medical school bill, but she could not afford to help him with his new business. *No, I would have to be the office nurse*, she mused before shaking herself from her reverie.

With her four-month assignment ending soon, Nancy hit on the right idea. She decided to apply for an OR position at Marshall's hospital. He would be leaving anyway, so there would not be any conflict or potential for embarrassment, but at least she would be in the same city. Moreover, maybe, after a few months, they could move in together. She decided not to mention this to him, fearful that he might misunderstand. *Men get so crazy when they think you are trying to get them to commit*, she reminded herself. She wanted to have the job and her own apartment ready before surprising him one evening with the good news.

Nancy took her cafeteria tray filled with a salad, soup, and tea and headed toward the group of nurses congregated at one of the tables. Her morning interviews with the medical staff at Marshall's hospital went well, and she now wanted to meet some of her potential coworkers. As a traveling nurse, Nancy enjoyed the chance to meet new people, work in new environments, and then move on before the insanity got to her. "Hi," she said, approaching the group. "Is this seat taken?"

"It's yours," responded Rhonda, the most senior person at the table, and the one with the most outgoing personality.

"Thanks," said Nancy, sitting down. "I'm Nancy R. I'll be starting in—"

"We know," interrupted Sally. "We get the scoop from HR on all the new travelers," she said, pointing to one of the women at the end of the table, who nodded. "Welcome."

As Sally made the introductions of those at the table, Nancy carefully noted their names, having learned early on that remembering coworkers' names was a critical first step to success at any location. Some staff nurses resented a traveler. Nancy was not sure why, but she always made it a policy to start on the best terms with everyone she met at her new assignments.

"Have you met the crazies yet?" asked Susie.

"Well, I was interviewed by Dr. S, who seemed real decent, and then Dr. H."

"Oh, those are the *normals*," interrupted Susie. "Wait until you meet the others!" Everyone at the table rolled their eyes.

"Does Dr. M work on the second shift?" she asked, her curiosity about Marshall getting the better of her.

"Haven't heard about that one," said Rhonda, puzzling. "Are you sure he works here?"

"Oh, well, I heard his name mentioned earlier today, and I was just wondering," said Nancy, hoping she had not said too much.

"We did have an M, Marshall M, on the third shift. He was a transporter, but he doesn't work here anymore," chimed in Sandra, the union rep for the nurses. A few of the women at the table visibly stirred at the mention of Marshall, but Sandra continued. "Got into a bit of trouble with one of the residents. Don't know any *doctor* by that name, though. You, Sally?"

"No, not since I've been here, which is going on twelve years," said a quiet, older nurse at the end of the table.

"Well, Marshall was a looker all right, did an okay job, but always fantasized about being a doctor someday. I think he moved to County General, not sure," added Rhonda.

"Oh, I must be mistaken," said Nancy, beginning to get nervous. She hurriedly finished her lunch and got up to make her exit. "I've got to see about my new apartment. Sorry, I have to run."

"So we'll see you next week?" asked Rhonda.

"Yes, yes, I'll be here!" chimed Nancy with a big smile.

As she got into her car, she picked up her cell phone. She decided to call Marshall to find out what was going on. His cell rang and rang. She realized that she did not have his address. As her anxiety grew, she decided to drive over to County General Hospital.

Nancy parked her car in County General's visitors' lot and walked to the main entrance. When her turn came, she said to the guard at the desk, "Hi. I'm here to see Dr. Marshall M. He's a surgeon."

The guard flipped the pages of his hospital phone directory and searched. "He's a doctor here?" he asked, puzzling over the list on his desk.

"Yes. He just started here, I heard."

"Oh," said the guard without looking up. He turned to the computer screen and typed. "Hmm. Are you sure about the name, miss?"

"Yes. Maybe he—"

"Well, we have someone by that name; looks like he just started on the night shift, but he's in maintenance." The guard looked up, adding, "Sorry. You might want to call your doctor's office to get the location. We have quite a few buildings here."

"Thanks," said Nancy, a tight smile across her face. "I'll do that." She headed for the parking lot and then stopped as a flush of panic swept over her. *What the . . . ?* she thought as she started her car and drove to her new apartment.

DISCUSSION QUESTIONS

- Is there some misunderstanding going on here or has Nancy been scammed?
- What lies did Marshall tell Nancy?
- What parts of Nancy's personality did Marshall play on?

- Have you ever been in a relationship with someone for a long time, thought you knew the person, and then found out that you didn't know him or her at all?

Psychopaths in Your Personal Life

Having a psychopath in your personal life is an emotionally draining, psychologically debilitating, and sometimes physically harmful experience. We have received numerous letters and emails from individuals who believe a psychopath has victimized them: many feel that their spouse or intimate partner is one; others believe a relative might be; and still others are confident they work for or with one. Their often detailed and pleading communications have given us a glimpse into the impact that psychopathic manipulation and abuse has had on their lives. In some cases, where the victim fears physical or financial harm, we have suggested they call the local police or civil authorities. In many cases, we referred them to qualified psychologists, psychiatrists, counselors, members of the clergy, or other professionals in their area who are best suited to provide the psychological and emotional help they need.

Over the years, we noticed that, much like psychopaths who operate through a parasitic-predator model of assessment-manipulation-abandonment, the targets and victims themselves seemed unwittingly to share a parallel response pattern. In this chapter, we will attempt to outline the development of the psychopath–victim relationship in such a way as to enlighten the reader to traps and pitfalls along the path. We believe the best defense against the dark art of psychopathic manipulation is to understand fully how psychopaths operate and to take every opportunity to avoid them.

BUT FIRST, A WORD OF CAUTION

In all cases, though, we suggest that you resist the temptation to label your antagonist a psychopath, especially if you lack formal training and qualifications to conduct psychological assessments. (The only exception might be when speaking with your lawyer, but we hope that you will not have to go down that road.) Clearly, it is "never wise to poke a snake"! The term *psychopath* has many negative connotations and once used, has a tendency to stick. Careless or inappropriate application of the label would be unfair and might (perhaps will) lead to lawsuits and other forms of retaliation (especially if your "diagnosis" is correct). Therefore, for most practical purposes, it is sufficient to be aware that a given individual appears to have many of the traits and behaviors that define psychopathy and act accordingly.

LEARN ALL YOU CAN ABOUT YOURSELF

"Know thyself" is perhaps one of the wisest bits of advice ever spoken. Self-knowledge will strengthen your immunity against psychopaths' games; it is crucial for your psychological, emotional, and, possibly, physical survival. Psychopaths feed on what they see as naiveté and innocence.

We are all somewhat reluctant to hear about our faults and weaknesses. Some people avoid going to the doctor because they do not want to know whether their aches and pains reflect something serious. Some avoid talking to psychologists because they fear they will learn something uncomfortable about themselves. Psychopaths are well aware of these concerns and capitalize on them. In effect, a perceptive psychopath may know you better than you know yourself.

The more you know who you are, the better able you will be to defend against psychopathic influence.

UNDERSTAND YOUR OWN UTILITY
TO PSYCHOPATHS

It can be difficult to appreciate what your worth might be to a psychopath, in part because society often requires us to play down our assets. A realistic assessment, however, supported by information and feedback from friends, family, and professional colleagues, can help you clarify your strengths and value to others. The most common types of utility attractive to psychopaths are money, power, fame, and sex, but in organizational life, this list grows to include access to information, communication, influence, authority, and so forth. Psychopaths target not only the rich and famous, but also others with more subtle value.

Psychopaths use various tactics to get you to share your assets with them, preying on your generosity, trusting nature, or sense of charity. They will play on your sense of pity if that feeling gets you to help them in some way or gets you to use your influence with others who could help them fulfill their needs. It is sometimes difficult to separate those in real need, whom you should help, from those who rely on psychopathic manipulation to get you to do so. A good defense is routinely to apply some common sense to social interactions, particularly those that involve people you do not know well. We all like compliments, but there is a difference between harmless social stroking and oily flattery designed to ingratiate and manipulate. The problem is that we do not always notice the difference, particularly if we do not have a realistic picture of who we are and if we are dealing with a psychopath skilled in painting the sort of picture we would like to see of ourselves. Excessive or incongruous compliments and flattery should be a signal for you to pay critical attention to what is coming next. It is prudent to create a list of the things you think your psychopath is using you for and be sensitive to manipulation techniques aimed at securing them from you. Ask yourself, "What does this person *really* want of me?"

UNDERSTAND YOUR TRIGGERS

We all have triggers that others can use to get the better of us. Triggers are those parts of our personality and temperament that stimulate emotional and psychological reactions, often beyond our ability to control or at least manage them. Here are the most common triggers that psychopaths use when playing head-games with victims.

HOT BUTTONS

Hot buttons are those things that provoke an automatic, emotional reaction from you, set you off (negative hot buttons), or get you excited (positive hot buttons). For example, you may react with envy and depression when the company promotes your colleague or with sudden frustration and anger when someone cuts you off in traffic, gets credit for your work, or is critical of the way you dress. You may react with pleasure and sometimes joy when complimented on your looks, when your political candidate is ahead in the polls, or when a player on your team scores. Hobbies are often hot-button topics and tend to provoke positive reactions out of most people. Likewise, passion for one's work can provoke intense energy and excitement, especially when someone takes an interest in what you do for a living.

When someone presses one of our hot buttons, two things happen: our attention shifts away from other, sometimes more important, things and the triggered feelings color our perceptions of the immediate social environment. This reflex-like tendency is not lost on the psychopath, who will push your buttons to stimulate positive feelings toward him or her and negative feelings against others. Another more insidious misuse of your hot buttons is to trick you into "acting out" (particularly negatively) in front of others.

It is difficult, except in the most blatant situations, to tell whether someone has purposely pushed your hot button or has inadvertently done so without any particular intent to manipulate or use you. In fact, many legitimate friendships start when someone has pushed a hot button in a genuine effort to befriend you (e.g., asking about your golf game, which is terrible). If you challenge a psychopath's attempt to use your hot buttons against you—for example, to make you lose control in front of someone of importance—he will quickly label it a mistake. You may even receive an apology. However, if the psychopath's goal was to embarrass or humiliate you in front of others, then the damage to your *reputation*, in the eyes of observers, has already occurred.

Often, the psychopath will press your buttons privately, convincing you that she understands and shares similar feelings—a ploy to build rapport. For example, you may complain that another employee has irritated or hurt you by some inconvenience, slight, or perceived insult. The psychopath need only say, "Oh, my God. She didn't!" and you will begin to feel that the psychopath understands and possibly even shares your feelings about the offending event or person. The astute psychopath will then listen to you let it all out about things, events, and people, thereby ingratiating himself with you and providing information that can potentially be used to manipulate you later on in the relationship.

Learning all you can about your hot buttons is a first defense against having them pushed unscrupulously. Unfortunately, it is far easier to become *aware* of one's hot buttons than to learn to *control* them. Feedback from others, including family members, close friends, or professional colleagues, is invaluable and with the assistance of a trusted friend or professional coach, you can learn to control or at least moderate your reactions. Eventually, you will improve your ability to recognize quickly a hot-button reaction as it starts, allowing you time to put on the brakes and to regain control of your reactions.

WEAK SPOTS

Like all predators, psychopaths perceive the weaknesses in potential victims. There are many types of human weakness and the astute psychopath knows most of them. For simplicity, we will focus on three common categories.

- **Flaws.** What is wrong with you—too heavy, too thin, or too shy? We often see flaws in ourselves that others do not see. Some are real, but many of these exist only in our imaginations. Psychopaths are adept at identifying those things that *you* like least about *yourself,* and then using them as levers or hooks to manipulate you. As discussed in an earlier chapter, a psychopath will try to convince you that he accepts you as you are, despite any flaws you think you have. This is a very powerful and reassuring message for someone to hear and is the foundation for the psychopathic bond. Then the psychopath will "reveal" that he shares the same flaws with you, deepening your sense of connectedness and anticipation that a strong personal relationship is in the works.

  Having a realistic picture of your flaws is important for your defense against psychopathic manipulation. This usually involves paring down the list in your mind to those that *really* matter, and then challenging those that remain on your list. You may decide to improve some and accept others. Once you make these assessments and decisions about your flaws, it becomes more difficult for others to manipulate you through them.

- **Lacks.** What is missing in your life—self-esteem, love, understanding, excitement, or a sense of purpose? Believing we have less of something than we should influences our thoughts, feelings, and behaviors; we often resent those who have more than we do. We begin to doubt our own abilities to provide and achieve, conclude we are failures, and desperately feel the need to fill the void, sometimes at any cost.

  Craving things that we lack leads to a vulnerable state, psychologically, emotionally, and sometimes physically. In this state, thoughts and dreams of fulfilling their desires consume some people, making them easy targets for psychopaths who are all too ready to "help." For example, promising to make you rich—but with no intention of delivering—is a common technique used in pyramid schemes and street games, such as three-card monte. Most economic scams lead you to believe that you can make a lot of money, but you usually lose everything before realizing how gullible you were. In another example, a psychopathic puppetmaster may entice you to join her in a criminal act to help pay a debt or to get even with someone. The crime may involve stealing money, supplies, or trade secrets from your company; damaging property belonging to others; or even hurting your own family members. This is especially seductive if the psychopath convinces you that you *never* will be caught, and that the victims are only getting what they deserve. If you succumb to this ploy, you will be forever indebted to the psychopath, plagued with guilt, and perhaps do prison time!

In general, it is good to understand totally your personal needs and wants, and to have a realistic appreciation of what steps it will take to achieve or get them. A good counselor or life coach sometimes can help. However, the best advice is age old: "If it's too good to be true, it probably is."

- **Fears.** What are you afraid of—intimacy, loneliness, or speaking in front of a group? All of us have fearful moments, times when we are plagued by questions and doubts. If these thoughts are not debilitating or if they do not intrude in our day-to-day lives, they are within the range of normalcy. Yet our fears, once identified by the psychopath, provide clues as to how we will react in certain situations and events and thus become potent tools for manipulation. Defense against this use of our fears is difficult, for they are the product of both nature and nurture, and therefore not easy to modify. A counselor or mental health professional may help you understand your fears and help you adopt protective strategies.

The Psychopathic Dance

The more that you understand about how psychopaths operate, the better prepared you will be to avoid manipulation. In an earlier chapter, we reviewed the phases that make up the parasitic lifestyle adopted by many psychopaths:

- *Assessment* of the individual's potential utility, weaknesses, and defenses.
- The use of impression management and *manipulation* to ingratiate themselves with the individual and then to siphon off resources.
- *Abandonment*, the phase in which the individual is no longer of use to the psychopath.

We have found repeatedly, in the cases reported to us in emails, letters, and interviews with victims, that *many did not know that they were dealing with a psychopath until it was too late*. While the specific details of each case may differ, the feelings, attitudes, behaviors, and outcomes the victims described seemed to form a pattern or process. In this section, we will review the phases that targets who ultimately become victims go through during manipulation. See S 11.2: *Politics and Poker: A License to Lie.*

PHASE 1: TEMPTED BY THE PSYCHOPATHIC FICTION

First impressions can be deceiving. Unfortunately, the first impressions you will have of a psychopath are positive. Their manifest charm, attractive appearance, verbal fluency, and adroit use of flattery and ego stroking are seductive. However, these impressions are similar to the promise contained in the jacket of a bad book. The unfortunate difference is that we seldom buy a book without first flipping through the pages or at least reading some reviews. Similarly, we would not buy a car or a TV without some careful research. On the other hand, we often accept the psychopathic façade at face value. With psychopaths, what you see is not what you get, but it may take a lot of pain before you realize this. Because not all psychopaths present themselves in the same way, they may victimize you more than once in your lifetime. It is prudent to exert at least a modicum of cautious, or even suspicious, evaluation of new social encounters, particularly those that potentially can have some long-range impact on your life. At the very least, you should reevaluate your first impressions as more information about the individual becomes available, and be prepared to make a speedy exit if things are not beginning to add up or if you are feeling uncomfortable.

PHASE 2: TAKEN IN BY THE PSYCHOPATHIC BOND

Subtle charm and manipulation techniques may convince you that a psychopath likes who you are. During long conversations or a series of meetings, he will try to convince you that he shares many of your likes, dislikes, traits, and attitudes. This typically is covert, not stated openly; in fact, psychopathic manipulation can be so subtle that you might arrive at this conclusion just by hearing the psychopath's life story. Of course, psychopaths create their stories carefully to take advantage of your hot buttons and weak spots. In all of the cases we have reviewed, a common theme was the victims' desire to find someone, a life partner, who shared their values, beliefs, and life experiences. You will feel excitement at this time, believing that the psychopath genuinely likes and respects you. You also may "know" that the relationship, whether personal or professional, will grow.

The psychopath will also convince you that his integrity is without question and that honesty and trust are the basis for the relationship. At this stage, most individuals report having shared a goodly amount of personal information with the psychopath, believing that the things they had learned about the psychopath's life were true and deeply personal. They did not suspect that this was blatant deception or that much of what they had heard was fabrication.

Psychopaths eventually guide you into believing that the two of you are unique, very special, and destined to be together. They portray themselves as the perfect friends, employees, or business partners and while the grooming will take considerable time and effort on their part, it will be subtle and persistent. At this point, you do not know that the psychopathic bond is a sham; it does not exist except in your mind.

Awareness of and sensitivity to the psychopathic bonding process is good preventive medicine. Be wary of falling for someone's story too quickly because solid relationships take time to develop and grow: apply critical thinking and careful assessment all along the way. If you feel that this person is *too* good to be true, try to prove yourself wrong.

PHASE 3: COLLUSION IN THE PSYCHOPATH'S GAME (THE PSYCHOPATHIC FICTION)

Once the psychopathic bond is firmly established, you will find that your hot buttons and weak spots are an easy means to gain your compliance and to reaffirm the relationship (although you will not be aware of this at this time). This is especially true in relationships in which you find yourself doing what the psychopath asks (even if it is not in your own best interest) in order to maintain the intense bond. Healthy relationships tend to be in balance, with each person giving and taking. Psychopathic relationships are one-sided; you give and the psychopath takes (money, a place to live, sex, power, and control).

Although in many cases, friends, family, and coworkers see what is going on and may try to warn you, you will not listen. Well-meaning comments such as, "He's no good for you," "Get out of that relationship," and "You can't trust her" often go unheeded or may lead to your estrangement from family and friends. The psychopath reinforces the isolation, and sometimes, as in the case of psychopathic cult leaders, demands it. Once you are isolated, you have little defense against the manipulative psychopath.

If your boss or coworker is dominating you, or if you are on an emotional roller coaster with a partner, seek outside confirmation. If you find that the interactions are damaging, it is time to end the relationship. Often, family, friends, and coworkers can assist you or provide you emotional support as you transition out. In abusive situations, you may need to get the advice and assistance of the authorities or other trained professionals.

PHASE 4: MANIPULATED BY SELF-DOUBT, GUILT, AND DENIAL

The opportunistic, deceptive, and manipulative behaviors of psychopaths can be as bewildering to the victims as they are devastating. Many victims blame themselves for whatever is happening, while others deny that there is any problem at all. In each case, doubts and concerns about the psychopaths in your life morph into *doubts about yourself.*

Unfortunately, it is very difficult to convince those in the grips of a psychopathic bond that they are being misled, or that they do not have a complete picture of what is going on. Even when data are presented to these victims (perhaps a suspicious motel receipt or a mysterious charge on a personal credit card), they exhibit denial. Like the psychopath, you may blame others for falsifying the information, you may slough it off as a misunderstanding, or you may even conclude others should not question the degree of trust you put in your "soul mate." When you are consumed with self-doubt, guilt, and denial, it is very difficult to help you. The best that family, friends, and coworkers can do is to help you get professional assistance, such as a referral to an employee assistance program or other counseling with a trained mental health professional.

The problem is particularly difficult when the psychopath has co-opted others and convinced them, including your family and close friends, that *you* are the cause of the problem! This can be devastating and may lead you to conclude that you must be, in fact, the crazy one. If you are lucky, others may still see the situation for what it really is, and you should seek out their advice. In an organizational setting, these can be coworkers with no utility to the psychopath, former victims, or the organizational police, many of whom are sensitive to the possibility of manipulation and deceit.

PHASE 5: ESCALATING ABUSE

Should victims raise questions to the psychopath about his or her behavior or decide to ask the psychopath about inconsistencies they have noticed, they risk retribution. At first, the psychopath may vehemently deny any improprieties and turn the game into an attack on the complainant. At this stage, most victims will feel ashamed that they doubted the psychopath and will come to doubt themselves even more. Should they persist in expressing doubt or concern, though, they will certainly suffer escalating abuse at the hands of the now irritated and angry psychopath. This abuse can take many forms but usually affects us in three ways: psychologically, emotionally, and physically.

Physical abuse, the most obvious, may appear as blackened eyes, bruises, cuts, and so on. Often, as in the case of abused spouses, physical aggression is unreported. Family members, friends, and astute coworkers may try to intervene, but often they can only stand by helplessly because you refuse their assistance. *Any* type of physical abuse is dangerous, as psychopaths—along with other abusers—tend to escalate their attacks over time: seeking help is mandatory.

It is much harder for outsiders to evaluate emotional and psychological abuse, which often leads to anxiety, distress, depression, inability to sleep, generalized fear, and post-traumatic stress disorder (PTSD). Individuals abused by psychopaths feel they are not themselves or something is wrong with *them*; they feel lowered self-esteem, feelings of unworthiness, self-doubt, and psychological pain. They often wonder, "What did I do wrong?" Because your thoughts and feelings affect how you behave, you may begin to do poorly on your job, being easily distracted, agitated, reticent, or overly emotional. Criticism ("You're too fat; nobody else will love you!"), threats ("I'm not putting up with this anymore, I'm leaving!"), or intimidation ("Don't make me hurt you!") are common manipulation and coercive techniques and, surprisingly, the resultant back-and-forth may strengthen rather than weaken the relationship.

If a victim of abuse, you should seek advice and counsel from those around you—friends, family members, or trusted colleagues—or, depending on the type of abuse, the authorities or human services providers dealing with these types of issues.

PHASE 6: REALIZATION AND INSIGHT

Eventually, the unexplained lies, inconsistencies, negative feelings, and feedback from friends and family reach a point when you will begin to realize that you have been a pawn in a psychopath's game. It will take a lot of validation and a lot of time for this realization to sink in, but once it happens, you have crossed the threshold to recovery.

Once you understand what has happened, it will upset you even more, as you may feel like a patsy or a fool. Many former victims report saying to themselves, "How could I have fallen for these lies?" or "I'm such a fool." This is a normal feeling, but it is not without its costs. People who feel like fools wish to hide their foolishness. Rather than seek out confirmation or validation of your new view of the psychopath, you may tend to avoid others. You may sometimes believe that others have not seen what is going on, and while this may be the case, it is far better to confide in trusted friends and family than to allow the perception of foolishness to fester. Talking about your experiences and writing in a journal are good ways to dissipate your humiliation. You may also want to begin documenting what transpired since you met the psychopath. Clearly, you should check your bank account, credit cards, personal documents, computer, cell phone, and other valuables. It is important that you distance yourself and take action to protect yourself from further contact and retribution, perhaps even posting your story (anonymously) on victim-support websites such as the one run by the Aftermath: Surviving Psychopathy Foundation (www.Aftermath-Surviving -Psychopathy.org). [Disclaimer: Both Drs. Babiak and Hare are on the Board of Directors of this non-profit organization dedicated to providing education and support for victims of psychopathy.]

PHASE 7: WORK THROUGH YOUR FEELINGS OF SHAME

Shame is a natural response to abuse. Because of this, many abusive situations go unreported. It is imperative that you discuss any feelings of shame with family, friends, or a trained professional. The first reason is that you do not deserve to feel shame, just as you did not deserve the abuse. It was not your fault; the psychopath is a predator and you were a target and victim. The second reason to seek help is that shame itself leaves you vulnerable to continued psychopathic manipulation. Consider some abused spouses who, despite beatings and verbal assaults, beg their abusive partners to take them back. Be aware, though, that it is just as easy for a psychopath to use your shame against you as it was to use your flaws, lacks, and fears in the first place. Do not let shame for being conned prevent you from seeking help and guidance; do not let the psychopath use it as a weapon against you.

PHASE 8: ANGER AND VINDICATION

By the time victims contact us, they are typically in this stage where they feel intense anger and rage toward the person who manipulated and abused them, and they want to get even. Anger and the need for vindication are normal emotional and psychological responses. The anger often comes from the residual feelings victims have had all along but could not express because of fear and submission. It is critical to work on angry feelings with a trained mental health professional as rumination over past events can be equally problematic, sometimes exacerbating the emotional pain.

Some individuals, in fact many, want to unmask and "out" the psychopath. It is *unwise* at this stage to broadcast your thoughts and feelings or to make accusations about the psychopath on social media, emails, texts, or a website. Consider your current emotional and psychological state of mind. You may be in the midst of intense thoughts and feelings that preclude you from acting rationally. You may be in a weakened state and unable to deal with any retaliation from the psychopath.

However, if a crime has been committed, certainly notify the authorities.

The need for vindication seems to be satisfied, at least for many people, by confirmation that the person who victimized them was truly a psychopath; the more they learned and understood about psychopathy, the better they felt. In addition, educating friends about the behaviors to watch out for can be useful and possibly save someone else from falling into a psychopath's web of deceit. Some victims have even written and published books about their experience with the psychopath.

DISCUSSION QUESTIONS

- What do you have that a psychopath might want?
- What triggers (hot buttons and weak spots) do you have?

- Has anyone tried to manipulate you through them?
- Were they successful?

What Can You Do? Next Steps to Recovery

Many readers have asked us, "What can I do?" Here is a brief, and necessarily general, list of suggestions of the best practices on how to handle the situation when you have been a victim.

COLLECT THE DATA
- Collect all of the documents you have related to your situation. This includes any journals or diaries you kept, including notes, emails, texts, or letters to/from the psychopath, banking and credit card records, transcriptions of telephone calls, and medical and court records.
- If you are on social media, stop posting immediately! Download or print out relevant information from your sites.

ASSESS THE DAMAGE
- Check your finances, including all credit cards statements, bank account balances, and deeds. Change all of your passwords or access codes, and phone numbers if necessary. Change beneficiaries or joint account holders if these include the psychopath. If necessary, close your accounts. If you find evidence of fraud, prepare a list for the authorities.
- Have your personal computer and cell phone professionally scanned for malware. (Several victims have told us that they uncovered tracking software on their phone and key-logging software on their computer!)
- See a mental health professional to assess your psychological and emotional state.

ASSESS YOUR FRIENDS AND SOCIAL CONTACTS

- Make a list of your friends and categorize them into those who warned you about the psychopath, those who seemed to side with him or her, and those who know nothing about the situation (and assess whether you think they would support you). Include your family members in the list.

WRITE OUT YOUR STORY

- Assemble all of your documentation in chronological order and organized by category (e.g., financial, social).
- Referring to your notes, write out the entire story of your relationship with the psychopath. The first draft will be necessarily a "stream of consciousness" report, rambling, vague at times, and filled with emotion.
- Edit your story, perhaps asking a friend to help, or better yet, a professional editor. The goal is to make your story "readable" to the lay reader, which might include the authorities or your legal counsel. It should be about two or three pages. The purpose at this point is to have a complete and accurate documentation of your experiences.

ASSESS YOUR FUTURE WITH AND WITHOUT THE PSYCHOPATH

- Is the psychopath still in your life? Will she be in your life for the near future? Some important facts that affect this: Are you married? Are there children involved? Do you have legal ties to the psychopath, such as a house? Is the psychopath a relative?
- If the psychopath has abandoned you, consider yourself lucky and focus on rebuilding your life.
- If you have legal ties to the psychopath, such as marriage, children, or property ownership, be prepared for a long, arduous battle. You will need help from professionals.

PLAN A STRATEGY AND TAKE THE
NEXT STEPS

- Visit a support group of psychopathy victims (such as www.Aftermath-Surviving-Psychopathy.org) and read the stories of others, as well as the well-researched support materials. If you post questions, do so anonymously, without any details that your psychopath can use to identify you.
- Call an abused-spouse shelter and/or local police authorities if you are in danger.
- Speak with a lawyer.

PREPARE FOR PSYCHOPATHIC RETALIATION

- **Taking hostages.** The psychopath may use your children or your house as weapons against you, typically forcing you to engage expensive legal counsel and then prolonging the battle. He may promise to co-parent but then not show up when scheduled (in order to mess up your schedule), or promise to take the kids on vacation (but never show up).
- **Siege.** As used in medieval warfare, the psychopath "surrounds" the victim in an attempt to starve him into submission. Typically this involves physical means (parking in front of the house late at night, stalking online or in person), financial means (instituting nuisance lawsuits or dragging out legal matters that drain the victim's resources), or social means (turning your friends against you or getting them to ostracize you). We have also heard of psychopaths convincing the victim's legal counsel to turn against them!
- **Sabotage.** The psychopath may call your employer in an attempt to have you fired. He or she may make overdrafts on your credit cards and checking account, and may also disparage you on social media. Do not take the

bait; rather, document everything he says or does, and stay quiet.

Your ultimate goal is to *release* yourself from any further contact (physical, emotional, or psychological) with the psychopath, which is necessary in order to *repair* the damage done and *regrow* your life without him or her.

S 12.1
Psychopathic Interviews: Computer
Analyses of Psychopathic Language

"If their speech is sometimes peculiar, why are psychopaths so believable, so capable of deceiving and manipulating us? Why do we fail to pick up the inconsistencies in what they say? . . . The oddities in their speech are often too subtle for the casual observer to detect, and they put on a good show" (p. 142).[1] In referring to this quotation by Hare, Le, and colleagues noted that computer-based analyses could provide some answers.[2]

Some two decades ago, Louth et al.[3] used a computer program to measure acoustic variables in the speech of psychopaths. We found that PCL-R psychopaths placed the same emphasis (voice amplitude) on emotional and neutral words, whereas other offenders placed more emphasis on emotional than on neutral words. Around the same time, one of Hare's students found that the narratives of psychopaths were rather odd[4] (see outlines of this and other linguistic research in Hare, *Without Conscience*). She conducted a content analysis of neutral and emotional narratives of offenders, and found that, compared with other offenders, psychopaths made many contradictory and logically inconsistent statements. They frequently "derailed," skipping from one topic to another, and giving contradictory and disjointed answers to simple questions, particularly those concerning emotional events.

Recently, several researchers have published a series of sophisticated computer analyses of psychopathic language. Because of space limitations, we describe only a few of these studies. Hare's colleagues, psychologists Hancock, Woodworth, and Porter,[5] used two text analysis tools to examine the crime-related narratives of offenders convicted of homicide. One tool analyzed parts of speech and semantic content, and the other tool examined emotional features. "We predicted that they would show unique linguistic patterns relating to their instrumental world view, primitive physiological (vs. higher level) needs, and profound affective deficit, when describing a major autobiographical event—a homicide for which they were responsible. The findings were generally consistent with our predictions; narratives by psychopaths included a higher level of instrumentality and more explanation themes, focused on self-preservation and bodily needs, and were more disfluent, past oriented, and had less emotional intensity relative to non-psychopathic offenders. Importantly, such stylistic differences likely are beyond conscious control and are difficult to alter intentionally in one's speech" (p. 110). PCL-R Factor 1 scores were behind the emotional aspects of the narrative.

Le and colleagues used text analysis software to examine the linguistic features of psychopathic speech. The material for the study was a set of PCL-R interviews provided by Hare. The results were consistent with other, similar research. Compared with other offenders, psychopaths used more disfluencies (e.g., "umm," "er"), fillers ("you know, "I mean"), and personal pronouns, made fewer references to other people (e.g., personal names, family), and were less emotionally expressive (anger- and anxiety-related words). The best predictors of PCL-R scores were a low frequency of anxiety-related words and more frequent use of personal pronouns.

Note: Most researchers have used offenders in their study of semantic and emotional speech by psychopaths. We do not know to what extent the findings will apply to more educated and successful corporate personnel, but the issue is intriguing and potentially of great use in understanding corporate psychopathy.

S 12.2
Dark Personalities in the Workplace[6]

Dark Triad and Career Choice

Research has found a link between entrepreneurial intentions (intention to start one's own business), narcissism,[7] and psychopathy.[8] Not surprisingly, for individuals scoring high on Dark Triad personalities, the motives for starting a new business may be destructive in nature (as a way to use others for their own gain and to receive attention and admiration).[9] A study on narcissism by Hill and Yousey[10] found that, of the occupations sampled, politicians scored highest on narcissism. Individuals high on Machiavellianism tend to choose business-related careers and to stay away from helping professions.[11] Dark Triad individuals value power, money, and social standing, and these values guide their career choices.

Dark Triad and Leadership

One way for Dark Triad personalities to gain power, money, and social standing is to seek out leadership positions. As leaders, narcissistic individuals are selfish, in the sense that instead of working for the good of the company, they work for themselves[12] and seem to lack moral sensibility.[13] Grijalva, Harms, Newman, Gaddis, and Fraley[14] conducted a meta-analysis of narcissism and leadership. They concluded: narcissism is associated with leader emergence but not with leader effectiveness; narcissism's association with leadership emergence may reflect the fact that they score high on extraversion. Although not confirmed by research on the other two Dark Triad personalities and leadership, we believe that similar results will apply to Machiavellianism and psychopathy. Dark personalities use abusive leadership behaviors[15,16] and have negative impacts on their employees. (For an in-depth review of Dark Triad personalities in the workplace, see LeBreton et al.[17])

Dark Triad and Employee Behavior/Attitudes

The workplace behaviors of all three Dark Triad personalities are counterproductive and toxic.[18] Furthermore, it seems that employees with Dark Triad personalities find pleasure and enjoyment in seeing coworkers suffer.[19]

And Then There Were Four: Dark Tetrad

This last result is interesting in that the author of *The Dark Triad* has recently introduced a fourth dark personality, sadism (taking pleasure in inflicting emotional or physical pain on others), forming what he now calls the Dark Tetrad.[20] It seems that all personalities in the Dark Tetrad are low on Honesty/Humility (deceitful, greedy, sly), and low on Agreeableness (competitive, with low empathy for others). Empirical studies on sadism in the workplace are not yet available; however, we believe that this fourth dark personality will also present very detrimental effects in the workplace, especially for employee well-being.

Some call them successful dark personalities, while others find that they might present an advantage in the workplace. It is important to remember that these individuals may display alluring traits, but they will inevitably cause harm to their colleagues and employees, and, eventually, to their organization.

Even More?

Although technically not dark *personalities*, Egoism, Moral Disengagement, Psychological Entitlement, Self-Interest, and Spitefulness have joined the pantheon of dark traits. Psychologists Moshagen, Hilbig, and Zettler[21] have proposed that all dark personalities and traits have, as their core, a *Dark Factor of Personality (D):* "A general tendency toward ethically, morally, and/or socially questionable behavior." Individuals with "high levels in D will generally aim to maximize their individual utility at the cost of others. Here, utility is used in the broad sense as a 'measure of extent of goal achievement . . . so that one's individual utility can take the form of visible gains such as a higher status or higher monetary payoffs, but also less tangible ones such as feelings of power, superiority, pleasure, or joy. Crucial for this aspect is that utility maximization is sought despite running contrary to the interest of others or even for the sake of such negative externalities." More succinctly, "D as the basic tendency to maximize one's own utility at the expense of others."

The Case of Dave

UNRAVELING THE PUZZLE

Frank arrived at John's office a little after 3 P.M., his arms loaded with files.

"Want some coffee?" asked John, standing at the credenza with a coffeepot in his hands.

"Yes, that would be great. I think we might be here a while," answered Frank, putting his files on the coffee table and walking over to John.

"What did you find out?" asked John.

"A lot, and it's not good. Apparently, the team problem is just the tip of the iceberg. I pulled Dave's personnel jacket, spoke at length with some of the folks on the team, and got an earful from some of the other department heads, including Tim in purchasing and Matthew in security."

"Security? Oh, boy, this is going to be good. Why don't you start at the top?"

"Well," began Frank, "while checking Dave's personnel file I noticed some discrepancy between his original letter, his résumé, and his application blank."

"Yes, what kind of discrepancy?" asked John, leaning forward.

"Apparently, he listed three different, although very similar, college degrees on these documents. I wasn't sure if this was intentional or just a clerical mistake, so I asked Melanie to check his education. Turns out that the university on his résumé was actually one of those online diploma mills. It's bogus."

"Why hadn't Melanie brought this to our attention before?" asked John with concern.

"Well, she hadn't checked his background because we offered the job to him on the spot, remember? She said that normally she follows up on these things once—"

"I remember, yes, we jumped the gun," said John, shaking his head. "What else did she find out?"

"He doesn't have a criminal record."

"That's nice to know," interrupted John.

"But he does have quite a few speeding tickets. Not really an issue, but since we're taking a closer look, I asked her to get everything she could." Frank sipped his coffee and continued. "I also found a note in his file from Tim asking Dave to—" Frank pulled out the note and read, " 'stop ordering supplies and equipment directly from suppliers.' " Frank looked up to find John staring at him. "Yes, apparently he's been using his signature authority to buy a new computer to use at home, some peripherals, and a few small things without going through channels. Eventually, one of the internal auditors questioned Tim and he followed up with a note to Dave."

"What did Dave say to Tim?" asked John.

"He said he was sorry, was new to the company, wouldn't do it again, et cetera."

"And nobody ever mentioned this to you?"

"No, Tim bought Dave's story and decided to put a copy of the note in his personnel file should anything ever come up about it," answered Frank. "Melanie also suggested I talk to Matt in security, and he told me that Dave had caused a scene one day when a guard wouldn't let him park up front."

"Well, Matt's group can sometimes blow things out of proportion," said John.

"It wasn't the only incident. Dave tried to enter the building after hours when he was new and didn't have card access. He apparently went ballistic on the young lady at the desk, threatened to have her fired, and so on. So she wrote it up. Eventually, he asked me for access, and now, according to Matt, Dave and this guard are 'best buddies.' "

"Please, let's not start any rumors about that kind of thing."

"I've got some more from Melanie."

"Okay," said John, pouring a second cup of coffee.

"She tried to check some of Dave's references and found that out of the four he listed, one no longer worked at the company, two would only give neutral comments, and one said he was a 'great guy.' However, Melanie said that when the phone was answered on the last one, it sounded more like a fraternity house than a company." John frowned, and Frank continued. "So she did some digging around and came up with two contacts at Dave's last two companies who agreed that he was trouble." Frank picked up his notes and read, "Quote, 'He's a loose cannon, always chewing people out, lies a lot, a back-stabbing ass-kisser,' unquote."

"Pretty much what your guys are telling you," stated John.

"Yes, the picture fits. And the new product project—"

"Yes?" said John, hesitantly.

"The whole idea, from concept to action plan, even the executive committee proposal presentation, was Dorothy's work. Dave just tapped into her and took her ideas as his own."

"You got that from Jerry?" asked John.

"Yeah, he never suspected, but Dorothy found a copy of the presentation on Dave's desk and saw that her name wasn't on it, so she confronted Dave in the meeting two days ago. He talked around it, telling her that I took her name off the slides. She then went to Jerry, who came to me this morning, but I had already gotten the story from my guy who wants off the team."

"What else?" asked John, finishing his coffee and putting down his cup.

"That pretty much sums it up; there are more incidents and other details, but the bottom line is Dave is not the guy we thought he was. He can't be trusted. I can't trust him."

"I agree, he doesn't belong here," said John, glancing at his watch. "I'm sure Melanie has left for the day; let's take a walk over to Jack's office and see if we can shut this operation down tonight. Dave's only been here about ten or eleven months, right?" Frank nodded. "Good, this shouldn't be much of a problem. Melanie can draw up the letter tomorrow."

Frank could see the lights were still on in the executive wing and felt relieved. As they headed down the hall, they ran into Victoria, Jack Garrideb's secretary, leaving for the day. "Hi," said John. "Is Jack still in?"

"You know he is, John," said Victoria with a smile. "Mr. Garrideb never gets out before the cleaning folks arrive."

"Yeah, you're right about that," said Frank, smiling. "Is he busy?"

"He has someone in his office. I didn't see who; they must have come in while I was at the copier. But you can hang out and wait if you like."

"I think we will," said Frank, smiling at Victoria as she left.

John and Frank took seats near Victoria's desk, positioning themselves so they could see when Jack finished his meeting and opened the door. They took the time available to review their material on Dave and strategize how they were going to inform Jack. Given what they now knew about Dave, there were few options. In fact, they saw only one. They agreed on what each would say, and Frank took notes.

Twenty minutes went by. Occasional sounds of laughter came from Jack's office. Frank and John smiled at each other, remembering the first time they heard Jack's laugh at a company function. Their attention then turned back to the door and the meeting they were waiting for.

Jack's voice got louder as he rose from behind his desk and was approaching the door to let his visitor out. Frank and John collected their notes and rose. "So we'll have that drink another time, right?" asked Jack, heftily patting his visitor on the back.

"You bet," said Dave, shaking Jack's hand vigorously, and turning to walk out of the office.

It was one of the slow-motion car-crash moments when their eyes met Dave's. Frank and John stood mute, barely keeping their mouths from dropping open. Dave paused, smiled broadly, and with a twinkle in his eyes said, "Hi, guys, always good to see you," before he walked past them out toward the corridor.

DISCUSSION QUESTIONS

- What should Frank and John say to Jack Garrideb?
- What would you say?

13

The Fifth Column

PSYCHOPATHS IN OUR MIDST

Several years ago, following a morning workshop and lunch with his host, Babiak took advantage of a free afternoon to tour a large metropolitan city, new to him. Tourists and locals filled the streets, and the weather was fine. He recalls:

> *At one point, the flow of the crowd slowed down when a group had bunched up ahead. As I moved toward the front, I witnessed the three-card monte game in progress that we described in Chapter 3. Although I had heard of them, I had never seen*

*one in action and I was amazed at how professional the oper-
ation seemed to be. I was amazed further still at the gullibility
of the tourists, in particular the poor young woman, with her
child, who had lost her rent money.*

*I continued my walk and enjoyed stopping in boutiques,
art galleries, coffee shops, and tourist stores, all the while taking
in the unique architecture of the downtown section. As evening
approached, I had to head back to attend a banquet for attendees and speakers given by my host. Taking a different route,
I was able to see more of the city until the crowd, swollen by
dinner-seekers, slowed down the pace. Getting past most, I came
upon a scene all too familiar. The three-card monte gang was
back on the street and enticing unsuspecting tourists with their
card table scheme. Quickly, one after another, tourists lost their
dollars to the fast-handed dealer. I was amused until I made
it to the front and saw a young woman, holding her baby in
her arms, step up and offer a hundred-dollar bill—her rent
money—to play.*

*The reader can guess what happened next: She lost, the
gang disappeared into the crowd, and she teared up. An elderly
woman in an old blue coat, the same one I had seen do this earlier, emerged from the crowd, patted the baby on the head and
handed our "victim" a ten-dollar bill. Several in the crowd also
handed the crying girl money; she received at least a hundred
dollars in total or more in my estimation.*

*Excited by my find, I rushed back to the hotel, took a seat
at the bar, ordered a drink, and proceeded to write up this case.
Two of the workshop attendees, both in federal law enforcement,
joined me and I excitedly recounted my tale. They glanced at
each other, turned back to me, and smiled.*

We receive many questions from the public about how to handle a psychopath in the workplace, whether they be a boss, peer,
subordinate, or coworker. Without a lot more information than we

typically receive, it is impossible to determine whether the individual described is truly psychopathic, although many times we believe it may be so.

In Chapter 11, we addressed how a company can strengthen its procedures for hiring and promotion to prevent hiring or promoting corporate psychopaths. In Chapter 12, we described the many ways you can fall victim to their manipulations. We believe that knowing how they operate makes them more transparent to you and thus somewhat easier for you to avoid, or at least to defend yourself against. We also described some general steps to take when a psychopath has already traumatized you in your personal life.

In this chapter, we will first focus on what you can do to minimize their ability to hurt you on the job, and then offer general steps to take if you have been unsuccessful.

Understand and Manage Your Reputation

Your reputation is your most prized possession on the job. Therefore, it is the most vulnerable to psychopathic attack because it is so visible to others and so fragile. Some researchers have said that it takes twelve "good" things said about you to counter just one "bad" thing. By stabbing you in the back vis-à-vis your competence and loyalty, the psychopath can neutralize any threat you pose and effect your ultimate demotion or termination. Hardening your reputation from attack is your first line of personal defense.

COMPETENCE

When your ability to perform tasks well suits their purpose, psychopaths will charm and groom you into helping them succeed in their own jobs. As long as you still have value, your competence does not pose a direct threat. However, if a psychopath sees you as *too* competent, that is, a rival, or if you balk at helping her, you will be attacked, often by being disparaged behind your back or, more formally, if your boss, in written performance reviews.

Because of the power differential and role expectations of managers versus subordinates, your company will take your boss's side in most disagreements over your performance. The best defense is always to perform up to your capabilities and do whatever tasks are assigned to you, unless they are clearly illegal, unethical, or violate safety or security procedures. In the hands of a psychopathic boss, your own less-than-optimal performance is a tool that can (and will) be used against you, and without additional support (see below) you will be left defenseless.

LOYALTY

Companies build and maintain loyalty by increasing feelings of pride (such as celebrating a major success in the marketplace), feelings of personal belongingness (through things like team achievement awards and company picnics), opportunities for personal and professional growth (through company-sponsored training programs and challenging assignments), or personal recognition (as in salary increases, promotions, and achievement bonuses). Psychopaths, on the other hand, just expect and demand loyalty and they offer nothing in return. Once they perceive you as disloyal, they will view you as a threat and will discard or attack you; you'll be "thrown under the bus," as they say. They do this by disparaging you to others in management, claiming you are disloyal to the company itself.

Should you try to complain about your psychopathic boss, you would find that she has poisoned the waters against you. Others will see every effort you make to remedy the situation as confirmation of the "disloyal" reputation that you now have. It is therefore incumbent on you to take *preventative measures* to assure that no one can question your competence and loyalty. Here are some suggestions:

Build and Maintain Relationships
with Upper Management

Take every opportunity to foster a reputation as a friendly, talented, competent, and loyal person. Seek out opportunities to interact with members of upper management. While they may not routinely visit your workplace, they will make occasional appearances to "mingle" with employees, where they are constantly on the lookout for talent. Take advantage of these impromptu meetings by preparing yourself with a serious question that is not embarrassing, confrontational, or self-serving; ask about the business, the competition, or a new product line.

The more maturity and practical understanding of business you demonstrate by your question, the more favorably the executives *will remember you in a positive light.* This will enhance your reputation and put you on their radar for the good. This can only help your career; it communicates competence and loyalty to someone who really matters and (most importantly) will raise doubts about any negative press you may receive from the psychopath.

WITH YOUR BOSS

Having a strong relationship with your own boss is necessary in order to deal with psychopathic coworkers and peers. Base this relationship on ready sharing of information about what is going on in the department and on projects. Make every effort to keep your boss in the loop: it is the loyal thing to do and it demonstrates competence.

There are many ways to keep the lines of communication open. Some bosses like to meet weekly with their staff members to review progress, project status, or issues, while others take a more relaxed approach, having lunch occasionally, or stopping by your desk to get the latest information. Take advantage of these opportunities to give

and receive information, particularly information about any potential problems.

WITH YOUR STAFF

While this is also part of being a good manager, it is so important
to handling psychopathic manipulation that it deserves mention on
its own. Psychopaths are good at setting people against each other,
particularly when the lines of communication are inadequate. The
more that you can keep open lines of communication between you
and your staff members, the more likely they will come to you when
they observe behaviors of the sort described in this book. This is the
heads-up needed to stay one step ahead of the psychopath.

You must keep an open mind, though. Sometimes subordinates
blow things out of proportion because they are important to them
but not necessarily to you. Nevertheless, it is just as likely that your
subordinates' reports are accurate because they have more contact
with their peers than you do. It is important to take all reports seriously and investigate to the best of your ability. At the very least, you
should keep detailed notes of all issues that come to your attention
and review them with your own boss during private meetings.

Understand the Rules

If you have not read your company policy manual, then do so! Many
companies distribute copies to their staff and may even offer orientation programs to answer questions. Be familiar with your obligations
to the company, as well as any policies or procedures in place to handle complaints and issues. For example, many American companies
have policies against sexual harassment and some have anti-bullying
provisions that you should also note. Do not be afraid to ask questions about policies and procedures you do not understand. You do
not want anyone to say you violated a company policy, and you want

to know your options should you have to use a policy to deal with an abusive, psychopathic boss or coworker.

Document Everything

This is tedious, indeed! However, experience tells us that access to contemporaneous notes of every interaction you have had on the job is invaluable should you eventually succumb to a psychopath's wrath. Certainly your lawyer (and you eventually might need one) will agree.

MEETINGS AND TELEPHONE CALLS

This need not be an onerous task, but instead can be part of your daily routine. Good notes include the following: Date, Names of participants, Issues discussed, Decisions agreed to, and Next Steps. Although you can probably do this on your smartphone, it is best to keep notes either in longhand or on your personal computer at home, where you can also add specific details about what the psychopath has said or done to you. Exact quotes are important to keep, especially if you were dressed down in front of others or otherwise verbally abused. This information will be invaluable when you want to reconstruct "what went wrong" after a corporate psychopath has targeted you.

GOALS AND OBJECTIVES

Many companies give assignments and objectives in writing. If this is not the case where you work, then you can always follow up each verbal directive with a written "memo of understanding." This memo should be short, well written, and focused. Simply state what you understand the assignment to be, the timetable, resource requirements, and assistance you expect from the boss or others working on the project. If possible, ask to meet with your boss to review it, take notes, and, of course, keep a copy of all documents for yourself.

OTHER THINGS

You should document other things as well. For example, note in your calendar or datebook any positive or negative feedback you receive from your boss. A simple note that documents the meeting, what people said, and your response should be sufficient. Note threats your boss or coworker makes, either in your datebook or in a "memo to file," which you should keep at home.

Make Good Use of Your Performance Appraisal

Most supervisors do not like writing or giving performance appraisals. Some find them time-consuming (especially if the supervisor has many employees to review), others find them hard to write properly, and still others do not like to give negative feedback to their staff members, even if it is valid. Because the performance review becomes a part of your *written record*, its contents are very critical to your career.

Unscrupulous bosses can use the review as a way to derail your career by including inaccuracies and distortions. Take the process seriously and try to participate as much as possible. For example, some companies allow employees to submit information to the supervisor—a self-assessment—to be used as notes as the supervisor writes the review. While no supervisor is required to accept a self-report of performance, it does help many to remember details they might have forgotten and may enlighten them to differences in understanding about objectives. Take advantage of this opportunity if it becomes available to you. However, remember to keep your self-evaluation focused, balanced, accurate, and succinct. This is also a good time to reflect on your developmental needs and be open to hearing about them during your review.

When you receive your performance review (face-to-face is typical), you will be better prepared to participate in the discussion if you have carefully reviewed your own performance. If something on your review is not clear, ask your boss to give you actual examples of any incidents or behaviors that it mentions. To the degree that your review is an accurate reflection of your true performance, the official record will better support your reputation for being competent and loyal.

Some performance review systems allow the employee to add written comments or submit an addendum for inclusion in the personnel file. Even if your review is outstanding, you should add a note. If your review contains inaccuracies, and especially if your boss does not want to modify the final document, then this may be your only chance to correct the record. Do not write something in haste. Instead, carefully write down your view of the events in question. Make sure your note is professional and without emotion or inflammatory language; stick to the facts. You may wish to have a friend read it and offer suggestions for improvement before you send it to human resources. Should anyone call into question your performance, reputation, or credibility, your performance reviews are the record the company will turn to first.

FOR SUPERVISORS

In some cases, performance reviews may be the only way to deal with a psychopathic subordinate. If you are a supervisor who has wanted to discipline or terminate an employee, human resources no doubt has asked you to demonstrate the employee's poor performance in a performance review. If you have not completed a review or have neglected to document performance deficiencies, you may not be able to move forward as quickly as you would like. In the case of psychopathic subordinates, the official performance record—written review and face-to-face discussion—is vital to managing them and, if necessary, terminating them.

Keep Improving Your Leadership and Management Skills

The more you know about leading and managing people, the better off you will be when handling a psychopath. There are two reasons for this. First, your informed management style will serve you in good stead when applied to others on your staff. They will be productive and quality conscious, deliver what you ask, and *have your back*. Second, your own boss will notice this, and it will go a long way toward building and maintaining your *reputation* as a good leader or manager. Remember that the psychopathic employee will attack your reputation, spread disinformation about your effectiveness and style, and sabotage your efforts to build and manage your team. If you can forestall this negative press by having a record of accomplishment and good management practices, you will receive better support from those above you in the organization.

Avoid Confrontations

Having a blowout with your boss in public is never a good idea; taking on a psychopathic boss can only lead to disaster. Psychopaths will set you up to explode—by pushing your hot buttons—when it suits their purpose. Do not take the bait. As hard as it may be, you should always remain cool and calm when being attacked, however unfairly. We are not suggesting that you be submissive, but rather that you rely on your strengths—through assertiveness, not aggressiveness— when confronted.

The safest, although not always practical, position is to minimize or avoid all contact with a boss you believe to be a psychopath. When you must interact, make sure there are others in the area who can witness your calm, professional stance while the psychopath is ranting. Then document the interaction in your datebook in accurate, unemotional terms.

Psychopaths will sometimes berate their subordinates in front of their superiors to demonstrate their own "leadership." Because they are uninformed about true leadership, they think that this will help their careers; in most cases, it does not. Seasoned executives know that berating subordinates in public is bad management. It shows them that the boss is not in control of himself or the situation, and this sign of weakness is not lost on those higher up. However, you should never get angry and retaliate against your boss (that is, take the bait) in these situations. Rather, defend your decisions, judgments, or results by stating the facts. If you are in the wrong, admit it, apologize, and ask for a chance to try again. If others are clearly at fault (for example, another department did not deliver material on time), mention it but do not come across as shifting blame to others. Make sure to note that you made every effort within your power (including asking for your boss's help) to achieve the goal or objective. To the best of your ability, you should come across as competent and loyal, even to the boss who just berated you in public.

You should also take good notes of what your boss says. Some non-psychopathic bosses and many psychopathic ones will use profanity. Many corporations do not tolerate this form of verbal abuse; it is almost never appropriate, except perhaps when someone is about to do something dangerous on the job (for example, push the wrong button on a nuclear reactor). In the majority of cases, however, the use of profane language works against the speaker, and you should note it verbatim in your datebook for future reference.

What to Do Once You Have Been Victimized

COLLECT THE DATA

Collect all of the documents you have related to your situation. This may include emails, texts or memos to/from the psychopath, transcriptions of telephone calls, your formal and informal performance appraisals, any other performance documents such as reports on goals and objectives, the human resources handbook, the company's

Code of Conduct, organization charts, your Day-Timer or calendar, and any and all personal notes you've made during this time.

If your antagonist is a business partner (a not uncommon occurrence), then collect all corporate records and documents, emails, texts, and other correspondence between you and the psychopath as well as with other investors/partners or employees.

If any of this information is on your smartphone, download it onto your personal computer at home.

ASSESS THE DAMAGE

Assess your employment situation, answering these questions: Do you have a poor performance review? Is your career derailed? Are you on probation? Have they given you notice?

The big questions are: Can you repair your reputation on the job, and what will it take to accomplish this? If others have suffered the same abuse from the psychopath, will they support you? Will management side with you or your antagonist? What are your career options with your current company? Is your résumé up to date, just in case?

ASSESS YOUR COLLEAGUES

Get a copy of your company's organization chart. If not available, make one, starting with yourself, adding in your peers, superiors (up to about three levels), and subordinates. Then assess each person according to your level of trust in them, whether they are a friend or associate of the psychopath, whether they are themselves victims, whether they socialize with the psychopath outside of work, whether there are any hidden intimate relationships in play, and so forth. Some areas of concern would be whether some coworkers stopped talking to you or started distancing themselves from you. Have others started spending more time (at the office and off-work hours) with the psychopath?

WRITE OUT YOUR STORY

This advice is similar to that for a psychopath in your personal life: Assemble all of your documentation in chronological order and organized by category (e.g., financial, social). Referring to your notes and documents, write out the entire story of your experiences with the psychopath. The first draft necessarily will be a "stream of consciousness" report, rambling, vague at times, and filled with emotion. Edit your story, perhaps with the help of a friend, or better yet, your spouse or partner. The goal is to make your story "readable" to the lay reader, which might include upper management, human resources, or your legal counsel. The purpose at this point is to have a complete and accurate documentation of your experiences that informs the reader in a convincing manner.

PLAN A STRATEGY AND TAKE THE NEXT STEPS

Visit a support group of psychopathy victims that includes information about corporate psychopaths (such as www.Aftermath -Surviving-Psychopathy.org) and read the stories of other victims as well as the well-researched support materials. If you post questions, do so anonymously, without any details that your company can use to identify you. Speak with a lawyer with expertise in employment law. Seek help from a mental health professional knowledgeable about psychopathy, especially if your dealings with the psychopath have affected your personal life. Also, speak with your closest friends, your spouse or partner, your life coach, or your religious/spiritual leader.

CONSIDER MAKING A COMPLAINT ABOUT YOUR BOSS

Before you make a formal complaint, you should assess your situation very carefully. What is the perception, *reputation*, and connection with the company's power hierarchy of the psychopathic boss? Do others report the same difficulties?

Understand and anticipate that the psychopath has already disparaged your reputation in the eyes of those same people. Now, consider your options. You may have to accept the fact that you cannot prevail in this situation. Your organization may have provisions for employees bringing issues to the attention of human resources or upper management. Read and understand these procedures carefully and weigh them against the abuse you have received. Some companies have anonymous hotlines or tip lines that encourage employees to call should they witness any illegal (such as stealing company funds or lying on production records) or abusive behavior (such as sexual harassment or bullying). Learn more about these options and the proper way to take advantage of them should the need arise for you to make a report.

It is important to understand that just because you complain, the company need not take action, or the action it takes may not be what you expected. Prepare yourself for the fact that the company has put trust in the boss's supervisory judgment. It will take a lot to change this. If you are dealing with a psychopath, he or she may be better entrenched (through a personal influence network) than you think. Your complaint may bring to the surface a history of your *own* poor performance or disloyalty, as carefully and consistently fabricated by your psychopathic boss. You may end up losing your own job in the process.

If you have been *personally* abused, seek advice from family, friends, or professionals outside the company (this is also a form of documentation), and then report the abuse to human resources or other avenues available at your company. Make sure you fully understand the proper procedure to use and the ramifications for yourself. Proceed with caution.

AN ANONYMOUS COMPLAINT

Confidentiality is an important part of organizational life. However, it is important to understand that *your record may not remain confidential* should you complain about your boss or coworker. If you feel threatened or fear retribution, you should make your report *anonymously*; you can always come forward later if you choose. However, keep in mind that some companies do not place much credence on anonymous complaints, considering them rumors or hearsay; your complaint may go unheard in these cases. Yet, sometimes multiple complaints about the same boss get attention.

If you observe illegal behavior or flagrant abuse of others, bring it to the attention of your (non-psychopathic) boss, but *only* if you have a strong, supportive relationship with the boss. Otherwise, send an anonymous letter to the boss. You may choose to make use of the company's reporting procedures, but do so anonymously, if you can. Many companies view the reporting of illegal, immoral, and abusive behaviors as a form of loyalty to the company, the industry, and in major cases, the country. However, do not assume that others will herald you as a hero, because psychopaths are constantly managing the perceptions of those around them. Recall that a successful corporate psychopath will already have established a strong influence network and will already have planted seeds of doubt about you.

CONSIDER OTHER CAREER OPTIONS

In the days of the psychological contract, employees expected to have jobs for life or at least until their retirement. Times have changed, and so should your approach to employment. It is wise to keep your résumé up-to-date, with a list of your completed projects, achievements, and performance reviews on hand. It is your security blanket. It might be fruitful to check the Internet occasionally for openings elsewhere. You do not have to be actively looking or even thinking of leaving; this is just good career management.

If you truly are working for a psychopathic boss, your best recourse may be to distance yourself by applying for a transfer. Many companies have job-posting bulletin boards on which they advertise positions in other departments and locations. Learn about the posting process and take advantage of it *early*. Should you apply for an internal transfer, keep in mind that the hiring manager will read your past performance reviews and seek a reference from your boss. It behooves you to try to maintain a good relationship with your boss—psychopath or not—for the length of your tenure. You may be surprised that your psychopathic boss may help you get the new job, especially if it seems to be an easy way to take care of a rival or threat. If you worked on interdepartmental teams, you should ask individuals from other areas to be internal references. If you received commendations for doing a good job, for instance, an employee-of-the-month award or a gain-share award, make sure these are in your personnel file. When you weigh your options—and only you know how you feel about your situation—you may opt for a lateral move rather than wait for a promotional position. If you have taken courses in a new field—for example, you currently work in the accounting department but are working toward a master's degree in marketing—then a junior-level position in the marketing department may be a good choice for you as well as for the company. The key is to keep your options open at all times and to keep tuned to changes in the perception that others have of you because of the machinations of your boss.

SEEK ADVICE FROM HUMAN RESOURCES

Many of the businesspeople who attend our talks and seminars are human resources professionals. Virtually all of them have recognized the traits and characteristics of the psychopath in one or more of their employees, in their current companies or in past jobs. They tell us that their hands "are tied" because of supervisors who do not come to them with issues early on. Others note that performance reviews are poorly written and do not measure up to the level of detail they need in order to handle (in their words) "disruptive," "counter-productive," "dysfunctional," or "problem" employees.

After your direct supervisor, the human resources professional is perhaps the best person to talk to about questionable or suspicious behavior. You need not label someone a psychopath, but you can document and report behavior that is abusive, counterproductive, or does not live up to the standards of performance, job requirements, or code of conduct expected of all employees. However, keep in mind that the human resources staff works for the company and their loyalty is to their employer. Ask your coworkers what they think about human resources before you give them a call.

BITE THE BULLET

If you cannot move to another job, department, or location, or if it is unlikely that the psychopath will move, then there may come a time when you decide that the best course of action is to leave your employer. Because this decision concerns your spouse and family as well, make sure you cover all bases before you act. The ideal situation is to have a new job lined up before you announce your intent to leave.

If *asked* to leave, then it is important that you understand the benefits due you at your termination. Things like termination pay, health insurance coverage, unemployment insurance, accrued vacation, and sick time pay may be due you. Your human resources representative has the responsibility to apprise you of these things.

You may be given the opportunity to resign, or you may ask for this opportunity, because having been fired can be problematic down your career road. In that event, the company likely will ask you to sign a release form. Always seek legal counsel before you sign anything, so that you fully understand to what you are agreeing.

They may ask you to give your reasons for leaving, usually during an *exit interview*. Here you must use good judgment, so seeking the

advice of legal counsel is not out of the question. It is always appropriate to state "personal reasons" and leave it at that. However, you
may feel the need to inform the company of the difficulties you have
had with your boss, subordinate, or peer. You may find that human
resources already knows about their behavior; they may even offer
you an incentive to stay if they realize that you have been competent,
loyal, and an asset to the company (do not count on this, however).
Always leave on good terms; do not burn any bridges.

Get On with Your Life and Career

Once you are out of the grips of the psychopathic relationship, you
will feel many things, some of which we described earlier. Most of
all you will feel relief, free of the burden on your back. Put your previous situation and the psychopath behind you. Seek counseling if
you need to, but move on with your life. Consider the experience as
one of life's hard lessons, and take on this new phase with enthusiasm
and eyes wide open.

Many types of people make up the world. Unfortunately, some
are psychopaths. In an ideal world, we would be able to get along
with others, and accept them as equals; our gut feeling tells us that
this is the right path to take. However, reality is often less than ideal
and our desires for an enlightened approach to business and professional relationships are often frustrated. It is our hope that this book
will help readers avoid psychopathic manipulation on and off the
job, and can assist those who have become embroiled in the psychopathic fiction to break free and get back on the path of a normal,
happy, and productive life.

The Case of Dave

THE RISE AND THE FALL

Dave sat on his deck admiring the trees in his backyard. He had called in sick that morning, deciding to lie low for a few days.

That branch needs to be cut, he thought, spotting a dead limb on an oak at the edge of the woods.

He watched his email most of the day for anything interesting and wondered what was going on back at the site. Finally, he typed a note to his secretary. "Denise, feeling a bit better, but still coughing," he wrote. "Anything going on I need to know about before the weekend?"

A few moments later he got the response he had been fishing for: "Frank has just been let go! Marge is in her office crying, and the rest of us are in shock," she wrote.

Dave smiled and picked up his phone and dialed. He practiced his cough as the tones went through. "Oh my God, Denise. They didn't!" he exclaimed, when Denise answered.

"Yes, Dave, it just happened. We don't know why," she said, holding back tears.

Dave asked what she had heard, and she told him all she knew. He had many questions and seemed to relish every detail Denise could provide. Dave assured her that things were going to be okay and then they hung up.

Dave breathed deeply, enjoying the fresh air, and then dialed Jack Garrideb. "Hi, Jack. How did it go?"

"As well as could be expected," answered Jack, wearily. "Word will travel fast, I'm sure."

"Yeah, Denise just called me—lots of folks in shock, apparently. Anything about me?" asked Dave in anticipation.

"Nothing yet. I'll have HR send you the draft announcement about your promotion for you to review. You may want to add in more about your background. Get it back to the communications department by Monday. We'll release it on Tuesday, after things quiet down a bit."

"Yes, certainly," assured Dave.

Dave hung up the phone and smiled. His wife brought him another glass of wine and they walked to the edge of the deck. He gazed out over his yard and silently toasted the oak with the dead limb.

"Sometimes you just have to cut out the deadwood," he said to his wife, taking a sip. "Life *is* good."

POSTSCRIPT

Frank accepted an enhanced "retirement" package and moved with his wife to their vacation home on a lake in the woods. He fishes as often as he can and enjoys spending time with their grandchildren.

Dave moved into his new position and continued his career, and became vice president after a year. Eventually the company merged with a competitor and Dave got himself selected to head the transition team, which meant he could decide who would go and who would stay. He cleaned house of all his rivals. He promoted Dorothy, who continued to work with him for another year until recruited by a competitor. Dave's wife divorced him after she discovered he was having an intimate relationship with his secretary. Dave eventually left Garrideb to start a consulting practice that, according to all accounts, is very successful. He also teaches as an adjunct professor at a large, very well-known university. His most popular course? *Business Ethics.*

ACKNOWLEDGMENTS

In the twenty-five years since I met my first corporate psychopath, a considerable amount of research has provided answers in response to many pressing questions. Based upon interesting case studies and exploratory theories of psychopaths' behaviors, we now have a field rich with applied research that continually advances our understanding of how these "invisible" human predators operate. Formerly skeptical organizations are now deeply interested in studying those rare but dysfunctional individuals who would undermine the success of these organizations in increasingly chaotic times. In this second, revised and updated edition of *Snakes in Suits*, we integrated the most important research findings that have contributed to our understanding.

After more than twenty-five years of collaboration and friendship, working with Bob on this second edition has only strengthened my respect for his scientific rigor, subtle wit, warm sense of humor, and genuine human kindness. Clearly, no one understands the mind of the psychopath as does Bob.

We thank John Silbersack, our agent, who helped us turn a rough manuscript about a somewhat controversial topic into a finished product, both the first time around and now for a second edition. Rebecca Raskin, our editor at HarperCollins, has been instrumental in helping us integrate the new research into this expanded edition; we appreciate her patience and diligence.

We are also thankful to the many readers of the first edition who contacted us to share their own stories of psychopaths in their professional lives. Many of their insights reaffirmed our thoughts about how psychopaths operate in organizations and deepened our understanding of the more nuanced tactics psychopaths use. It has been very rewarding to work with some readers toward resolution of their personal situations. I can say that it is possible, with diligence, to overcome the psychopath in one's life despite the odds against this outcome.

I am indebted and forever grateful for the support of Joan, my wife, friend, and life partner, who made writing this second edition far easier than I had expected by unselfishly giving me the love, support, and encouragement I needed at a time when there were more pressing issues of life to deal with at home. Her love for life, open acceptance of people of all kinds, and deep understanding of the human mind made every day an adventure. I am forever grateful for her undying love; I miss her every day.

—Paul Babiak,
New York, 2019

During my years of research on psychopathy, I have had the privilege of working with many outstanding students and colleagues. I thank them all. Particularly helpful in writing this book were Drs. Cynthia Mathieu, Craig Neumann, Dan Jones, and Andreas Mokros. Since I began work in this area five decades ago, things have changed dramatically. Instead of a few academics and clinicians working in isolation, there now are many hundreds of researchers around the world, many in contact with one another and all dedicated to understanding the nature and implications of psychopathy for society. A significant event was the 2005 formation of the Society for the Scientific Study of Psychopathy (SSSP), an organization that does much to facilitate international and interdisciplinary collaboration in the study of psychopathy and its impact on society.

Scientific research and debate and their applications to mental health and criminal justice certainly are important, but at the same time, the public must learn as much as it can about psychopathy. It was for this reason that I wrote *Without Conscience: The Disturbing World of the Psychopaths Among Us.* While writing the book, I had my first discussions with Paul Babiak. He had provided me with a case study that I included in a chapter on "White Collar Psychopaths." Since then, I have had the great pleasure of working with Paul, as a colleague and friend, on a number of projects, one of which is this book. His vast and insightful experience as an industrial-organizational psychologist is evident in every chapter of this volume.

I would like to thank Kylie Neufeld, who, for two decades, was invaluable for her able assistance with my research and writing, for organizing and maintaining my web page, and for her work with Darkstone. Our agent, John Silbersack, provided wise counsel during our work on this and the first edition of the book. We thank him for his guidance and efforts on our behalf. We owe a special debt to our editor, Rebecca Raskin, for her insightful editing and her cogent comments and suggestions, and for her patience in dealing with our tardiness in submitting the final product.

My wife and best friend, Averil, for more than five decades, continues to provide me with a loving, nurturing environment, sound counsel, trenchant insights, and enlightened debates about things of importance. Her career as a social worker, field consultant for child abuse, neglect, and Director of Inspections and Standards for the BC Ministry of Family Services brought her into daily contact with the best and worst of people and situations. Her experiences and our discussions had a great influence on my work.

Our late, beloved daughter, Cheryl, who was admissions officer for the Faculty of Medicine at UBC, taught us much about courage, dignity, and grace in the face of adversity. She remains deeply embedded in our hearts.

—Robert D. Hare,
Vancouver, 2019

APPENDIX

IS THERE A PSYCHOPATHIC BRAIN?

Early Days

In *Without Conscience*, Hare (p. 1)[1] referred to an article that he and his students had submitted to the journal *Science*. The editor rejected the submission with the following comment: "Frankly, we found some of the brain wave patterns depicted in the paper very odd. Those EEGs [electroencephalograms] couldn't have come from real people." Actually, they came from a sample of psychopathic offenders who took part in a laboratory study of behavioral and brain responses to letter strings flashed briefly on a computer screen. The letter strings were neutral, positive, negative, and nonwords. The participant had to press a button as quickly as possible if what he saw was a word. Most participants responded more quickly, and exhibited larger and more prolonged brain responses (event-related potentials; ERPs), when the words were emotional than when they were neutral. Psychopaths, on the other hand, responded to all words as if they were neutral.

Fortunately, another major journal published the study,[2] which was the first to support Cleckley's hypothesis of a lack of integration of the semantic and affective components of psychopathic language. That is, their words lacked emotional coloring. There have been many literal and conceptual replications of this finding, using both ERPs and neuroimaging.[3,4,5]

Neuroimaging

In the early 1990s, Joanne Intrator, newly in charge of a brain-imaging unit at the Bronx Veterans Affairs Medical Center, and Hare's group conducted what may have been the first imaging study of psychopathy, with substance abuse patients rated on the PCL-R as participants. Injection of a radioactive tracer allowed the researchers to determine which parts of the brain became most active during the task, based on Williamson et al.[6] The results clearly indicated that psychopathic patients used relatively little emotional resources, and different parts of the brain, to process neutral and emotional words. An intriguing finding was that while processing emotional words the psychopathic patients showed unusual activation in areas of the brain associated with semantic and decision-making processes.

In the mid-1990s, one of Hare's graduate students, Kent Kiehl—now a major player in the neurobiology of psychopathy—coordinated collaborative research among Hare's lab, Peter Liddle in psychiatry, and Bruce Forster in radiology. The result was the first in a series of functional magnetic resonating (fMRI) studies that showed that the parts of the brain associated with emotional processing had little impact on the language, cognitions, and behaviors of psychopaths.[7]

Overview of Current Findings

Since these early studies, research on the neuroscience of psychopathy has exploded, and now includes the neurobiology of language, moral behavior, decision-making, reward and punishment, executive functions, response inhibition, error monitoring, emotional processing, cognitive-emotional integration, empathy, social cognition, and perspective-taking, to name but a few areas. An outline of research findings is well beyond the scope of this book. Detailed reviews of the neuroscience of psychopathy are available in a number of books and articles written for the public[8,9,10], and for the scientific community[11,12,13,14] (see a recent study by Espinoza et al.[15]).

We note that the dominant instruments for most of this research are the PCL-R and its derivatives, the PCL: SV (see Chapter 2) and the PCL: YV.[16,17] Their importance stems from the fact that they are the standards for the assessment of psychopathy, but also because they each have the same four-factor structure. Why is the latter important? Because the psychopathy-neurology associations often depend on the factor involved (see review by Poeppl et al.[18]). The result is a more nuanced picture of psychopathy than we could obtain with total psychopathy scores alone. For example, Wolf et al.[19] noted, "Moreover, the right uncinate fasciculus [the major white-matter tract connecting ventral frontal and anterior temporal cortices] finding was specifically related to the interpersonal features of psychopathy (glib superficial charm, grandiose sense of self-worth, pathological lying, manipulativeness), rather than the affective, antisocial, or lifestyle features. These results indicate a neural marker for this key dimension of psychopathic symptomatology."

Importantly, researchers have managed to relate, in theoretically meaningful ways, many of the traits and behaviors of psychopathy to various brain structures, functions, and networks. For example, Kiehl[20] has described the *paralimbic system*, a group of interconnected brain structures involved in emotion processing, goal-seeking, motivation, and self-control. Based on an extensive body of research, he and his colleagues have identified some of the brain structures and processing features related to criminal psychopathy. In most cases, the evidence indicates that, on average, psychopaths show decreased activity and smaller volumes in brain areas involved in emotional processing, but increased activity and greater volumes in areas related to reward and its anticipation.

Poeppl et al.[21] conducted a meta-analysis of 28 fMRI studies and 155 experiments. In general, their results were consistent with those described above. The meta-analysis revealed "aberrant" brain activity associated with psychopathy converging in frontal, insular, and limbic regions: decreased activity in regions crucial for semantic language processing, action execution, pain processing, social cognition, and *emotional* reward processing. There was increased activity in a region for *cognitive* reward processing and another region associated with semantic language and pain processing. Interestingly, the increased activity in regions associated with semantic language processing is consistent with the results of early studies described above, indicating that psychopaths tend to use linguistic resources to process emotional material.

Of course, brain regions are interdependent and interactive, and an important line of research is concerned with functional circuits, networks, and connectivity. In this work, researchers measure functional connectivity during a resting state (no task), a procedure that uncovers the relations among the neuronal activation patterns of anatomically separated brain regions, and describes the organization, interrelationship, and integrated performance of functionally coupled brain regions (p. 36).[22] Espinoza and colleagues (p. 2634) suggested "that the affective and interpersonal symptoms of psychopathy (Factor 1) are associated with aberrant connectivity in multiple brain networks, including paralimbic regions."[23,24,25]

Attentional Models

Hamilton and Newman[26] argued that the cognitive/affective models of psychopathy, discussed above, are consistent with *attentional* (cognitive) models in which it is possible to explain the results of behavioral and brain-imaging studies of psychopathy in terms of selective attentional processes. They present a *response modulation hypothesis* in which a "bottleneck" in the lateral prefrontal cortex blocks emotion and inhibitory information when the attentional focus is on goal-directed information.

A Psychopathic Brain?

So, after this long discourse, is there a psychopathic brain? Scores of empirical studies with offenders, many of which show the same things, suggest that there is something different about the structure and function of the brains of psychopaths, at least at the group level. (Many psychopaths show the anomalies described above, but many others do not.) We believe that, as a group, they *are wired* up differently, but for reasons that are unclear. Most researchers use terms such as *damaged, dysfunctional,* or *deficit,* whereas it is possible that the differences are not evidence of deficit but of adaptive evolutionary processes. Certainly, it is difficult to understand how high-functioning psychopathic executives might be the product of erroneous, faulty wiring of the brain. Moreover, this raises an important issue that we cannot address at this time. Are the structure and functioning of the brains of psychopathic corporate and other professionals similar to those of psychopathic offenders?

Neurolaw

These issues are not simply academic. They have serious implications for determining legal culpability and responsibility. There already has been at least one attempt to use imaging as a mitigating factor in a death penalty hearing.[27,28] The attempt failed, but the legal and scientific arguments will continue for a long time.[29,30,31]

NOTES

Introduction

1 Hare, R. D. (1999). *Without conscience: The disturbing world of the psychopaths among us.* New York, NY: Guilford Press.

2 For a detailed discussion of these issues, see Lilienfeld, S. O, Watts, A. L. Smith, S. F. (2015). Successful psychopathy: A scientific status report. *Current Directions in Psychological Science,* 24, 298–303. doi: 10.1177/0963721415580297.

3 Babiak, P., & Hare, R. D. (2006). *Snakes in suits: When psychopaths go to work.* New York, NY: Harper Collins.

Chapter 1: The Case of the Pit Bull

1 The authors wish to thank Dr. Michael Walton, a UK-based chartered psychologist, for providing material for this case.

Chapter 2: Who *Are* These People?

1 Hare, R. D. (1999). *Without conscience: The disturbing world of the psychopaths among us.* New York, NY: Guilford Press. See recent em-

pirical accounts by Hare, R. D., Neumann, C. S., & Mokros, A. (2018). The PCL-R assessment of psychopathy: Development, properties, debates, and new directions. In C. Patrick (Ed.), *Handbook of psychopathy* (2nd ed., pp. 26–79). New York, NY: Guilford Press.

2 This book is about adult psychopaths. We discuss the origins of psychopathic traits in S 2.1: *Nature? Nurture? Both!* It is important to note that many studies in developmental psychopathology clearly indicate that heredity and environmental factors related to psychopathy find expression very early in life. In a recent large sample, longitudinal study, the authors reported that teacher ratings of the traits and behaviors that define adolescent and adult psychopathy are evident in middle childhood (ages 6–8). Their findings "confirm that interpersonal, affective, and lifestyle/ antisocial traits can be observed in youth as early as six years of age. These findings suggest a somewhat similar structure to psychopathic traits in middle childhood to the construct of psychopathic traits identified in adolescence and adulthood." The traits were based on the Psychopathy Checklist: Youth Version (see Table 2.1, Note 2 in Chapter 2, and Notes 13 and 14 in the Appendix). Gorin et al., (2019). Psychopathic traits in middle childhood. *Journal of psychopathology and Behavioral Assessment.* Advance online publication. https:// doi.org/10.1007/s10862-019-09733-2.

Also see Salekin, R. T. (2016). Psychopathy in childhood: Toward better informing the DSM-5 and ICD-11 conduct disorder specifiers. *Personality Disorders: Theory, Research, and Treatment,* 7, 180–191.

3 American Psychiatric Association. (1994). *Diagnostic and statistical manual of mental disorders* (4th ed., DSM-IV). Washington, DC: Author. DSM-5: American Psychiatric Association. (2013). *Diagnostic and statistical manual of mental disorders* (5th ed., DSM-5). Arlington, VA: Author. See diagnostic overviews by Johnson, S. A. (2019. Understanding the violent personality. Antisocial personality disorder, psychopathy, & sociopathy explored. *Forensic Research & Criminology International Journal,* 7, 76–88.

4 "Since the publication of DSM-III, there has been a recurrent criticism of the APA diagnostic manual for failing to be fully commensurate with the conceptualization of psychopathy by Cleckley . . . and/or

the PCL-R" (Crego, C., & Widiger, T. A., 2015, p. 52). Psychopathy and the DSM. *Journal of Personality, 83*, 665–677. "Cleckley and Hare are well-known authors who defined how psychopathy is currently conceptualized; neither was referenced in the DSM-5 rationale" (Blashfield, R. K., & Reynolds, S. M., 2012, p. 826). An invisible college view of the DSM-5 personality disorder classification. *Journal of Personality Disorders, 26*, 821–829. Similarly, "DSM-IV criteria for [ASPD] consist almost exclusively of behavioral indicators, neglecting the affective-interpersonal features that appear to reflect much of the notion of a distinct personality type as described by Cleckley [1941/1976]. To address these issues, Hare and colleagues revived the construct of psychopathy, operationally defined by the Psychopathy Checklist, presently available in a revised version" (Minzenberg, M. J., & Siever, L. J., 2006). Neurochemistry and pharmacology of psychopathy and related disorders. In C. J. Patrick (Ed.), *Handbook of psychopathy* (pp. 251–277). New York, NY: Guilford Press.

5 Lykken, D. T. (2018). Psychopathy, sociopathy, and antisocial personality disorder. In C. J. Patrick (Ed.), *Handbook of psychopathy* (2nd ed., pp. 22–32). New York, NY: Guilford Press. His first publication was Lykken, D. T. (1957). A study of anxiety in the sociopathic personality. *Journal of Abnormal and Social Psychology, 55*, 6–10.

6 Hare, R. D. (1999). *Without conscience: The disturbing world of the psychopaths among us.* New York, NY: Guilford Press. See recent empirical accounts by Hare, R. D., Neumann, C. S., & Mokros, A. (2018). The PCL-R assessment of psychopathy: Development, properties, debates, and new directions. In C. Patrick (Ed.), *Handbook of psychopathy* (2nd ed., pp. 26–79). New York, NY: Guilford Press.

7 Douglas, K. S., Vincent, G. M., & Edens, J. F. (2018). Risk for criminal recidivism: The role of psychopathy. In C. Patrick (Ed.), *Handbook of psychopathy* (2nd ed., pp. 682–709). New York, NY: Guilford Press. Verona, E., & Vitale, J. (2018). Psychopathy in woman: Assessment, manifestations, and etiology. In C. Patrick (Ed.), *Handbook of psychopathy* (2nd ed., pp. 509–528). New York, NY: Guilford Press.

8 Blais, J., Solodukhin, E., & Forth, A. E. (2014). A meta-analysis exploring the relationship between psychopathy and instrumental ver-

sus reactive violence. *Criminal Justice and Behavior, 41,* 797–821. doi: 10.1177/0093854813519629.

9 Sewall, L. A., & Olver, M. E. (2019). Psychopathy and treatment outcome: Results from a sexual Violence Reduction Program. *Personality Disorders: Theory, Research, and Treatment,* 10, 59–69. Hare, R. D., & Neumann, C. S. (2008). Psychopathy as a clinical and empirical construct. *Annual Review of Clinical Psychology, 4,* 217–246.

10 De Oliveira-Souza, R., Ignácio, F. A., Moll, J., & Hare, R. D. (2008). Psychopathy in a civil psychiatric outpatient sample. *Criminal Justice and Behavior,* 35, 427–437.

11 Hare, R. D. (1985). Comparison of the procedures for the assessment of psychopathy. *Journal of Consulting and Clinical Psychology,* 53, 7–16.

12 Westen, D., & Weinberger, J. (2004). When clinical description becomes statistical prediction. *American Psychologist, 59,* 595–613.

13 Lilienfeld, S. O., Watts, A. L., Patrick, C. J., & Hare, R. D. (2018). Hervey Cleckley (1903–1984): Contributions to the study of psychopathy. *Personality Disorders: Theory, Research, and Treatment. 9,* 520–520. doi:10.1037/per0000306.

14 Cleckley, H. (1976). *The mask of sanity* (5th ed.). St. Louis, MO: Mosby. This book is available as a free download from the Internet, courtesy of Cleckley's second wife, Emily Cleckley.

15 Lilienfeld, S. O., Watts, A. L., Patrick, C. J., & Hare, R. D. (2018). Hervey Cleckley (1903–1984): Contributions to the study of psychopathy. *Personality Disorders: Theory, Research, and Treatment. 9,* 520–520. doi:10.1037/per0000306.

16 Initially, these ratings were rather crude (Low, Medium, and High psychopathy). Later, Hare and his students rated offenders on a 7-point scale, with 6–7 indicative of psychopathy. Although agreement among the raters was very good, other researchers and journal editors were never certain about what the ratings meant, with respect to the traditional concept of psychopathy. As a result, Hare commented in *Without Conscience* that he and his team "spent more than ten years improving and refining our procedures for ferreting the psychopaths out of the general prison population."

17 Hare, R. D. (1980). A research scale for the assessment of psychopathy in criminal populations. *Personality and Individual Differences, 1,* 111–119.

18 Hare, R. D. (1991). *The Hare Psychopathy Checklist–Revised.* Toronto, ON: Multi-Health Systems. Hare, R. D. (2003). *Manual for the Revised Psychopathy Checklist* (2nd ed.). Toronto, ON, Canada: Multi-Health Systems.

19 Gacono, C. B. (Ed.). (2016). *The clinical and forensic assessment of psychopathy: A practitioner's guide* (2nd ed.). New York, NY: Routledge.

20 Hare, R. D., Black, P., & Walsh, Z. (2013). The PCL-R: Forensic applications and limitations. In R. P. Archer & E. M. A. Wheeler (Eds.), *Forensic uses of clinical assessment instruments* (2nd ed., pp. 230–265). New York, NY: Routledge.

21 Hart, S. D., Cox, D. N., & Hare, R. D. (1995). *The Hare Psychopathy Checklist: Screening Version.* Toronto, ON: Multi-Health Systems. Hare and his team developed the PCL: SV for use in the MacArthur Violence Risk Assessment Study, which evaluated 133 potential predictors of inpatient violence. The PCL: SV was the strongest of these predictors (Steadman, H. J., Silver, E., Monahan, J., Appelbaum, P. S., Clark Robbins, P., Mulvey, E. P., Grisso, T., Roth, L. H., & Banks, S., 2000). A classification tree approach to the development of actuarial violence risk assessment tools. *Law and Human Behavior, 24,* 83–100.

22 Neumann, C. S., & Hare, R. D. (2008). Psychopathic traits in a large community sample: Links to violence, alcohol use, and intelligence. *Journal of Consulting and Clinical Psychology, 76,* 893–899.

23 Kelsey, K. R., Rogers, R., & Robinson, E. V. (2015). Self-report measures of psychopathy: What is their role in forensic assessments? *Journal of Psychopathology and Behavioral Assessment, 37,* 380–391. doi:10.1007/s10862-014-9475-5.

24 Hare, R. D. (2003). *Manual for the Revised Psychopathy Checklist* (2nd ed.). Toronto, ON, Canada: Multi-Health Systems.

25 Rosner, B. (1990). *Swindle.* Homewood, IL: Business One Irwin.

26 Civil Action No. 08-495-KSF.

27 Personal communication from B. Rosner to R. Hare, December 12, 2018.

Supplemental S 2.1: Nature? Nurture? Both!

28 Waldman, I. D., Rhee, S. H., LoParo, D., & Park, Y. (2018). Genetic and environmental influences on psychopathy and antisocial behavior. In C. J. Patrick (Ed.), *Handbook of psychopathy,* (2nd ed., pp. 335–353). New York, NY: Guilford Press.

29 Powledge, T. (2011). How nature shapes nurture. *Bioscience, 61,* 588–592. doi:10.1525/bio.2011.61.8.4.

30 Verona, E., Hicks, B. M., & Patrick, C. J. (2005). Psychopathy and suicidality in female offenders: Mediating influences of personality and abuse. *Journal of Consulting and Clinical Psychology, 73,* 1065–1073. doi:10.1037/0022-006X.73.6.1065

31 Blonigen, D. M., Sullivan, E. A., Hicks, B. M., & Patrick, C. J. (2012). Facets of psychopathy in relation to potentially traumatic events and post-traumatic stress disorder among female prisoners: The mediating role of borderline personality disorder traits. *Personality Disorders: Theory, Research, and Treatment, 3,* 406–414. doi:10.1037/a0026184.

32 Graham, N., Kimonis, E. R., Wasserman, A. L., & Kline, S. M. (2012). Associations among childhood abuse and psychopathy facets in male sexual offenders. *Personality Disorders: Theory, Research, and Treatment, 3,* 66–75. doi:10.1037/a0025605.

33 Dargis, M., Newman, J., & Koenigs, M. (2016). Clarifying the link between childhood abuse history and psychopathic traits in adult criminal offenders. *Personality Disorders: Theory, Research, and Treatment, 7,* 221–228. doi:10.1037/per0000147.

34 A detailed review of the role of family and other early forces in the development of psychopathy is available in Farrington, D. P., & Bergstrøm, H. (2018). Family background and psychopathy. In C. Patrick (Ed.), *Handbook of psychopathy* (2nd ed., pp. 354–379). New York, NY: Guilford Press.

35 Glenn, A. L., Kurzban, R., & Raine, A. (2011). Evolutionary theory and psychopathy. *Aggression and Violent Behavior, 16,* 371–380. doi:10.1016/j.avb.2011.03.009.

36 Meloy, J. R., Book, A., Hosker-Field, A., Methot-Jones, T., & Roters, J. (2018). Social, sexual, and violent predation: Are psychopathic

traits evolutionarily adaptive? *Violence and Gender, 5,* 153–165. doi:10.1089/vio.2018.0012.

37 Mealey, L. (1995). The sociobiology of sociopathy: An integrated evolutionary model. *Behavioral and Brain Sciences, 18,* 523–540. doi:10.1017/S0140525X00039595. In *Without Conscience,* Hare described Diane Downs as a chilling example of maternal psychopathy. (For detailed accounts, see Ann Rule's 1987 book *Small Sacrifices.* New York: New American Library. Also revealing is the 1989 book by Diane Downs, *Best Kept Secrets.* Springfield, OR: Danmark Publishing.) Downs often would leave her young children alone when there was no babysitter available. Neighbors described the children, ranging in age from fifteen months to six years, as hungry, emotionally starved, and generally neglected. Downs professed to love her children, but her callous indifference to their physical and emotional welfare argues otherwise. She shot her children in 1983 (killing one) because the man with whom she was having an extramarital affair did not want children. Sentenced to life plus fifty years, she has a parole hearing in 2020.

38 Book, A. S., & Quinsey, V. L. (2004). Psychopaths: Cheaters or warrior hawks? *Personality and Individual Differences, 36,* 33–45. doi:10.1016/S0191-8869(03)00049-7.

39 PBS: https://ihavenotv.com/mischief-spy-in-the-wild.

40 Krupp, D. B., Sewall, L. A., Lalumière, M. L., Sheriff, C., & Harris, G. T. (2013). Psychopathy, adaptation, and disorder. *Frontiers in Psychology, 4,* article 139. doi:10.3389/fpsyg.2013.00139.

41 Hare, R. D. (2013). Foreword. In K. Kiehl & W. Sinnott-Armstrong (Eds.), *Handbook on Psychopathy and Law* (pp vii–ix). New York, NY: Oxford University Press.

Supplemental S 2.2: Psychopathy and Lethal Violence

42 Neumann, C. S., Hare, R. D., & Pardini, D. A. (2015). Antisociality and the construct of psychopathy: Data from across the globe. *Journal of Personality, 83,* 678–692.

43 DeLisi, M. (2009). Psychopathy is the unified theory of crime. *Youth Violence and Juvenile Justice, 7,* 256–273. doi:10.1177/1541204009 333834.

44 Fox, B., & DeLisi, M. (2019). Psychopathic killers: A meta-analytic review of the psychopathy-homicide nexus. *Aggression and Violent Behavior, 44,* 67–79. doi:10.1016/j.avb.2018.11.005.

45 O'Connell, D., & Marcus, D. K. (2019). A meta-analysis of the association between psychopathy and sadism in forensic samples. *Aggression and Violent Behavior, 46,* 109–115. Also see Darjee, R. (2019). Sexual sadism and psychopathy in sexual homicide offenders: An exploration of their associates in a clinical sample. *International Journal of Offender Therapy and Comparative Criminology.* Advance online publication. doi: 10.1177/0306624X19836872.

46 Fox, B., & DeLisi, M. (2019). Psychopathic killers: A meta-analytic review of the psychopathy-homicide nexus. *Aggression and Violent Behavior, 44,* 67–79. doi:10.1016/j.avb.2018.11.005.

47 O'Connell, D., & Marcus, D. K. (2019). A meta-analysis of the association between psychopathy and sadism in forensic samples. *Aggression and Violent Behavior, 46,* 109–115. Also see Darjee, R. (2019). Sexual sadism and psychopathy in sexual homicide offenders: An exploration of their associates in a clinical sample. *International Journal of Offender Therapy and Comparative Criminology.* Advance online publication. doi: 10.1177/0306624X19836872.

48 Lalumière, M. L., Mishra, S., & Harris, G. T. (2008). In cold blood: The evolution of psychopathy. In J. Duntley & T. K. Shackelford (Eds.), *Evolutionary forensic psychology* (pp. 176–197). Oxford: Oxford University Press.

49 Woodworth, M., & Porter, S. (2002). In cold blood: Characteristics of criminal homicides as a function of psychopathy. *Journal of Abnormal Psychology, 111,* 436–445. doi:10.1037/0021-843X.111.3.436.

Supplemental S 2.3: The Dark Triad

50 Paulhus, D. L., & Williams, K. M. (2002). The dark triad of personality: Narcissism, Machiavellianism, and psychopathy. *Journal of Research in Personality, 36,* 556–563. doi:10.1016/S0092-6566(02)00505-6.

51 Jones, D. N., & Figueredo, A. J. (2013). The core of darkness: Uncovering the heart of the dark triad. *European Journal of Person-*

ality, 27, 521–531. doi:10.1002/per.1893. Also, see Jones, D. N., & Hare, R. D. (2016). The mismeasure of psychopathy: A commentary on Boddy's PMMRV. *Journal of Business Ethics, 138*, 579–588. doi:10.1007/s10551-015-2584-6.

52 Moshagen, M., Hilbig, B. E., & Zettler, I. (2018) The dark core of personality. *Psychological Review, 125*, 656–688. doi.org/10.1037/rev0000111. Also see Jonason, P. K., Webster, G. D., Schmitt, D. P., Li, N. P., & Crysel, L. (2012). The antihero in popular culture: Life history theory and the dark triad personality traits. *Review of General Psychology, 16*, 192–199. http://dx.doi.org/10.1037/a0027914.

Supplemental S 2.4: Gender, Ethnicity, Culture

53 Murphy, J. (1976). Psychiatric labeling in cross-cultural perspective. *Science, 191*, 1019–1028. She noted, "Similar kinds of disturbed behavior appear to be labeled abnormal in diverse cultures" (p. 1019). She described an Eskimo (now Inuit) term, "*kunlangeta*, which means 'his mind knows what to do but he does not do it.' This is an abstract term for the breaking of many rules when awareness of the rules is not in question. It might be applied to a man who, for example, repeatedly lies and cheats and steals things and does not go hunting and, when the other men are out of the village, takes sexual advantage of many women—someone who does not pay attention to reprimands and who is always being brought to the elders for punishment" (p. 1026).

54 Fanti, K. A., Lordos, A., Sullivan, E. A., & Kosson, D. S. Cultural and ethnic variations in psychopathy. In C. Patrick (Ed.), *Handbook of psychopathy* (2nd ed., pp. 529–569). New York, NY: Guilford Press. This is a very detailed and current review of the literature on racial, cultural, and ethnic differences in psychopathy and its measurement.

55 Verona, E., & Vitale, J. (2018). Psychopathy in women. In C. J. Patrick (Ed.), *Handbook of psychopathy* (2nd ed., pp. 509–528). New York, NY: Guilford Press.

56 Thomson, D., Bozgunov, K., Psederska, E., & Vassileva, J. (2019). Sex differences on the four-facet model of psychopathy predict physical, verbal, and indirect aggression. *Aggressive Behavior*. DOI: 10.1002/ab.21816.

57 Book, A. S., Forth, A. E., & Clark, H. J. (2013). The Hare Psychopathy Checklist–Youth Version. In R. P. Archer & E. M. A. Wheeler (Eds.), *Forensic uses of clinical assessment instruments* (2nd ed., pp. 266–290). New York, NY: Routledge.

58 Verona, E., & Vitale, J. (2018). Psychopathy in women. In C. J. Patrick (Ed.), *Handbook of psychopathy* (2nd ed., pp. 509–528). New York, NY: Guilford Press.

59 Bolt, D. M., Hare, R. D., Vitale, J. E., & Newman, J. P. (2004). A multigroup item response theory analysis of the Psychopathy Checklist-Revised. *Psychological Assessment, 16,* 155–168.

60 Fanti, K. A., Lordos, A., Sullivan, E. A., & Kosson, D. S. Cultural and ethnic variations in psychopathy. In C. Patrick (Ed.), *Handbook of psychopathy* (2nd ed., pp. 529–569). New York, NY: Guilford Press. This is a very detailed and current review of the literature on racial, cultural, and ethnic differences in psychopathy and its measurement.

61 Olver, M. E., Neumann, C. S., Sewall, L. A., Lewis, K., Hare, R. D., & Wong, S. C. P., (2018). A Comprehensive Examination of the Psychometric Properties of the Hare Psychopathy Checklist-Revised in a Canadian Multisite Sample of Indigenous and Non-Indigenous Offenders. *Psychological Assessment, 30,* 779–792. doi: 10.1037/pas0000533. Kosson, D., Neumann, C. S., Forth, A. E., Hare, R. D., Salekin, R. T., & Sevecke, K. (2013). Factor structure of the Hare Psychopathy Checklist: Youth Version (PCL: YV) in adolescent females. *Psychological Assessment, 25,* 71–83. Vachon, D. D., Lynam, D. R., Loeber, R., & Stouthamer-Loeber, M. (2012). Generalizing the nomological network of psychopathy across populations differing on race and conviction status. *Journal of Abnormal Psychology,* 121, 263–269.

62 Bolt, D. M., Hare, R. D., & Neumann, C. S. (2007). Score metric equivalence of the Psychopathy Checklist-Revised (PCL-R) across criminal offenders in North America and the United Kingdom: A critique of Cooke, Michie, Hart, and Clark (2005) and new analyses. *Assessment, 14,* 44–56.

63 Neumann, C. S., Schmitt, D. S., Carter, R., Embley, I., & Hare, R. D. (2012). Psychopathic traits in females and males across the globe. *Behavioral Sciences & the Law, 30,* 557–574. doi:10.1002/

bsl.2038. Participants rated each item (e.g., *I like to con others*; *Rules are meant to be broken*) on a 5-point scale from 1 (disagree strongly) to 5 (agree strongly). A mean item score of 3.5 defined high psychopathy. The eleven regions are: North America, Central/South America, Northern Europe, Eastern Europe, Southern Europe, Middle East, Africa, Oceania, South/South East Asia, and East Asia. The study was part of the *International Sexuality Description Project-2*, a collaborative research effort involving the administration of anonymous surveys to men and women throughout the world. For details, see Schmitt, D. P. (2010). Romantic attachment from Argentina to Zimbabwe: Patterns of adaptive variation across contexts, cultures, and local ecologies. In Ng, K. & P. Erdman (Eds.), *Cross-cultural attachment across the life-span* (pp. 211–226). New York: Routledge.

64 Paulhus, D. L., Neumann, C. S., & Hare, R. D. (2016). *Manual for the Self-Report Psychopathy Scale—Fourth Edition (SRP-4)*. Toronto, ON: Multi-Health Systems. The SRP-E was labeled the experimental version of the SRP, but is the same as the SRP-III.

Chapter 3: What You See May Not Be What You See

1 American Psychiatric Association. *Diagnostic and statistical manual of mental disorders,* 5th ed. Arlington, VA.

2 Babiak, P. (2008, February). "Psychopath" or "narcissist": The coach's dilemma. *Worldwide Association of Business Coaches eZine.* http:// www.wabccoaches.com/blog/psychopath-or-narcissist-the-coaches -dilemma-by-paul-babiak-phd/.

Supplemental S 3.2: Red-Collar Criminals

3 Perri, F. S. (2016). Red collar crime. *International Journal of Psychological Studies, 8,* 61–84. doi: 10.5539/ijps.v8n1p61.

4 Perri, F. S., & Lichtenwald, T. G. (2008). The arrogant chameleons: Exposing fraud detection homicide. *Forensic Examiner, 17,* 26–34. Also see the extensive and detailed account of white-collar crime by Perri. F. S. (2019). *White-collar crime, organizational misconduct, and fraud examination: An accounting, behavioral, and criminological approach.* Rockford, IL.

Chapter 5: Enter the Psychopath, Stage Left

1 Psychopaths are skilled at faking mental illness when it is in their interests to do so. In many cases, it is difficult for clinicians to determine if such a patient is "mad" or "bad," often with dire consequences. Several decades ago, staff at a major American Forensic Psychiatric Hospital granted a patient special ward privileges, allowing him to move freely throughout the hospital. He killed a staff member, and the ensuing investigation determined that he had a very high score on the PCL-R. The hospital adopted a policy in which patients with a high PCL-R score and a history of violence required special permission from the director in order to receive ward privileges.

Supplemental S 5.2: The Dark Triad and Face-to-Face Negotiations

2 Jonason, P. K., Slomski, S., & Partyka, J. (2012). The Dark Triad at work: How *toxic* employees get their way. *Personality and Individual Differences, 52,* 449–453. doi:10.1016/j.paid.2011.11.008.

3 Crossley, L., Woodworth, M., Black, P. J., & Hare, R. D. (2016). The dark side of negotiation: Examining the outcomes of face-to-face and computer-mediated negotiations among dark personalities. *Personality and Individual Differences, 91,* 47–51. doi:10.1016/j.paid.2015.11.052.

4 Jones, D. N., & Hare, R. D. (2016). The mismeasure of psychopathy: A commentary on Boddy's PMMRV. *Journal of Business Ethics, 138,* 579–588. doi:10.1007/s1055.

5 Paulhus, D. L., Neumann, C. S., & Hare, R. D. (2016). *Manual for the Self-Report Psychopathy Scale—Fourth Edition (SRP-4).* Toronto, ON: Multi-Health Systems.

Chapter 7: Darkness and Chaos

Supplemental S 7.1: Opportunity Knocks

1 https://www.quora.com/What-is-the-meaning-of-the-Chaos-is-a-ladder-quote-from-Game-of-Thrones.

2 Michael Deacon, April 7, 2019.

Chapter 8: I'm Not a Psychopath, I Just Talk and Act Like One

1 Halpin, A. W., & Winer, B. J. (1957). A factorial study of the leader behavior descriptions. In R. M. Stogdill & A. E. Coons (Eds.), *Leader behavior: Its description and measurement.* Columbus, OH: Bureau of Business Research, Ohio State University.

2 Babiak, P., Neumann, C. S., & Hare, R. D. (2010). Corporate psychopathy: Talking the walk. *Behavioral Sciences and the Law, 28,* 174–193. doi:10.1002/bsl.925. Download the article from www .hare.org.

3 Mokros, A., Hare, R. D., Neumann, C. S., Santtila, P., Habermeyer, E., & Nitschke, J. (2015). Variants of psychopathy in adult male offenders: A latent profile analysis. *Journal of Abnormal Psychology, 124,* 372–386. doi:10.1037/abn0000042.

Chapter 9: A Unique Empirical Study of Corporate Psychopathy

1 Parts of this chapter are adapted from Babiak, Neumann, & Hare (2010), Mokros and colleagues (2015), and from recent analyses by Craig Neumann.

2 Lowman, R. L. (1989). *Pre-employment screening for psychopathology: A guide to professional practice.* Sarasota, FL: Professional Resource Series. Professional Resource Exchange, Inc.

3 Hare, R. D., & Neumann, C. S. (2008). Psychopathy as a clinical and empirical construct. *Annual Review of Clinical Psychology, 4,* 217–246. doi:10.1146/annurev.clinpsy.3.022806.091452.

4 Hare, R. D. (2003). *Manual for the Revised Psychopathy Checklist* (2nd ed.) Toronto, ON: Multi-Health Systems.

5 Babiak, P., Neumann, C. S., & Hare, R. D. (2010). Corporate psychopathy: Talking the walk. *Behavioral Sciences and the Law, 28,* 174–193. doi:10.1002/bsl.925. Download the article from *www.hare.org.*

6 Neumann, C. C., & Hare, R. D. (2008). Psychopathic traits in a large community sample: Links to violence, alcohol use, and intelligence. *Journal of Consulting and Clinical Psychology, 76,* 893–899. doi:10.1037/0022-006X.76.5.893. The sample was part of the MacArthur Violence Risk Assessment Study to identify predictors of inpatient violence. See Chapter 2, Note 20.

7 Coid, J., Yang, M., Ullrich, S., Roberts, A., & Hare, R. D. (2009). Prevalence and correlates of psychopathic traits in the household population of Great Britain. *International Journal of Law and Psychiatry, 32*, 65–73. doi:10.1016/j.ijlp.2009.01.002.

8 Babiak, P., Neumann, C. S., & Hare, R. D. (2010). Corporate psychopathy: Talking the walk. *Behavioral Sciences and the Law, 28*, 174–193. doi:10.1002/bsl.925. Download the article from *www.hare.org*.

9 Babiak, P., Neumann, C. S., & Hare, R. D. (2010). Corporate psychopathy: Talking the walk. *Behavioral Sciences and the Law, 28*, 174–193. doi:10.1002/bsl.925. Download the article from *www.hare.org*.

Supplemental S 9.1: Economic and Corporate Fraud

10 PriceWaterhouseCoopers. (2018). Pulling fraud out of the shadows: *Global Economic Crime and Fraud Survey, 2018.* www.pwc.com/fraudsurvey.

Supplemental S 9.2: The Mismeasure of Corporate Psychopathy

11 Boddy, C. R. (2014). Corporate psychopaths, conflict, employee affective well-being and counterproductive work behaviour. *Journal of Business Ethics, 121*, 107–121. doi:10.1007/s10551-013-1688-0.

12 Boddy, C. R., Ladyshewsky, R. K., & Galvin, P. (2010). Leaders without ethics in global business: Corporate psychopaths. *Journal of Public Affairs, 10*, 121–138. doi:10.1002/pa.352.

13 Boddy, C. R., Ladyshewsky, R. K., & Galvin, P. (2010). Leaders without ethics in global business: Corporate psychopaths. *Journal of Public Affairs, 10*, 121–138. doi:10.1002/pa.352.

14 Deutschman, A. (2005). Is your boss a psychopath? *Fast Company Magazine*, July, 2005. Retrieved from http://www.fastcompany.com /magazine/96/openboss-quiz.html.

15 Jones, D. N., & Figueredo, A. J. (2013). The core of darkness: Uncovering the heart of the Dark Triad. *European Journal of Personality, 27*, 521–531. doi:10.1002/per.1893.

16 Jones, D. N., & Hare, R. D. (2016). The mismeasure of psychopathy: A commentary on Boddy's PMMRV. *Journal of Business Ethics, 138*, 579–588. doi:10.1007/s10551-015-2584-6.

17 Jones, D. N., & Hare, R. D. (2016). The mismeasure of psychopathy:
    A commentary on Boddy's PMMRV. *Journal of Business Ethics, 138,*
    579–588. doi:10.1007/s10551-015-2584-6.

Supplemental S. 9.3: The Wall Street "Ten Percenters"
18 Babiak, P., Neumann, C. S., & Hare, R. D. (2010). Corporate psy-
    chopathy: Talking the walk. *Behavioral Sciences and the Law, 28,* 174–
    193. doi:10.1002/bsl.925. Download the article from www.hare.org.
19 Personal communication from J. Grohol to R. D. Hare, May 3, 2012.
20 http://psychcentral.com/blog/archives/2012/03/06/untrue-1-out-of
    -every-10-wall-street-employees-is-a-psychopath/.

Chapter 10: The B-Scan

1 https://www.nytimes.com/2004/12/12/magazine/psychopathic-ceos
   .html.
2 Kelsey, K. R., Rogers, R., & Robinson, E. V. (2015). Self-report
   measures of psychopathy: What is their role in forensic assessments?
   Journal of Psychopathology and Behavioral Assessment, 37, 380–391.
   doi:10.1007/s10862-014-9475-5.
3 Sellbom, M., Lilienfeld, S. O., Fowler, K. A., & McCrary, K. L.
   (2018). The self-report assessment of psychopathy: Challenges, pitfalls, and promises. In C. J. Patrick (Ed.), *Handbook of psychopathy*
   (2nd ed., pp. 211–258). New York, NY: Guilford Press.
4 Babiak, P. (1995). When psychopaths go to work: A case study of an
   industrial psychopath. *Applied Psychology: An International Review,*
   44, 171–188. doi:10.1111/j.1464-0597.1995.tb01073.x.
5 Mathieu, C., Hare, R. D., Jones, D. N., Babiak, P., & Neumann, C. S.
   (2013). Factor structure of the B-Scan 360: A measure of corporate psychopathy. *Psychological Assessment, 25,* 288–293. doi:10.1037/a0029262.
6 Paulhus, D. L., Neumann, C. S., & Hare, R. D. (2016). *Self-Report*
   Psychopathy Scale 4th Edition (SRP-4). Toronto, ON: Multi-Health
   Systems.
7 Mathieu, C., & Babiak, P. (2016b). Validating the B-Scan Self: A self-
   report measure of psychopathy in the workplace. *International Journal of*
   Selection and Assessment, 24, 272–284. doi:10.1111/ijsa.12146.

8 LeBreton, J. M., Shiverdecker, L. K., & Grimaldi, E. M. (2018). The dark triad and workplace behavior. *Annual Review of Organizational Psychology and Organizational Behavior, 5,* 387–414. doi:10.1146 /annurev-orgpsych-032117-104451.

9 Coid, J., Yang, M., Ullrich, S., Roberts, A., & Hare, R. D. (2009). Prevalence and correlates of psychopathic traits in the household population of Great Britain. *International Journal of Law and Psychiatry, 32,* 65–73. doi:10.1016/j.ijlp.2009.01.002.

10 Lynam, D. R., Gaughan, E. T., Miller, J. D., Mullins-Sweatt, S., & Widiger, T. A. (2010). Assessing basic traits associated with psychopathy: Development and validation of the Elemental Psychopathy Assessment. *Psychological Assessment, 23,* 108–124. doi:10.1037 /a0021146.

11 Neumann, C. C., & Hare, R. D. (2008). Psychopathic traits in a large community sample: Links to violence, alcohol use, and intelligence. *Journal of Consulting and Clinical Psychology, 76,* 893–899. doi:10.1037/0022-006X.76.5.893.

12 Verona, E., & Vitale, J. (2018). Psychopathy in women. In C. J. Patrick (Ed.), *Handbook of psychopathy* (2nd ed., pp. 509–528). New York, NY: Guilford Press.

13 Mathieu, C., & Babiak, P. (2016b). Validating the B-Scan Self: A self-report measure of psychopathy in the workplace. *International Journal of Selection and Assessment, 24,* 272–284. doi:10.1111/ijsa.12146.

14 Mathieu, C., Babiak, P., & Hare, R. D. (2019). *Use of the B-Scan in a large sample of public employees.* Manuscript in preparation.

15 Raver, J. L., & Nishii, L. H. (2010). Once, twice, or three times as harmful? Ethnic harassment, gender harassment, and generalized workplace harassment. *Journal of Applied Psychology, 95,* 236. doi:10.1037/a0018377.

16 Andersson, L. M., & Pearson, C. M. (1999). Tit for tat? The spiraling effect of incivility in the workplace. *Academy of Management Review, 24,* 452–471. doi:10.5465/AMR.1999.2202131.

17 Skarlicki, D. P., Folger, R., & Tesluk, P. (1999). Personality as a moderator in the relationship between fairness and retaliation. *Academy of Management Journal, 42,* 100–108. doi:10.2307/25687.

18 Douglas, S. C., & Martinko, M. J. (2001). Exploring the role of individual differences in the prediction of workplace aggression. *Journal of Applied Psychology, 86,* 547–559. doi:10.1037//0021-9010.86.4.547.

19 Lee, K., Ashton, M. C., & Shin, K. H. (2005). Personality correlates of workplace anti-social behavior. *Applied Psychology, 54,* 81–98. doi:10.1111/j.1464-0597.2005.00197.x.

20 Hershcovis, M. S., Turner, N., Barling, J., Arnold, K. A., Dupré, K. E., Inness, M., Leblanc, M. M., & Sivanathan, N. (2007). Predicting workplace aggression: a meta-analysis. *Journal of Applied Psychology, 92,* 228–238. doi:10.1037/0021-9010.92.1.228.

21 Hoel, H., Cooper, C. L., & Faragher, B. (2001). The experience of bullying in Great Britain: The impact of organizational status. *European Journal of Work and Organizational Psychology, 10,* 443–465. doi:10.1080/13594320143000780.

22 Mathieu, C., & Babiak, P. (2016c). Workplace harassment: The influence of corporate psychopathy and the HEXACO model of personality. *Personality and Individual Differences, 101,* 298. doi:10.1016/j.paid.2016.05.225.

23 Mathieu, C., Fabi, B., Lacoursière, R., & Raymond, L. (2015). The role of supervisory behavior, job satisfaction and organizational commitment on employee turnover. *Journal of Management & Organization, 22,* 1–17. doi:10.1017/jmo.2015.25.

24 Mathieu, C., Neumann, C., Babiak, P., & Hare, R. D. (2015). Corporate psychopathy and the full-range leadership model. *Assessment, 22,* 267–278. doi:10.1177/1073191114545490.

25 Avolio, B. J., & Bass, B. M. (2004). *Multifactor leadership questionnaire: Manual and sampler set.* Redwood City, CA: Mind Garden Incorporated.

26 Judge, T. A., Piccolo, R. F., & Ilies, R. (2004). The forgotten ones? The validity of consideration and initiating structure in leadership research. *Journal of Applied Psychology, 89,* 36–51. doi:10.1037/0021-9010.89.1.36.

27 Sosik, J. J., & Godshalk, V. M. (2000). Leadership styles, mentoring functions received, and job-related stress: A conceptual model and preliminary study. *Journal of Organizational Behavior, 21,*

365–390. doi:10.1002/(SICI)1099-1379(200006)21:4:AID-JOB14:3.0.CO;2-H.

28 Barling, J., Weber, T., & Kelloway, E. K. (1996). Effects of transformational leadership training on attitudinal and financial outcomes: A field experiment. *Journal of Applied Psychology, 81*, 827–832. doi:10.1037/0021-9010.81.6.827.

29 Lim, B.-C., & Ployhart, R. E. (2004). Transformational leadership: Relations to the five-factor model and team performance in typical and maximum contexts. *Journal of Applied Psychology, 89*, 610–621. doi:10.1037/0021-9010.89.4.610.

30 Arnold, K. A., Turner, N., Barling, J., Kelloway, E. K., & McKee, M. C. (2007). Transformational leadership and psychological well-being: The mediating role of meaningful work. *Journal of Occupational Health Psychology, 12*, 193–203. doi:10.1037/1076-8998.12.3.193.

31 Mathieu, C., & Babiak, P. (2015). Tell me who you are, I'll tell you how you lead: Beyond the Full-Range Leadership Model, the role of corporate psychopathy on employee attitudes. *Personality and Individual Differences, 87*, 8–12. doi:10.1016/j.paid.2015.07.016.

32 Tepper, B. J. (2000). Consequences of abusive supervision. *Academy of Management Journal, 43*, 178–190. doi:10.2307/1556375.

33 Tepper, B. J., Duffy, M. K., Henle, C. A., & Lambert, L. S. (2006). Procedural injustice, victim precipitation, and abusive supervision. *Personnel Psychology, 59*, 101–123. doi:10.1111/j.1744-6570.2006.00725.x.

34 Mathieu, C., & Babiak, P. (2016a). Corporate psychopathy and abusive supervision: Their influence on employees' job satisfaction and turnover intentions. *Personality and Individual Differences, 91*, 102–106. doi:10.1016/j.paid.2015.07.016.

35 The authors wish to thank Dr. Cynthia Mathieu, Université du Québec à Trois-Rivières, for her collaboration, extensive contributions to this chapter, and her research, contained herein.

Chapter 11: Enemy at the Gates

1 Book, A., Methot, T., Gauthier, N., Hosker-Field, A., Forth, A., Quinsey, V., & Molnar, D. (2015). The Mask of Sanity revisited: Psychopathic traits and affective mimicry. *Evolutionary Psychological Science, 1*, 91–102. doi:10.1007/s40806-015-0012-x.

2 *The Brock News*, Thursday, December 2, 2018.

Supplemental S 11.1: Does Practice Make Perfect?

3 Cleckley, H. (1976). *The Mask of Sanity* (5th ed.). St. Louis, MO.

Supplemental S 11.2: Politics and Poker: A License to Lie

4 Gillstrom, B. J., & Hare, R. D. (1988). Language-related hand gestures in psychopaths. *Journal of Personality Disorders, 2*, 21–27. doi:10.1521/pedi.1988.2.1.21.

5 ten Brinke, L., Porter, S., Korva, N., Fowler, K., Lilienfeld, S. O., & Patrick, C. J. (2017). An examination of the communication styles associated with psychopathy and their influence on observer impressions. *Journal of Nonverbal Behavior, 41*, 269–287. doi:10.1007/s10919-017-0252-5.

6 Gunnery, S. D., & Ruben, M. A. (2016). Perceptions of Duchenne and non-Duchenne smiles: A meta-analysis. *Cognition and Emotion, 30*, 501–515. doi:10.1080/02699931.2015.1018817.

7 ten Brinke, L., Porter, S., Korva, N., Fowler, K., Lilienfeld, S. O., & Patrick, C. J. (2017). An examination of the communication styles associated with psychopathy and their influence on observer impressions. *Journal of Nonverbal Behavior, 41*, 269–287. doi:10.1007/s10919-017-0252-5.

Chapter 12: Personal Self-Defense

Supplemental S 12.1: Psychopathic Interviews

1 Hare, R. D. (1999). *Without conscience: The disturbing world of the psychopaths among us.* New York, NY: Guilford Press.

2 Le, M., Woodworth, M., Gillman, L., Hutton, E., & Hare, R. D. (2017). The linguistic output of psychopathic offenders during

a PCL-R interview. *Criminal Justice and Behavior, 44,* 551–565. doi:10.1177/0093854816683423.

3 Louth, S. M., Williamson, S., Alpert, M., Pouget, E. R., & Hare, R. D. (1998). Acoustic distinctions in the speech of male psychopaths. *Journal of Psycholinguistic Research, 27,* 375–384. doi:10.1023 /A:1023207821867.

4 Williamson, S. (1991). Cohesion and coherence in the speech of psychopaths. *Unpublished doctoral dissertation.* University of British Columbia, Vancouver, Canada.

5 Hancock, J., Woodworth, M., & Porter, S. (2011). Hungry like the wolf: An analysis of the language of human predators. *Legal and Criminological Psychology, 18,* 102–114. doi:10.1111/j.2044 -8333.2011.02025.x.

Supplemental S 12.2: Dark Personalities in the Workplace

6 We thank Dr. Cynthia Mathieu for her extensive contributions to this Supplemental.

7 Mathieu, C., & St-Jean, É. (2013). Entrepreneurial personality: The role of narcissism. *Personality and Individual Differences, 55,* 527–531. doi:10.1016/j.paid.2013.04.026.

8 Akhtar, R., Ahmetoglu, G., & Chamorro-Premuzic, T. (2013). Greed is good? Assessing the relationship between entrepreneurship and subclinical psychopathy. *Personality and Individual Differences, 54,* 420–425. doi:10.1016/j.paid.2012.10.013.

9 Hmieleski, K. M., & Lerner, D. A. (2013). The Dark Triad: Narcissism, psychopathy, and Machiavellianism as predictors of entrepreneurial entry (summary). *Frontiers of Entrepreneurship Research, 33,* Article 6. Retrieved from https://digitalknowledge.babson.edu/fer/vol33/iss4/6.

10 Hill, R. W., & Yousey, G. P. (1998). Adaptive and maladaptive narcissism among university faculty, clergy, politicians, and librarians. *Current Psychology, 17,* 163–169. doi:10.1007/s12144-998-1003-x.

11 Fehr, B., Samsom, D., & Paulhus, D. L. (1992). The construct of Machiavellianism: Twenty years later. In C. D. Spielberger & J. N. Butcher (Eds.), *Advances in personality assessment* (vol. 9, pp. 77–116). Hillsdale, NJ: Erlbaum.

12 Hornett, A., & Fredericks, S. (2005). An empirical and theoretical exploration of disconnections between leadership and ethics. *Journal of Business Ethics, 59*, 233–246. Retrieved from http://www.jstor.org /stable/25123556.

13 Blair, C. A., Hoffman, B. J., & Helland, K. R. (2008). Narcissism in organizations: A multisource appraisal reflects different perspectives. *Human Performance, 21*, 254–276. doi:10.1080/0895928080 2137705.

14 Grijalva, E., Harms, P. D., Newman, D. A., Gaddis, B. H., & Fraley, R. C. (2015). Narcissism and leadership: A meta-analytic review of linear and nonlinear relationships. *Personnel Psychology, 68*, 1–47. doi:10.1111/peps.12072.

15 Mathieu, C., & Babiak, P. (2016a). Corporate psychopathy and abusive supervision: Their influence on employees' job satisfaction and turnover intentions. *Personality and Individual Differences, 91*, 102–106. doi:10.1016/j.paid.2015.07.016.

16 Wisse, B., & Sleebos, E. (2016). When the dark ones gain power: Perceived position power strengthens the effect of supervisor Machiavellianism on abusive supervision in work teams. *Personality and Individual Differences, 99*, 122–126. doi:10.1016/j.paid .2016.05.019.

17 LeBreton, J. M., Shiverdecker, L. K., & Grimaldi, E. M. (2018). The dark triad and workplace behavior. *Annual Review of Organizational Psychology and Organizational Behavior, 5*, 387–414. doi:10.1146 /annurev-orgpsych-032117-104451.

18 O'Boyle, E. H., Jr., Forsyth, D. R., Banks, G. C., & McDaniel, M. A. (2012). A meta-analysis of the Dark Triad and work behavior: A social exchange perspective. *Journal of Applied Psychology, 97*, 557–579.

19 James, S., Kavanagh, P. S., Jonason, P. K., Chonody, J. M., & Scrutton, H. E. (2014). The Dark Triad, schadenfreude, and sensational interests: Dark personalities, dark emotions, and dark behaviors. *Personality and Individual Differences, 68*, 211–216. doi:10.1016/j .paid.2014.04.020.

20 Buckels, E. E., Jones, D. N., & Paulhus, D. L. (2013). Behavioral confirmation of everyday sadism. *Psychological Science, 24*, 2201–2209. doi:10.1177/0956797613490749.

21 Moshagen, M., Hilbig, B. E., & Zettler, I. (2018) The dark core of personality. *Psychological Review, 125,* 656–688. doi.org/10.1037 /rev0000111.

Appendix: Is There a Psychopathic Brain?

1 Hare, R. D. (1993). *Without conscience: The disturbing world of the psychopaths among us.* New York, NY: Simon & Schuster (Pocket Books). Paperback published in 1993 and reissued in 1999 by Guilford Press.

2 Williamson, S. E., Harpur, T. J., & Hare, R. D. (1991). Abnormal processing of affective words by psychopaths. *Psychophysiology, 28,* 260–273. doi:10.1111/j.1469-8986.1991.tb02192.x.

3 Kiehl, K. A., Smith, A. M., Hare, R. D., Mendrek, A., Forster, B. B., Brink, J., & Liddle, P. F. (2001). Limbic abnormalities in affective processing by criminal psychopaths as revealed by functional magnetic resonance imaging. *Biological Psychiatry, 50,* 677–684. doi:10.1016 /S0006-3223(01)01222-7.

4 Poeppl, T. B., Donges, M., Mokros, M., Rupprecht, Fox, P. T., Laird, A. R., Bzdok, D., Langguth, B., & Eickhoff, S. B. (2018). A view behind the mask of sanity: Meta-analysis of aberrant brain activity in psychopaths. *Molecular Psychiatry.* Advance online publication. doi:10.1038/s41380-018-0122-5.

5 Kiehl, K. A., Bates, A. T., Laurens, K. R., Hare, R. D., & Liddle, P. F. (2006). Brain potentials implicate temporal lobe abnormalities in criminal psychopaths. *Journal of Abnormal Psychology, 115,* 443–453. doi:10.1037/0021-843X.115.3.443.

6 Williamson, S. E., Harpur, T. J., & Hare, R. D. (1991). Abnormal processing of affective words by psychopaths. *Psychophysiology, 28,* 260–273. doi:10.1111/j.1469-8986.1991.tb02192.x.

7 Kiehl, K. A., Smith, A. M., Hare, R. D., Mendrek, A., Forster, B. B., Brink, J., & Liddle, P. F. (2001). Limbic abnormalities in affective processing by criminal psychopaths as revealed by functional magnetic resonance imaging. *Biological Psychiatry, 50,* 677–684. doi:10.1016 /S0006-3223(01)01222-7.

8 Haycock, D. A. (2015). *Murderous minds: Exploring the criminal psychopathic brain: Neurological imaging and the manifestation of evil.* New York, NY: Pegasus Books.

9 Kiehl, K. A. (2015). *The psychopath whisperer: The science of those without conscience.* New York, NY: Random House. This is a personal account of the experiences of one of Hare's students, who was instrumental in the initiation of MRI and fMRI research with psychopaths. http://kentkiehl.com/home/.

10 Raine, A., & Glenn, A. L. (2014). *Psychopathy: An introduction to biological findings and their implications.* New York, NY: NYU Press.

11 Kiehl, K. A., & Buckholtz, J. W. (2010). Inside the mind of a psychopath. *Scientific American Mind,* September. Retrieved from https://www.scientificamerican.com/article/inside-the-mind-of-a-psychopath/.

12 Kiehl, K. A., & Sinnott-Armstrong, W. P. (Eds.). (2013). *Handbook on psychopathy and law.* New York, NY: Oxford University Press.

13 Patrick, C. J. (Ed.). (2018). *Handbook of psychopathy* (2nd Ed.). New York, NY: Guilford Press.

14 Thijssen, S., & Kiehl, K. A. (2017). Functional connectivity in incarcerated male adolescents with psychopathic traits. *Psychiatry Research: Neuroimaging, 265*, 35–44. doi:10.1016/j.pscychresns.2017.05.005.

15 Espinoza, F. A., Vergara, V. M., Reyes, D., Anderson, N. E., Harenski, C. L., Decety, J., Calhoun, V. D. (2018). Aberrant functional network connectivity in psychopathy from a large (N = 985) forensic sample. *Human Brain Mapping, 39*, 2634-2634. doi: 10.1002/hbm.24028.

16 Forth, A. E., Kosson, D., & Hare, R. D. (2003). *The Hare Psychopathy Checklist: Youth Version.* Toronto, ON: Multi-Health Systems.

17 Book, A. S., Forth, A. E., & Clark, H. J. (2013). The Hare Psychopathy Checklist: Youth Version. In R. P. Archer & E. M. Archer (Eds.). *Forensic uses of clinical assessment instruments* (2nd ed., pp. 266–290). New York, NY: Routledge.

18 Poeppl, T. B., Donges, M., Mokros, M., Rupprecht, Fox, P. T., Laird, A. R., Bzdok, D., Langguth, B., & Eickhoff, S. B. (2018). A view behind the mask of sanity: Meta-analysis of aberrant brain activity in psychopaths. *Molecular Psychiatry.* Advance online publication. doi:10.1038/s41380-018-0122-5.

19 Wolf, R. C., Pujara, M. S., Motzkin, J. C., Newman, J. P., Kiehl, K. A., Decety, J., Kosson, D. S., & Koenigs, M. (2015). Interpersonal traits of psychopathy linked to reduced integrity of the uncinate fasciculus. *Human Brain Mapping, 36*, 4202-9. doi:10.1002/hbm.22911.

20 Kiehl, K. A. (2006). A cognitive neuroscience perspective on psychopathy: Evidence for paralimbic system dysfunction. *Psychiatry Research, 142*, 107–128. doi:10.1016/j.psychres.2005.09.013.

21 Poeppl, T. B., Donges, M., Mokros, M., Rupprecht, Fox, P. T., Laird, A. R., Bzdok, D., Langguth, B., & Eickhoff, S. B. (2018). A view behind the mask of sanity: Meta-analysis of aberrant brain activity in psychopaths. *Molecular Psychiatry*. Advance online publication. doi:10.1038/s41380-018-0122-5.

22 Thijssen, S., & Kiehl, K. A. (2017). Functional connectivity in incarcerated male adolescents with psychopathic traits. *Psychiatry Research: Neuroimaging, 265*, 35–44. doi:10.1016/j.pscychresns.2017.05.005.

23 Baskin-Sommers, A. R., Neumann, C. S., Cope, L. M., & Kiehl, K. A. (2016). Latent-variable modeling of brain gray-matter volume and psychopathy in incarcerated offenders. *Journal of Abnormal Psychology, 125*, 811–817. doi:10.1037/abn0000175.

24 Waller, R., Gard, A. M., Shaw, D. S., Forbes, E. E., Neumann, C. S., & Hyde, L. W. (2018). Weakened functional connectivity between the amygdala and the ventromedial prefrontal cortex is longitudinally related to psychopathic traits in low-income males during early adulthood. *Clinical Psychological Science*. Advance online publication. doi:10.1177/2167702618810231.

25 Espinoza, F. A., Vergara, V. M., Reyes, D., Anderson, N. E., Harenski, C. L., Decety, J., Calhoun, V. D. (2018). Aberrant functional network connectivity in psychopathy from a large (N = 985) forensic sample. *Human Brain Mapping, 39*, 2634-2634. doi: 10.1002/hbm.24028.

26 Hamilton, R. K. B. & Newman, J. P. (2018). The response modulation hypothesis. In C. Patrick (Ed.), *Handbook of psychopathy* (2nd ed., pp. 80–93). New York, NY: Guilford Press.

27 Haederle, M. (2010, Feb. 23). A mind of crime: How brain-scanning technology is redefining criminal culpability. *Pacific Standard*. Retrieved from https://psmag.com/social-justice/a-mind-of-crime-8440.

28 Saks, M. J., Schweitzer, N. J., Aharoni, E., & Kiehl, K. A. (2014). The impact of neuroimages in the sentencing phase of capital trials. *Journal of Empirical Legal Studies, 11*, 105–131. doi:10.111..1/jels .12036.

29 Hare, R. D. (2013). Forward. In K. Kiehl & W. Sinnott-Armstrong (Eds.), *Handbook on Psychopathy and Law* (pp vii–ix). New York, NY: Oxford University Press.

30 Harenski, C., Kiehl, K., & Hare, R. D. (2011). Neuroimaging, genetics, and psychopathy: Implications for the legal system. In L. Malatesti & J. McMillan (Eds.), *Interfacing law, psychiatry and philosophy* (pp.125–154). New York, NY: Oxford University Press.

31 Malatesti, L., & McMillan, J. (Eds.), *Responsibility and psychopathy: Interfacing law, psychiatry and philosophy*. New York, NY: Oxford University Press. http://ukcatalogue.oup.com/product/9780199551637.do.

SOME RECOMMENDED DOCUMENTARIES

DOCUMENTARIES

A *Google* and *YouTube* search will reveal hundreds of movies, documentaries, and websites that feature, describe, or comment on what are, or purportedly are, psychopaths. Unfortunately, far too many of these presentations and commentaries are wildly inaccurate, misleading, or even bizzare. A distressing number of websites have used the PCL-R as a basis for constructing "tests" for determining if you or someone you know might be a psychopath. Others present psychopaths as heroes or as "movers and shakers." We ask the reader to evaluate these sites critically, and to focus on the legitimate science of psychopathy. Several websites and Internet sources provide up-to-date information on developments in the study of psychopathy (e.g., see www.sssp.com; www.hare.org; aftermath-surviving-psychopathy .org; www.snakesinsuits.com). Many of the researchers to whom we refer in this text have their own websites. Below are several recommended documentaries.

The Psychopath Next Door. https://www.cbc.ca/doczone/episodes/the-psychopath-next-door. A Canadian Broadcasting Corporation (CBC) documentary by Jeremy Torrie, November 27, 2014. The film received the *Aftermath Media Award* in 2015. This fascinating hour-long film documents the impact of people with psychopathic traits on those around them. https://aftermath-surviving-psychopathy.org/index.php/2015-aftermath-foundation-media-award-winner/.

Bad Bosses: The Psycho-path to Success? https://edition.cnn.com/2012/01/19/business/psychopath-boss/index.html. A CNN segment and article on psychopathic bosses, January 20, 2012. It made the same mistake about the percentage of psychopathic senior managers as described in S 9.3: *The Wall Street "Ten Percenters."*

I, Psychopath. https://www.youtube.com/watch?v=jKvhKI6Kxew. An excellent documentary by Australian Ian Walker, following a self-proclaimed narcissist/suspected psychopath on a disturbing journey into diagnosis and a session in an imaging laboratory in Germany. Hare warned the producer that he was in for a rough time, and that he would not come away from the venture psychologically unscathed. Revealing "off camera" video clips validated this warning.

Psychopath. https://www.youtube.com/watch?v=60vK6Uw9sSE. A great UK Channel 4 Equinox documentary by Rosalind Arden, with over 5 million views on YouTube. For a transcript of the program, see http://www.hare.org/links/equinox.html. The subject of the program later was released, found with a gun in his car on the way to kill his wife, and died in prison.

I am Fishead: Are Corporate Leaders Psychopaths? https://topdocumentaryfilms.com/i-am-fishead-are-corporate-leaders-psycho

paths/. A compelling documentary by Misha Votruba and Vaclav Dejcmar, and narrated by Peter Coyote. The first half is about psychopathy, and the second half about Big Pharma. The producers stated, "We have coined the term Fishead as a metaphor for the fundamental devastating wrongs our society faces today. Fishead is synonymous with these words: problem, devastating, fundamental, selfish, disregard, irresponsible, uncaring, lack of empathy, psychopathic, wrong, mindless, and apathy."

The Criminal Mind. https://www.youtube.com/watch?v=NJ7 ck8Q_RII. A pilot documentary by Tony Wade for a potential series with the Canadian Broadcasting Corporation. Not picked up.

Psychopath MRI. https://www.youtube.com/watch?v=oaTfdKY budk. A detailed account by Hare of the first SPECT (single proton emission tomography) imaging study of psychopathy (Intrator, J., Hare, R.D., Stritzke, P., Brichtswein, K., Dorfman, D., Harpur, T., Bernstein, D., Handelsman, L., Schaefer, C., Keilp, Rosen, J., & Machac, J. (1997). A brain-imaging (single photon emission computerized tomography) study of semantic and affective processing in psychopaths. *Biological Psychiatry*, 42, 96-103).

INDEX

Abandonment phase, of
    manipulation, 61–62, 288
    confrontation, 139–41
    in corporate environment,
        138–39
    irresponsibility and, 60
    lacking empathy, 52–53
    lacking guilt/remorse, 58–59
    the patsies, 138–39
    psychopathic traits evident in,
        61–62, 85
Ablow, Keith, 75
Abuse. *See also* Physical abuse
    documenting and reporting,
        292–93, 298, 319, 325–27
    intimidation deterring
        reporting, 51

psychopathy and abusive
    leadership, 228–29
    victim response to, 292–93,
        294, 295, 323
Adolescence, psychopathic traits
    in, 26, 348n
Advertising jobs, 236
Affective domain, 21, 26
Affinity fraud, 93–97, 108–9
Aggression (aggressive behavior),
    20–21, 34
    Classic (Aggressive) profile,
        185–86, *186*, 210, 222
    Corporate Bullies, 182–83,
        184
    gender and, 39
    inability to accept blame, 260

Aggression (aggressive behavior)
(*cont.*)
  inability to act without, 262
  reporting, 292–93
Aging, and psychopathy, 29–31
Agreeableness, 124, 223, 225,
  302
Amazon Mechanical Turk
  (MTurk), 202, 222–23
American Psychiatric Association
  (APA), 18, 19
Anger/vindication, 295
Anonymous complaints, 327
Antagonists, 136–37
Antisocial behaviors, 20, 25, 26,
  28, 33
Antisocial personality disorder
  (ASPD), 17, 18–19
Ascension phase, 141
Assessing psychopathy. *See*
  Psychopathic traits
Assessment centers, 251–53
Assessment phase, of
  manipulation, 54–57, 288
  in corporate environment,
  126–30
  forging bonds in, 81–85
  identifying pawns and patrons,
  128–30
  messages communicated in,
  81–85
  the power base, 127–28
Attentional models, 345
Attributed personality
  (reputation), 80–81, 83,
  315–16

Background checks, 232, 240–41,
  246, 308
"Bad" bosses, 176–78
"Bad" coworkers, 178–80
Bad Seed, The (movie), 263
Behavioral genetics, 31–32
Bird, Anne, 75
Black Sails (TV series), 193
Blame. *See* Responsibility,
  avoiding
Blood Brother (Bird), 75
Bonds, with psychopaths
  avoiding, 289–90
  Dave case study, 89–91
  forging process, 77, 81–85,
  289–90
Bosses. *See also* Leadership;
  Managing
  "boss from hell," 176–78
  employee retention and
  psychopathic, 226
  handling psychopathic, 317–18
  supervisory styles and
  psychopathy, 177–78,
  227–29
Brain. *See* Psychopathic brain
B-Scan 360. *See* Business-Scan
  360
Bullies (bullying). *See also*
  Aggression; Corporate
  psychopaths; Corporate
  psychopaths, handling
  non-psychopathic, 187–91
  traits of, 182–83, 184
  understanding company
  policies about, 318–19

Bureaucracies
  deterring psychopaths, 99–101
  succession planning and, 252
  transitioning away from, 154–
    156, 158, 252
Bush, George W., 190
Business organizations, 97–99. *See
    also* Bureaucracies; Corporate
    psychopaths; Hiring
    psychopaths
  corporations as psychopaths,
    98–99
  entrepreneurial environment,
    157–59
  evolution of, 154–57. *See also*
    Change
  goals and objectives, 100
  honeymoon period, 127–28
  managing growth, 98–99
  manipulation in, 97–99
  organizational police, 136–38
  psychological employment
    contracts, 153–54, 158–59
  reasons psychopaths attracted
    to, 99–101
  Ron case study, 117–23
  secrecy, 161–62
  trusting environments, 123–25
Business-Scan 360 (B-Scan 360),
    219–25
  building, 221–23
  corporate psychopathy and
    gender, 224–25
  employees and bosses, 226
  leadership and, 227–29
  origins of, 220–21

research studies using, 224
Self-Report, 222, 223
workplace harassment, 225

Caesar, Julius, 189–90
Callousness, 32, 33, 34, 37, 38,
    39, 61, 181–82, 222
Calmness, lack of, 261–62
Calvin and Hobbes (comic), 263
Canadian Police Association,
    201–2
Career goals, 62, 100, 212
Celebrities, 54, 55
Chameleons. *See* Social
    chameleons
Change, 154–62
  attracting psychopaths, xii,
    159–61
  embracing, 156–57
  entrepreneurial environment
    and, 157–59
  negative effects of, 155–56
  positive effects of, 154–55
  psychological employment
    contracts and, 153–54,
    158–59
  responses to, 154–56
  secrecy and, 161–62
Chaos, opportunity from, 163–64
Charisma/Presentation Style, 206,
    207, *209*
Charismatic leadership, 188
Charm, 23, 51, 54, 57–58, 108,
    212
Cheater-hawk strategy, 34
Cheater strategy, 34

Child abuse, 32–33
Classic (Aggressive) psychopath, 185–86, *186*
Cleckley, Hervey, 19, 22–24, 25, 54, 104, 342
Cold-blooded, 37
Collusion, avoiding, 290–91
Communication networks, 132, 156
Communications, documenting, 319–20
Communication skills, 83
    facilitating lying, 50, 51, 59, 107
    PCL assessments, 205, 209
Company policies, 318–19
Competence
    assessing in hiring, 241–42, 244
    conscientiousness and, 179–80, 223
    handling challenges, 254
    psychological employment contract and, 153
    psychopaths attacking, 315–16, 317
    succession planning and, 251
Competency domains, in PCL-R, 205–7, 209
Complaints
    anonymous, 327
    formal, 325–26
Computer analyses of psychopathic language, 299–300
Condescension. *See* Grandiosity
Confidentiality, 327

Confrontation, of psychopaths, 139–41
    avoiding, 322–23
Cons, 181–82, 184
Conscience, and emotional emptiness, 18, 56, 190
Conscientiousness, 179–80, 223
Consideration scale, 177, 180
Consistency and reputation, 80
Contracts
    entrepreneurial psychological, 158–59
    psychological employment, 153–54, 158–59
Corporate Bullies, 182–83, 184
Corporate Cons, 181–82, 184
Corporate psychopaths, x–xii, 101–5
    aging and, 29–31
    assessing power base, 127–28
    B-Scan measure of. *See* Business-Scan 360
    bullies. *See* Bullies
    carrying workload of, 134
    change and, 159–61
    Classic (Aggressive) profile, 185–86, *186*
    common career progression of, 102–3, 105
    confronting, 139–41
    covert operation of, 101
    detractors of, 135–36
    empirical study using PCL-R, 204–12
    experience of, without knowing, 105–8

exposure of, 138–41. *See also*
  Abandonment phase, of
  manipulation; Revealing
  psychopaths
extras and, 135–36, 137–38
four-factor model of, 26, *27,*
  28, 185–86, *186*
gender and, 224–25
good leaders vs., 187–91
handling. *See* Corporate
  psychopaths, handling
hiring/not hiring. *See* Hiring
  practices; Hiring psychopaths
honeymoon period, 127–28
interactions with, 49–51
low-utility observers of, 135–37
manipulating management and
  coworkers, 130–35
mimicking good performers,
  125–26, 263–65
mismeasurement of, 214–15
mixed reactions to, 136–37
nature-nurture issue, 31–32,
  348*n*
organizational police and,
  136–37
orientation/socialization
  process, 123–24
patrons of. *See* Patrons
pawns of. *See* Pawns
power and. *See* Power/strength
public and media interest in,
  201, 203–4, 215–17
red flags, 137–38. *See also* Red
  flags
rise of, 152–53

secrecy and, 82, 132–33,
  161–62
statistics on, 175–76
styles of, 181–85
supporters of, 128–30, 135–36
Wall Street's "Ten Percenters,"
  215–17
Corporate psychopaths, handling,
  313–30. *See also* Victim
  responses
assessing colleagues, 324
assessing employment situation,
  324
avoiding confrontations,
  322–23
bosses, 317–18
building and maintaining
  relationships, 317–18
building and managing
  reputation, 315–16
collecting data, 323–24
considering other career
  options, 327–28
coworkers, 318, 324
documenting, 319–20
filing anonymous complaints,
  327
filing formal complaints, 325–26
improving leadership and
  management skills, 322
leaving on own terms, 329–30
seeking HR advice, 328–29
understanding company rules,
  318–19
using performance appraisals,
  320–21

"Corporate Psychopathy: Talking the Walk," 208–10
Corporate Puppetmasters, 183–185, 191–92
Corporations. *See* Business organizations
Coworkers, psychopathic
  handling, 318
  manipulation of, 130–35
"Coworkers from hell," 178–80
Creativity/innovation, 205
Credit sharing, 257
Criminal psychopaths. *See also* Fraud; Scams
  aggression/violence of, 20–21, 36–37, 74–77
  Andrew Cunanan, 74–76
  avoiding responsibility, 60
  brain structures and, 344
  empirical study, 201–2, 205
  lacking long-term goals, 62
  manipulation and, 58
  PCL assessments, 104, 105
  recidivism of, 21
  red-collar criminals, 64–65
  scientific literature on, xi–xii
  Scott Peterson, 75–76
  statistics on, 152–53
"Crown prince/ princess approach," 253
Cultural factors, 39–40, 355–56n
Cunanan, Andrew, 74–76

Dark Factor of Personality (D), 302–3
Dark personalities, 37–38, 301–3

Dark Tetrad, 202, 302
Dark Triad, 28, 37–38, 202
  face-to-face negotiations and, 109–10
  leadership and, 301
  in the workplace, 301–3
Dave case study, xii–xiii
  attracted to "employee of the month" power, 69, 71
  dissent and incongruities, 269–72
  doubts dance away, 197–200
  first day on job, 43–45
  forging bonds, 89–91
  hiring process, 3–6
  parking-lot grandiosity, 69–71
  plagiarizing for gain, 113–16
  questionable actions, 145–47, 167–69
  successful coup, 333–35
  uncovering the truth, 307–11
DeCovny, Sherree, 215–16
DeLisi, Matt, 36–37
Denial, 291–92
Deresiewicz, William, 216
Detractors, 135–36
  red flags, 137–38
Diagnostic and Statistical Manual of Mental Disorders (DSM), 18, 19, 52, 53
Diamond smuggling, 63–64
Disinformation, spreading, 59, 132–33, 253, 322
Documentaries, recommended, 373–75

Documenting communications,
    319–20
Documenting interview, 247–48
Double life, 74–76
Downs, Diane, 353n
Duchenne smiles, 263, 264–65

Eichler, Alexander, 215–16
Embezzlement, 37, 65, 204, 211
Empathy/emotions, lack of
    abandoning victims and,
        61–62
    conscience and, 18, 56, 190
    genetic continuity and, 33–34
    loyalty and, 128
    mistaken for calmness, 261–62
    murders, 36–37, 65, 74–76,
        75–76, 191–92
    PCL assessments and, 32, 33,
        34, 182
    research finding, 52–53
Employee retention, 226
Employment contracts,
    psychological, 153–54,
    158–59
Entitlement, sense of, 52–53, 57
Entrepreneurial environment,
    157–59
Entrepreneurial psychological
    contracts, 158–59
Environmental factors, 31–32,
    348n
Epigenetics, 32
Erratic behavior, 261
Ethnic factors, 39–40, 355–56n
Evolution, 18, 33–36

Excuses. See Responsibility,
    avoiding
Executive recruiters, 107
Executives, hiring. See Hiring
    practices
Exit interviews, 329–30
Expert power, 127
Extras, 135–36
    red flags, 137–38

Facades. See Charm; Impression
    management
Failure to report, 85
Fears, of victim, 287–88
Feelings. See Empathy/emotions,
    lack of
Fiction. See Impression
    management; Lying;
    Psychopathic fiction
First impressions, 57–58, 80,
    288–89
Flaws, of victims, 286
Forensic hospitals, 97
Formal complaints, 325–26
Forster, Bruce, 343
Four-factor model of psychopathy,
    26–28, 27, 185–86, 186
Fraud, 204, 213–14. See also
    Criminal psychopaths;
    Scams
    affinity fraud, 93–97, 108–9
    Pit Bull case study, 13–16
    probation officer case, 149–52
    "Sammy the Slimeball," 93–95
Frustration tolerance, 56–57, 62,
    157

Full Range Model of leadership, 227–28

Functional magnetic resonating (fMRI), 343, 344

"Future leader," 129–30, 211–12

Game of Thrones (TV series), 163

Gender, 33, 38–39, 224–25

Genetic continuity, 33–34

Genetic factors, 17–18, 31–32, 348*n*

Giuliani, Rudolph, 190

Global Economic Crime and Fraud Survey, 213–14

Goals, lacking, 62, 100, 212

"Gold watch," 153

Google Scholar, 237

Grambling, John, Jr., 29–31

Grandiosity, 52, 57, 180, 212
Dave case study, 69–71

"Greed is good," x, 193

Grohol, John, 215–16

Group dynamics
affinity fraud, 93–97, 108–9
business organizations, 97–99
in prisons/forensic hospitals, 97

Gruber, Peter, 225

Guilt/remorse, lack of
abandoning victims and, 58–59
identifying/assessing victims and, 20, 29, 33, 56
Scott Peterson and, 75–76
victim response and, 291–92

Halo effects, 188

Hard tactics, 110

Hare Psychopathy Checklist—Revised. *See* Psychopathy Checklist—Revised

Hiding psychopathic traits. *See* Impression management

"High-status" interviewers, 249

Hiring executives, 250
evaluating competencies, 241–242, 244
executive recruiters, 107
internal vs. external candidates, 251–54
job descriptions, 250
succession planning systems, 251–54

Hiring managers, 235–36, 239, 243–44

Hiring practices, 235–50. *See also* Résumés
advertising jobs, 236
asking for work examples, 245
behavioral concerns. *See* Red flags
clarifying details, 246
the close, 243–44
evaluating feelings/emotional responses, 246–47
executive hiring and promotion, 250
face-to-face screening interviews, 239–42
focusing on action and behavior, 245
follow-up on concerns, 242–43

job descriptions, 236, 250
learning about yourself,
    249–50
note taking, 247–48
providing information about
    job and company, 242
retaining control of interview,
    244
selection committee, 248–49
telephone screening interview,
    238–39
Hiring psychopaths
avoiding. *See* Hiring practices
charm and, 108
Dave case study, 3–6
decision-time case study,
    231–34
honesty and, 124
manipulation and, 105–8,
    123–24
mistaking psychopathic traits
    for leadership, 187–91
perceiving "potential" skills
    and, 107–8
Pit Bull case study, 9–10
typical pattern, 123–25
Histrionic personality disorder,
    52, 53
Honeymoon period, 127–28
Hostage taking, 298
Hot buttons, 284–85
Human resources (HR), 328–29

"Ideal employees," 244, 248–49
"Ideal leaders," 129–30, 191,
    211–12

Immodesty, 260
Impression management
charm and, 23, 51, 54, 57–58,
    108, 212
masking psychopathic traits,
    49–51, 74–77, 241–42
pawns for. *See* Pawns
Pit Bull case study, 11–13
politics and poker, 264–65
psychopathic dance. *See*
    Psychopathic dance
psychopathic fiction and,
    57–62, 125–28
recognizing manipulation and,
    75–77
social chameleon skills and,
    49–51, 125–26
style trumpeting substance,
    192–93
threats, coercion, intimidation,
    and violence, 51
Impulsive psychopaths, 180–81,
    189
Influence networks, 140,
    252–53
Informal power, 55, 127
Initiating structure scale, 177–78,
    180
Interpersonal factors, 33, 39
Intimidation
failure to report fraud and, 51
manipulation through, 51
Pit Bull case study, 10–13
Intrator, Joanne, 342
Irresponsibility. *See* Responsibility,
    avoiding

"Jingle fallacy," 28
Job descriptions, 236, 250
Job interview. *See* Hiring
  psychopaths; Screening
  interviews
Julius Caesar, 189–90

Kidman, Nicole, 263
Kiehl, Kent, 342–43, 344
Knowledge power, 127

Labels, avoiding, 282, 329
Lacks of victims, 286–87
Laissez-Faire Leadership, 227–28
Leadership. *See also* Bosses; Hiring
  executives; Managing
  behaviorial concerns. *See* Red
    flags
  building and maintaining
    relationships, 317–18
  charisma and, 188, 206, 207
  consideration and initiating
    structure, 177–79, 180
  continuously improving skills,
    322
  Dark Triad and, 301
  employee retention and, 226
  influencing and persuading
    others, 188
  mistaking psychopathic traits
    for, x–xi, 187–91
  psychopathic traits and, 227–
    229
  strategic thinking, 188–89, 205
  styles of, 177–78, 227–29
  two-factor model of, 177–78

Liddle, Peter, 342–43
Life goals, 62, 100, 212
Lifestyle domain, 26, 33
Loneliness, 55, 287
"Low-status" interviewers, 249
Low-utility observers, 135–37
Loyalty, 128, 316
  entrepreneurial environment
    and, 158
  psychological employment
    contracts and, 153–54,
    158–59
Lying (lies), 58–60
  Dave case study, 113–16
  decision-time case study,
    231–34
  detecting, 235–37
  embezzlement case, 64–65
  manipulation and, 58–60
  as red flag, 259
  screening résumés, 236–37
Lykken, David, 19–20, 25

Machiavellianism, 28, 37–38,
  109–10, 223
Macho psychopaths. *See* Bullies
Malice (movie), 263
Managing. *See also* Bosses;
  Leadership
  building relationships, 317–18
  change, 154–62
  competencies for, 315–16
  documenting communications,
    319–20
  employee retention and, 226
  handling challenges, 254

performance appraisals and, 320–21

reputation, 315–16

seeking HR advice, 328–29

Manipulation, 57–62, 73–85, 288

abandonment phase, 61–62, 138–39

abuse and. *See* Abuse

ascension phase, 141

assessment phase, 54–57, 126–28

basics of personality, 78–81

Caroline case study, 63–64

charm for, 23, 51, 54, 57–58, 108, 212

confrontation, 139–41

Dan case study, 131–34

the Extras, 135–36

forging bonds for, 77, 81–85

handling. *See* Corporate psychopaths, handling

hearts and minds, 131–35

identifying pawns and patrons, 128–30

lying and, 58–60

management and coworkers, 130–35

mind tricks, 81–85

phases overview, 288

power and. *See* Power/strength

in prisons/forensic hospitals, 97

psychopathic dance and. *See* Psychopathic dance

psychopathic fiction and, 57–62, 125–28

recognizing, 75–77

secrecy and, 82, 132–33, 161–62

social chameleons and, 49–51, 125–26

Ted case study, 73–74

using what you have, 63–64

Manipulator subtypes, 181–84, 186, *186*

Masking personalities. *See* Impression management

Mask of Sanity, The (Cleckley), 19, 23–24

Mathieu, Cynthia, 225, 226, 227–28

Meetings, documenting of, 319

"Memo of understanding," 319–20

Mentors. *See* Patrons

#MeToo movement, 225

Mimicking, 49–51, 96, 110, 125–26, 263–65

in screening interviews, 246–47

Minard, Richard Bryan, 108–9

Mind tricks, of psychopaths, 81–85

Misinformation, spreading, 59, 132–33, 253, 322

Mission-critical rules, 157

Modesty, inability to experience, 260

Murders, 36–37, 65, 74–76, 75–76, 191–92

Narcissism, 37, 51–54, 109–10, 134

Narcissistic managers,
  manipulating, 134–35
Narcissistic personality disorder,
  52–53
Nature-nurture issue, 31–32,
  348n
Neuroimaging, 342–43
Neurolaw, 346
New York Times, 216, 219,
  224
Novel stimulation, 56–57

Oral communication skills,
  83
  facilitating lying, 50, 51, 59,
    107
  PCL assessments, 205, 209
Organizational police, 136–37
  red flags, 137–38
Ouston, Rick, 109
Overt answers, 241, 242

Paralimbic system, 344
Parasitic lifestyles, 55–56, 105,
  288
Parasitic-predator model, 281
Passive aggression, 181
Patrons
  abandonment, 138–39
  ascension, 141
  assessment (identifying),
    128–30, 252
  influence networks, 252–53
  red flags, 137–38, 257
Patsies, 138–39, 176
Paulhus, Del, 37–38, 65, 224

Pawns, 128–30
  abandonment, 138–39
  confrontation, 139–41
  identifying, 128–30
  manipulation, 130–35
  as patsies, 138–39, 176
  psychopathic fiction and,
    125–28
  red flags, 137–38
  responding to realization,
    293–94
  Ron case study, 117–23
Performance appraisals, 320–21
Perri, Frank, 65
Persona, 80–81
  fictitious. See Impression
    management
  perceptions of. See Reputation
  psychopaths using mind tricks,
    81–85
Personality, x, 78–81
  attributed. See Reputation
  conscientiousness, 179–80, 223
  mind tricks, 81–85
  private self, 78–79, 80–81
  public self. See Persona
  self-report inventories, 202–3
Personal self-defense. See Victim
  responses
Person-oriented approach, 185
Peterson, Scott, 75–76
Phases, psychopathic. See
  Abandonment phase, of
  manipulation; Ascension
  phase; Assessment phase, of
  manipulation; Manipulation

Physical abuse, 292–93, 294, 295, 298

Pit Bull (Helen) case study, 7–16
   fraud, 13–16
   hiring, 9–10
   impression management, 11–13
   intimidating/disrespecting staff, 10–13

"Players," 62

Poker, 77, 264–65

Politics and poker, 264–65

Ponzi schemes, 204

Post-traumatic stress disorder (PTSD), 32–33, 292–93

Potentially traumatic events (PTE), 32–33

Power/strength
   building power base, 127–28
   case study, 131–34
   informal power, 55, 127
   pawns/patrons and, 128–30

Premise of book, xi

Pretenders
   in entrepreneurial environment, 157–59
   secrecy empowering, 161–62

Prisons, x, 97

Privacy laws, 203

Private self, 78–79, 80–81
   mind tricks, 81–85

Professional credentials, 56, 237

Promiscuity, 39

Promotions, 247, 250
   succession planning, 251–54

"Psyche out," 77

Psychological employment contracts, 153–54, 158–59

Psychopath's drama, roles in, 125. See pawns; patsies; organizational police

Psychopathic brain, 34–35, 36, 341–46
   early days of research, 341–42
   nature-nurture issue, 31–32, 348n
   neuroimaging, 342–43
   neurolaw, 346
   overview of current finding, 56, 343–44

Psychopathic criminals. See Criminal psychopaths; Fraud

Psychopathic dance, 288–95
   phase 1: tempted by the psychopathic fiction, 288–89
   phase 2: taken in by psychopathic bond, 289–90
   phase 3: collusion in psychopath's game, 290–91
   phase 4: manipulated by self-doubt, guilt, and denial, 291–92
   phase 5: escalating abuse, 292–93
   phase 6: realization and insight, 293–94
   phase 7: working through feelings of shame, 294
   phase 8: anger and vindication, 295

Psychopathic fiction, 57–62, 125–28
assessing power base, 127–28
collusion in the game, 290–91
first impressions and, 288–89
identifying pawns and patrons, 128–30
manipulation and, 57–62, 288–89
in screening interview, 244
Psychopathic labels, avoiding, 282, 329
Psychopathic language, computer analyses of, 299–300
Psychopathic lifestyle, 192–93
Psychopathic manipulation. *See* Manipulation
Psychopathic retaliation, 298–99
Psychopathic traits, x–xi, 20–21, 28–29, 175–76. *See also specific traits*
assessment challenge, 180–81
in assessment phase, 54–57
avoiding taking responsibility, 60
B-scan assessment, 221–22
cons, bullies, and puppetmasters, 181–85, 191–92
emulating the style, 192–93
examples. *See* Psychopathic trait examples
good leaders vs. corporate psychopaths, 187–91
Hervey Cleckley view, 19, 22, 23–24, 25, 54, 104, 342

hiding. *See* Impression management
in manipulation phase, 57–62, 73–85
mistaking, for leadership, 227–29
nature-nurture issue, 31–32
PCL: SV assessment for, 26–29, *27,* 104, 343
PCL-R assessment for, 25–28, 184–85, 204–12
recognizing, 75–77
social chameleons, 49–51, 125–26
statistics on, 175–76
varied expressions of, 185–86
Psychopathic trait examples. *See also* Charm; Empathy/ emotions, lack of; Guilt/ remorse, lack of; Lying
avoiding responsibility, 60, 260
manipulation and, 60
needing novel stimulation, 56–57
parasitic lifestyles, 55–56
taking unethical shortcuts, 56–57
Psychopathic-like traits
assessment challenge, 180–81
avoiding psychopath labels, 282, 329
"boss from hell," 176–78
case study illustrating, 171–74
"coworkers from hell," 178–80
difficult people vs. psychopaths, 187–91
pervasiveness of, 175–76

Psychopathy, 17–31
abusive leadership and, 228–29
aging and, 29–31
antisocial personality disorder
vs., 18–19
clinical/forensic measurement
of, 25–28. *See also*
Psychopathy Checklist—
Revised
from clinical to empirical study
of, 22–25
conscientiousness and, 179–80,
223
corporate. *See* Corporate
psychopaths
criminality and. *See* Criminal
psychopaths
Dark Triad and. *See* Dark
Triad
defined, x, 17–18
four-factor model of, 26–28,
27, 185–86, *186*
gender, ethnicity, culture,
38–40, 224–25
genetic continuity and, 33–34
as multidimensional
continuum, 28–29
narcissism and, 37, 51–54,
109–10
responding to. *See* Corporate
psychopaths, handling;
Victim responses
rise of, 152–53
sociopathy vs., 19–20
statistical estimates of, 175–76,
184–85

traditional clinical construct of,
20–22
Psychopathy Checklist: Screening
Version (PCL:SV), 26–29,
27, 104, 343
Psychopathy Checklist: Youth
Version (PCL: YV), *27*, 343
Psychopathy Checklist—Revised
(PCL-R), 25–29, 184–86,
186, 204–12, 343
comparison with community
samples, 207–8, *208*
competency domains, 205–7
corporate variations, 210–11,
211
Dark Triad and, 38
four-factor model, 26–28, *27*,
185–86, *186*, 222
psychopathy scores, 25–26, 207
talking the walk, 208–10
Psychopathy Measure—
Management Research
Version (PM—MRV),
214–15
Public self. *See* Persona
Puppetmasters, 183–85, 191–92,
287

R.D. Hare Lifetime Achievement
Award, 25
Reactions, to psychopaths. *See*
also Corporate psychopaths,
handling; Victim responses
initial impressions, 135–36
mixed, 136–37
"Reading people," 49–50

Realization and insight, 293–94
Red-collar criminals, 64–65
Red flags
    discrepant views of coworkers,
        137–38
    disparate treatment of staff,
        257–59
    inability to accept blame, 260
    inability to act consistently and
        predictably, 261
    inability to act without
        aggression, 262
    inability to be modest, 260
    inability to form teams, 255–56
    inability to react calmly,
        261–62
    inability to share, 256–57
    inability to tell the truth, 259
Relationships
    building and maintaining,
        317–18
    forging, for manipulation, 77,
        81–85
Religious groups
    affinity frauds and, 93–97,
        108–9
    Richard Bryan Minard, 108–9
Remorse. See Guilt/remorse, lack
        of
Reputation, 80–81, 83
    formation of, 80–81
    protecting. See Corporate
        psychopaths, handling;
        Victim responses
    understanding and managing,
        315–16

Resource power, 127
Responsibility, avoiding
    blaming others, 60, 102, 150,
        181, 182–83, 258–59
    elevating self/disparaging others
        by, 60
    endless excuses for, 60, 259
    manipulation and, 60
    as red flag, 260
Résumés, 106–7
    considering other career
        options, 327
    lies on, 4, 5, 62, 103, 107, 150,
        308
    note taking during interview,
        247–48
    screening, 236–37
Revealing psychopaths. See also
        Abandonment phase, of
        manipulation
    detractors and, 135–36
    discrepant views, 137–38
    exposure and confrontation,
        138–41
Richards, Bryan, 108–9
"Right and wrong," ix–x
Risk taking
    conscientiousness and, 179
    in entrepreneurial environment,
        156, 157
    of great leaders, 189–90
    of psychopaths, 28, 39, 57,
        160
Ron, sales psychopath, case study,
        117–23
Rosner, Brian, 29–31

Rotational assignments, 252
Rule breaking, 22, 99, 160

Sabotage, 298–99
"Sammy the Slimeball" fraud case,
    93–95
"Saviors," 161
Scams. *See also* Criminal
    psychopaths; Fraud
    affinity fraud, 93–97, 108–9
    diamond smuggler, 63–64
    Pit Bull case study, 13–16
    three-card monte, 47–49,
        313–14
Screening interviews
    asking for work examples, 245
    clarifying details, 246
    the close, 243–44
    evaluating feelings/emotional
        responses, 246–47
    face-to-face, 239–42
    focusing on action and
        behavior, 245
    follow-up on concerns,
        242–43
    learning about yourself,
        249–50
    note taking, 247–48
    providing information about
        job and company, 242
    résumés, 236–37
    retaining control, 244
    selection committee, 248–49
    telephone, 238–39
    training programs for, 240–41
Secondary psychopaths, 20

Secrecy
    of corporate psychopaths, 82,
        132–33
    of organizations, 161–62
Self-actualization, 153–54
Self-confidence, 79, 188, 212,
    260
Self-defense. *See* Victim responses
Self-doubt, 56, 59, 138, 286,
    291–92
Self-esteem, 177, 286, 293
Self-image, 79
Self-knowledge, 249–50, 282
September 11 attacks (2001), 190
Sex-role expectations, 39
Sexual abuse, 32–33, 292–93
Sexual harassment, 225, 318
Sexual relationships, 33–34, 39
Shame, 139, 294
Siege, and psychopathic
    retaliation, 298
Social chameleons, 49–51, 125–
    126. *See also* Mimicking
Sociopathy, 19–20, 75
Soft tactics, 110
"Soul mates," 85, 131, 291
Spouses as psychopaths, 281
Stimulation-seeking, 20, 33,
    56–57
Strategic thinking, 188–89, 205
Strength. *See* Power/strength
Structure scale, 177–78, 180
Style vs. substance, 192–93
"Successful psychopaths," x–xi
Succession planning, 251–54
"Success lists," 157

Sullenberger, Chesley "Sully,"
    190–91
Superfluous rules, 157
Superiority. See Grandiosity
Swindle (Rosner), 30–31

Team-based models of
    management, 154
Teams (teamwork)
    "coworkers from hell," 178–80
    inability to form, 255–56
    inability to share, 256–57
    performance appraisals and,
        321
    psychopaths in, 99–100,
        102–3. See also Corporate
        psychopaths, handling;
        Victim responses
    references from teammates, 328
    screening applicant affinity for,
        206, 209
Telephone calls, documenting,
    319
Telephone screening interviews,
    238–39
"Tells," 77, 264
Temptation, avoiding, 288–89
"Ten Percenters," 215–17
Tepper, Bennett, 228
Thigpen, Corbett, 23–24
Three-card monte swindle, 47–49,
    313–14
Three Faces of Eve, The (Cleckley
    and Thigpen), 23–24
Thrill-seeking, 57, 126, 131, 160,
    189, 190

Time-management, 231–32
Todd, Douglas, 109
Traits. See Psychopathic traits
Transactional Leadership,
    227–28
Transformational Leadership,
    227–28
Transitioning organizations. See
    Change
Triggers, 284–88
Trust, 59–60, 123–25

"Unified theory of crime," 36–37
Unpredictably, 261
US Airways Flight 1549, 190–91

Variable-oriented approach, 185
Versace, Gianni, 74–76
Victim responses, 139, 275–99
    to abuse, 292–93, 294, 295,
        323
    after realizing truth, 293–94
    anger/vindication, 295
    avoiding collusion with
        psychopath, 290–91
    avoiding psychopathic bonds,
        289–90
    avoiding psychopathic labels,
        282, 329
    avoiding temptation, 288–89
    dealing with self-doubt, guilt,
        and denial, 291–92
    handling corporate
        psychopaths, 323–27
    learning about psychopathy,
        281–82

learning about yourself, 282
Nancy and Marshall, case study,
    275–80
next steps to recovery, 296–99
psychopathic dance. *See*
    Psychopathic dance
understanding manipulation
    process, 288
understanding own triggers,
    284–88
understanding own value to
    psychopaths, 283
understanding own weaknesses,
    284–88
working through shame, 294
Victim support groups, 294, 298,
    325
Violence, 51, 74–76
    psychopathy and, 36–37
Visionary thinking, 188–89

Wall Street's "Ten Percenters,"
    215–17
Warrior-hawk strategy, 34
Washington, George, 159
Watterson, Bill, 263
Weaknesses
    psychopaths assessing victims,
        49–50, 55, 62, 83–84
    targets understanding own,
        284–88
Weak spots, 285–88
Weinberger, Joel, 22–23
Westen, Drew, 22–23
Without Conscience (Hare),
    20–21, 29–30, 65, 175, 264,
    341–42
Work ethic, 100, 124–25
"Working the system," 56
Workplace harassment, 225, 318
Work portfolios, 245

About the Authors

PAUL BABIAK, PH.D., is a New York–based industrial and organizational psychologist, and president of HRBackOffice, an executive coaching and consulting firm specializing in helping executives deal with possible psychopaths hiding within their organizations. He and his collaborators have conducted some of the most influential original research on corporate psychopaths. Newspapers, business magazines, and documentaries have featured his work, and he has been a guest on many radio and television talk shows. His clients have included executives in business, academia, law enforcement, government, insurance, medicine, finance, and intelligence, and he speaks about the corporate psychopath at professional conferences and business meetings. Paul is vice president of the *Aftermath: Surviving Psychopathy Foundation*, a non-profit organization providing information and support for victims of psychopathy.

ROBERT D. HARE, PH.D., is Emeritus Professor of Psychology, University of British Columbia, where he taught and conducted research for more than forty years, and is president of Darkstone Research Group Ltd. He was a pioneer in the empirical study of psychopathy, and has devoted most of his academic career to the investigation of the construct, its nature, assessment, and implications for mental health and criminal justice. He is the author of several books, including *Without Conscience*, and more than two hundred chapters and scientific articles on psychopathy, and is the developer of the *Psychopathy Checklist–Revised* (PCL-R), the international standard for the clinical/forensic assessment of psychopathy. He and his colleagues (see Appendix) were among the first to conduct systematic research on the neurobiology of psychopathy using structural and functional brain imaging. He is the recipient of many awards and honors, including induction into the Order of Canada in 2010. As a point of interest, prior to starting his studies for a Ph.D., he worked for eight months as the sole psychologist in a maximum security penitentiary in British Columbia.